Voyage
through Time

Voyage
through Time

Walks of Life
to the Nobel Prize

Ahmed Zewail

The American University in Cairo Press
Cairo — New York

Dar el Kutub No. 7150/01
ISBN 977 424 677 2

Designed by the AUC Press Design Center/Andrea El-Akshar
Printed in Egypt

To Egypt

You lit the beacon of civilization

You deserve a brilliant future

May my voyage light a candle of hope for your youth

———

Contents

Illustrations

Between pages 212 and 213

Maha's graduation from Caltech, 1994

Amani's graduation from San Marino High School in 1997

Halloween trick or treating with my sons

Dema Faham on the occasion of the awarding of the King Faisal
    International Prize in March of 1989

Wedding photo of Dema and me, with family, at Caltech's
    Athenaeum, 1989

Professor Bengt Nordén introducing me at the Nobel awards ceremony

My family and friends at a reception in Stockholm

With Naguib Mahfouz in Cairo, 2000

Dema and I with Nabeel and Hani

Nabeel and Hani, demonstrating their fishing skills in Cairo

Omar Batisha and I at al-Fishawi cafe in Cairo in 1997

My family on board a yacht on the Nile, December, 1999

In the Tea Garden of the Semiramis

With Mme. Amal Fahmy in West Lost Angeles, 1988

Walking with Linus Pauling on the Caltech campus

Dick Bernstein and I sharing coffee and points of view in 1987

Street scene in Desuq at the dedication of a street in my name in 1998

At the head of the street named for me in Damanhur, 1998

Dr. Ahmed Zewail Square in Alexandria

My wife and I, with Nabeel and Hani, at the Zewail Square open
    museum wall in Alexandria

The souvenir photograph taken at the Athenaeum, January, 2000

Groundbreaking ceremony for the University of Science and
    Technology on January 1, 2000

Prologue

A telephone call at dawn on October 12, 1999, shook my inner being just as an earthquake does in California. In Pasadena, California, I received the news at 5:30 A.M. from the secretary-general of the Swedish Academy of Sciences, congratulating me on the award of the 1999 Nobel Prize in Chemistry. He read the citation of the academy and indicated that I was receiving the prize unshared. After three other members of the academy praised the contribution for which the prize was awarded, the secretary-general came back on the line and said: "In twenty minutes we will be announcing it to the world—these are the last twenty minutes of peace in your life." The secretary-general was right. My life has changed, and in the years to come there will be opportunities to reflect on these changes following the Nobel prize.

The award was for research on atoms and molecules, which have an enormously complex "sociology." Ever since their discovery, scientists have been concerned with their behavior in matter—why atoms and molecules sometimes like or attract each other and sometimes don't. This love and hate dynamic is extremely important—it determines why substances exist in different shapes and phases, and how they transform to other substances. And, like humans, the only way to find out how they behave is to watch them in action. However, the entire time span of the journey during any transformation is a billion trillion times shorter than the human lifespan. That is why for twenty-four centuries, since its conception, the atom's motion in real time was invisible.

For atoms and molecules, the scale of time involved is awesome—its unit is the *femtosecond*. A femtosecond is a millionth of a billionth of a second, a quadrillionth of a second; it is one second divided by ten raised to the power of fifteen (10^{-15}), or 0.000 000 000 000 001 second. Put in comparative terms, a femtosecond is to a second as a second is to 32 million years. In one second, light travels about 186,000 miles (300,000 kilometers), almost from here to the moon; in one femtosecond, light travels 300 nanometers (0.000 000 3 meter), the dimension of a bacterium, or a small fraction of the thickness of a human hair. With femtosecond timing, the atom's motion becomes visible.

The call from Stockholm was for our contribution to the science of *time* and *matter*—the development, with laser strobes, of femtosecond timing techniques, making possible the observation of matter's dynamics with atomic-scale resolution. With the shutter speed of the "camera" more than one million million times faster than a normal one, we can now freeze the motion of atoms and resolve the transition states in the journey of molecular reactions. The discovery of phenomena and the development of concepts allow us to understand the behavior and the forces in this microuniverse of atoms and molecules, with the prospect of taming matter. The new field of science was named *femtochemistry*, and the coining of this word was appropriate—it captured the interconnection between the time scale (femtosecond) and the molecular change (chemistry). By this ideal marriage between time and matter, femtochemistry ends the race against time for all molecules of nature, including those of life.

At exactly 6:00 A.M. Pacific Standard Time the prize announcement was posted on the Internet, and, concurrently at 3:00 P.M. Stockholm time, the Academy held a press conference. My family and I saw the press release on the Internet on our home computer and read the citation, which says, in part:

This year's laureate in Chemistry is being rewarded
for his pioneering investigation of fundamental chemical reactions, using ultra-short laser flashes. . . .
Professor Zewail's contributions have brought
about a revolution in chemistry and adjacent sciences. . . . Zewail's technique uses laser flashes of
such short duration that we are down to the time
scale on which the reactions actually happen—
femtoseconds (fs). . . . We can now see the movements of individual atoms as we imagine them.
They are no longer invisible. . . . With the world's
fastest camera available, only the imagination sets
bounds for new problems to tackle.

At the ceremony that followed two months later, Professor Bengt
Nordén, a member of the Nobel Committee, introduced me with more
descriptive words:

Zewail's use of the fast laser technique can be
likened to Galileo's use of his telescope, which he
directed towards everything that lit up the vault of
heaven. Zewail tried his femtosecond laser on literally everything that moved in the world of molecules. He turned his telescope towards the frontiers
of science.

The Nobel recognition of scientific achievements is the highest honor
for any scientist, but for me this recognition adds a new dimension—it
represents pride in the world from which I came. The 1999 Nobel Prize
in Chemistry was the first in chemistry, physics, or physiology or medicine that Egypt and the Arab world can claim. Egypt has had a Nobel
Prize for Peace, awarded to President M. Anwar al-Sadat, and a Nobel
Prize in Literature, awarded to the renowned novelist Naguib Mahfouz.
However, in the sciences, over the past one hundred years of the exis-

tence of the prizes, the Islamic world—which represents more than one billion of the Earth's six billion in population—can claim only Abdus Salam from Pakistan, cowinner of the 1979 Nobel Prize in Physics, and myself. Nearly all of the prizes in science and medicine have been awarded to the Western world.

If the Nobel prizes had existed 6,000 years ago, when Egypt's civilization began, or even 2,000 years ago, when the famous Library at Alexandria was established, Egypt would have garnered many of them in the scientific fields. A millennium ago, the Arab and Islamic civilization, which made major, seeding contributions to the European Renaissance and to science and literature, would surely have had an equally large share on account of the work of many scholars, such as Avicenna (Ibn Sina), Averroës (Ibn Rushd), Geber (Jabir Ibn Hayyan), Alhazen (Ibn al-Haytham), and others.

The situation is different today, and one can understand why the announcement of my Nobel Prize in Chemistry made millions of Arabs and, I believe, the developing world at large more hopeful about the future and more confident in their people's ability to achieve noteworthy advances in science, the hallmark of the Western world. These sentiments were evidenced in the thousands of messages I received over the days that followed. The Egyptians were full of joy. President Mubarak called me at home, and in December I received from the president the highest state honor, the Grand Collar of the Nile. The hope is that this first science prize will inspire younger generations to think positively and for governments to develop new programs for science and technology.

At Caltech (the California Institute of Technology) the news was welcomed with much appreciation. Caltech had already had twenty-seven Nobel prizes credited to its faculty and alumni, but every new one merits gala celebrations as it reaffirms Caltech's preeminence in science and its contributions through science to the betterment of humankind—this also adds to Caltech's fame. There were many parties, and one was held at the Athenaeum, our faculty club, with about five hundred persons present. This grand gathering was scheduled after my visit to the White

House in Washington, D.C., and after the award ceremony in Stockholm. In the evening at the Athenaeum, I spoke of the greatness of the place that allowed our team to make the scientific contributions cited by the Nobel committee only ten years after my arrival on campus as a beginning assistant professor, but I didn't forget to speak about my plans for the future.

For this journey on the road to the Nobel prize, I have been asked several times to write a biography, or at least a biographical summary of my life. I declined these invitations. I was of the opinion that a traditional biography should represent a lifetime of work and experience and much effort and time are needed to do it well. In July of 1997 while on a trip to Cairo this strong feeling softened to a more moderate one. I was stimulated to ask a few questions by two books I was reading, one titled *A History of Knowledge* by Charles van Doren and the other *Making Waves* by Charles Townes. How did I acquire knowledge? Why did I become a scientist? What are the forces that have determined the walks of my own life? What are the meanings of faith, destiny, and luck? In the attempt to answer such complex questions, I began to sketch my thoughts.

I was sitting in the Tea Garden of the Semiramis Intercontinental Hotel, in the grip of the fantastic panorama of the Nile. On its banks, three major epochs of Egypt's history seemed symbolized: a pharaonic obelisk, a minaret of a mosque, and the giant modern postrevolutionary structures of the Cairo Tower and Opera House. Scanning the landscape unfolded events of the past, bringing back memories and reflections on the history of the land, the eternity of the Nile, and my transition to the land of opportunity in America. I decided to write, thinking it would be a few pages long. I ended up filling eight notebooks (made of papyrus!) in a few days, and for some reason the pen would not stop. In fact, one of my secretaries, Jeanne, noted that what I wrote was not a draft—it was written with few corrections. In the background, the music of Umm Kulthum, the great singer of Egypt, kept me going.

This book, in its ten chapters, describes my journey from Egypt to America; it is a voyage through time. I use "walks of life" purposely as a term to reflect the apparently random nature of walks and the incidents and surprises that may change such walks to define one's path through life. The book encapsulates six stations of the journey: childhood, which began on the banks of the Nile and was shaped by the love and confidence of my parents; admission to the Faculty of Science in Alexandria, which defined my science career as well as my engagement to a science student; the scholarship in America, which opened up a whole new world for me; the years of scientific discovery at Caltech, which have changed the way we think about the science of time and matter; the receipt of the King Faisal International Prize, which was the first major prize to recognize my group's contribution and which ultimately provided me with a new family; and the receipt of the Nobel prize, which led to a place in the history of science.

The book focuses not only on my walks of life. It is also about time and matter. It gives an exposition of the scientific development and the path to discovery in the femtouniverse. It ends with my concerns about the new world disorder and with hopes for the future, with focus on Egypt and America. As such, the book highlights three elements: life, science, and vision. Chapters one through four recount stations of my life; chapters five through seven overview the scientific work; and chapters nine and ten present a personal perspective on the prospect for world order through science and on my wish for the two cultures that I share. Chapter eight is special in that it describes the festivities and "fairy tales" that were happy moments for my family; some details about awards are included more for those not familiar with the prize culture of science.

Throughout the book, I emphasize the human dimension of my experience and the many walks that led to the appearance of a defined path on this landscape of the voyage. I found that faith, destiny, serendipity, and intuition were forces influencing this complex path. Perhaps one of the most valuable gifts for scientists (and artists) is to have intuition or insight, the direct knowing or learning of something without the conscious use of reason. Faith can provide strength and guides people toward ethical and moral behavior, unless it is wrongly exploited. In Islam, the faith of about one sixth of the world's population, the real message is clearly and unequivocally expressed in the

Holy Quran. Islam and other religions provide high standards for the life of their adherents and success becomes an integral part of the betterment of humankind.

Many might think that one can orchestrate success only with endowed intelligence or genius. In my case, I did not walk the course of my life easily—there were many challenges and obstacles. From the beginning, though, I knew the strength of passion for my work. I also knew that I am an optimist and perhaps endowed with the good genes that brighten insights. American journalists frequently ask how I could rise to such heights of success in spite of what they perceive to have been a restricted and resourceless environment. My birth in Egypt was not an obstacle to my achievement, and my life's path would not necessarily have been any easier had I grown up in any other country. Egypt planted the seeds properly and America gave me the opportunity.

I came to America for my Ph.D. education and to have a taste of science at the frontiers. Struggling to learn the English language and to overcome scientific, cultural, and political barriers, I never thought that I could one day be a faculty member at Caltech, one of America's premier universities. After being at Caltech, a science village full of giants, I didn't expect, as an assistant professor, that one day I would be honored with the Linus Pauling Chair, named after the winner of two Nobel prizes. Caltech is truly unique and I have been fortunate to have begun my scientific journey at this institution.

It is my hope that in this book the reader will find that the saga told here reflects the human experience of a person who was born, educated, and worked not only in the right place at the right time but also with passion and optimism. I also hope that through the knowledge of how discoveries are made and of what it takes to contribute to world science, this book will inspire young people to gain confidence and to feel that *it is possible!* As Sir Humphrey Davy eloquently said in 1825: "Fortunately, science, like that nature to which it belongs, is neither limited by time nor by space. It belongs to the world, and is of no country and of no age."

With this in mind, my goal here is to address the general public of both the developing and the developed world, and not specifically the specialist or select intellectuals. Most intellectuals and scientists do not like to give personal details or discuss their own achievements—it is considered poor taste. I follow this tradition in my professional practice and in my office—my awards are in my desk drawers! But here I follow a different route. I take the opportunity to describe the path to discovery, to popularize the science and its beauty, and to be explicit about the human dimension. Throughout, I mention some discoveries and contributions and the scientists behind them, and, in the hope of stimulating young people, I also mention the crowning of these achievements by the Nobel and other prizes. Naturally, I cannot list all players as this book is not intended for such a purpose.

———

This book would not have been completed without the support of a great many people. Although the subjects covered are in large part based on my science work, public lectures, and other writings, the final product came about as a result of the enthusiastic overtures of Mark Linz, the Director of the AUC Press, with whom I had many wonderful and persuasive discussions. The Press also provided me with a gifted editor, Mary Knight, who, through "oral history" sessions, has managed to kindle my interest in completing the work. I am grateful to Mary for her devotion and genuine interest to produce a high-quality book. I am also thankful to other members of the AUC Press staff, especially Neil Hewison, the Managing Editor, for his care and thoroughness, and Andrea El-Akshar for her careful and elegant design. In preparing the text, my office assistants went through several draft versions, and I wish to thank them all: Janet Davis, Sylvie Gertmenian, and Mary Sexton, and toward the end, Karen Hurst.

The science story would not have been told without the teamwork effort of members of my research group, past and present, at Caltech. I hope that they will find this saga reflects the exciting time of discovery and their days in Femtoland. Science and nonscience friends have been a continuous source of support and encouragement and to them I owe a debt of gratitude. Over the years, many have given their unqualified support. I wish to thank Spencer Baskin of Caltech and Hesham El Ashmawy in Cairo for their special care over the past few years.

Last but not least, my family has always been the source of love and enjoyment in my life. To them I owe more than words can describe. In my immediate family, my wife, Dema, has made my work possible by her understanding of my passion and by her critical support. Forever I am grateful. My daughters, Maha and Amani, and my sons, Nabeel and Hani, have given life a real joy, and with their happiness and success surely the mind can be free to write *our* story that I told here.

1

First Steps
On the Banks of the Nile

D amanhur, where I was born in 1946, is a sprawling Delta town, which now has some 200,000 inhabitants. Only 60 km southeast of Alexandria, it lies on the main agricultural road between Cairo and Alexandria and is the chief town of the Governorate of Behira. The name has changed little from its ancient pharaonic days, when it was called *Dmi-n-Hr*, "The Town of Horus," the sun god. I assume the city got its name not just because there was a temple to Horus here, but also because the sun so generously blessed the area with a good climate and bountiful harvests.

Some might say that Horus continues to watch over his city, since the sun is still generous to Damanhur, with sweet fruit like mangoes, oranges, grapes, and guavas abounding in its open-air markets. Furthermore, people in Damanhur, like most people throughout Egypt, radiate sunshine from within—they are kind and joyous, and they see the bright side of things, even when they receive bad news. In this sense, because I was touched at birth by the sun of Horus, I think I am an optimist and a true son of Damanhur.

I was born in Damanhur by chance, however, and what I remember of Damanhur comes from a later time, when I lived there and went to the university in Alexandria. My mother, Rawhia Rabi'e Dar, and father, Hassan Ahmed Zewail, were living in Desuq, a charming and serene town on the east bank of the Nile's Rosetta branch. Desuq is not far from Damanhur—it is some 20 km to the northeast. There was regular transportation by train and by car between the two towns, which made it easy to visit Damanhur. On a visit to her mother and one of her brothers in Damanhur, my mother gave birth to her first child, a son named Ahmed Hassan Zewail, on February 26. Forty days later, on *al-arba'in* as it is called, she went back to Desuq. My arrival after five years of marriage was the reason I was nicknamed *Shawqi*, "my desired one." Everyone called me by this name until I went to the university, where I became Ahmed, not Shawqi.

I don't know the true origins of my family or our name. Some believe that our roots are in ancient Egypt, others think that they are Arab in origin, especially since there is a famous gateway called Bab Zeweila, or "the gate of Zeweila," near al-Azhar University in Cairo. After the announcement of the Nobel prize, the Sudanese claimed me, because to them my name apparently derives from *Zuwel*, meaning the "man of *zuq*" (good taste) or "gentleman." Whatever the origin, I know that I am an Egyptian to the bones.

My father was born in Alexandria, on September 5, 1913, one of eight children, four boys and four girls. World War II played a key role in his destiny.

The war was felt in Alexandria along the North African front. By May 1941, the Axis Forces were already in Sallum and Mersa Matruh on the Egyptian western frontier, and Egypt was deeply involved in the conflict—on the one hand, Egypt was supposed to be Britain's ally, as dictated by the Anglo-Egyptian Treaty of 1936, and on the other hand, Egyptians under the reign of King Farouk were unhappy with Britain's occupation. By November of 1942, Field Marshal Bernard Montgomery and his army had defeated Field Marshal Erwin Rommel's army in one of the war's bloodiest battles—at al-Alamein, 110 km from Alexandria. Together with the Russian triumph at Stalingrad shortly afterwards, it marked the turning point of the war. Winston Churchill wrote: "Before Alamein we survived; after Alamein we conquered." Today there is a huge cemetery in al-Alamein, which stands as a memorial for the thousands of German, Italian, and British and Commonwealth soldiers killed in this battle.

It was during this time that the economic situation in Egypt deteriorated and people panicked. There was a run on groceries and banks and many began to leave Alexandria and Egypt. My father decided to migrate, leaving what the Egyptians call the "Bride of the Mediterranean Sea," Alexandria, for peaceful Desuq. There, he started what was then a unique business of importing and assembling bicycles and motorcycles, and later he was appointed a government official. After settling down in Desuq, he became well known in the town and was ready to get married. Rawhia, my mother, was about ten years younger than Hassan, and they were married in a traditional wedding. My mother did not see the prospective groom in person until he had formally asked for her hand from her family. They remained together for fifty years until my father died on October 22, 1992, at the age of 79.

The Zewail family is very large but concentrated mostly in Damanhur and Alexandria. In Damanhur, they are known for their cotton factories. In these two cities there are more than 120 Zewails now occupying such notable positions as university professors, judges, CEOs of both small and large businesses, and the like. I met some of them when the country was celebrating the awarding of the Nobel prize, although many of them I did not know before moving to the United States.

My mother's family is relatively small and they are mostly from Desuq and other neighboring cities. She had a sister and three brothers; after my arrival, she gave birth to three girls. My sisters were named after our grandmothers and the sisters of my parents, as I was named after my grandfather. These old given names were replaced with modern nicknames—Hanem for Nafisa, Seham for Khadra, and Nana for Nema. According to Egyptian tradition, our middle name is our father's first name, Hassan.

Desuq was the home of the immediate family, but we had a much bigger family—the people of Desuq. Families knew each other well, shared in happy and difficult times, and valued interdependence, socially and financially. I do not recall there being a bank in Desuq; instead, people formed a group called a *gam 'iya*, pooling their money to help each family in turn, using a rotation process. My family, like others, were sensitive to the feelings of the community. We were forbidden, for example, to have the sound of a radio loud enough to be heard outside our rooms for forty days following a death in the town. These community feelings and interests were clearly important parts of my first steps in Desuq.

What is so special about Desuq is that it is on the Nile, and the Nile is part of Egypt's ancient heritage. There is still a saying that after you've drunk water from the Nile, you will always return to Egypt. This is a descriptive expression, because it reveals both the nation's sense of community and its willingness to open its hearts and homes to people from outside Egypt. Egypt is the gift of the Nile, as the Greek historian Herodotus said many centuries ago, in about 450 BC. The Nile is a spectacular river that has flowed for eons with the same regularity, and it is this eternity that defines the Egyptian character.

As a child in Desuq, I used to walk along the road that was parallel to the Nile. This is a special road. It follows the Nile all the way to Rosetta, where the famous stone was found in 1799. The stone, now in the British Museum in London, records the gratitude of the chief priests of Egypt to the pharaoh at the time (early in the second century before Christ), Ptolemy V. It's a remarkable monument because it's in two languages, Egyptian and Greek, and three scripts, hieroglyphs, demotic, and Greek. (Demotic is a "shorthand" form of hieroglyphs, developed in the later pharaonic period.) The stone was recovered by a French officer during Napoleon's expedition, and ultimately supplied Jean-François Champollion with the key to the decipherment of the ancient Egyptian language in 1822—he compared the words in Greek to the Egyptian hieroglyphic and demotic signs, and from this study he decoded the Egyptian signs and words. Rosetta is also an important port city, and thousands of traders and government officials and other travelers used to arrive in Egypt at Rosetta. They would then travel up the Nile by boat—

or along the road I just mentioned—to Cairo and other places. These visitors would stop along their journey up the river at Desuq to take a rest or to do business.

Much of that importance of the place still remains and there is more—it has spiritual depth. In the center of the town is the mosque of Sidi Ibrahim al-Desuqi, "Mr. Ibrahim of Desuq." Sidi Ibrahim was an Egyptian scholar and a sufi. He was a student of another famous sufi, Ahmed al-Badawi, who is celebrated, especially in Tanta, where there is a mosque in his name. Some say the word *sufi* comes from the Arabic root with the letters *sad/fa/waw*, and thus is related to words like *safw*, which mean "clarity, pureness, or sincerity"; it is also related to the word *Mustafa*, which is a name for the Prophet Mohammed, meaning "the chosen one, the choicest, best, most perfect." Most Arabic-language experts claim the word is derived from the root *sad/waw/fa*, transposing the final two root letters, which also makes sense, because *suf*, with the long *u*, means "wool," and sufis originally wore woolen garments.

The Sidi Ibrahim al-Desuqi mosque was very important in my life because it defined my early childhood. As children, we used to gravitate to the mosque. We would go at dawn and study. When I look back at my life, I realize that this mosque was the nucleus for scholarship at that age. By this I mean that we used to go to the mosque to *study*, which is traditional in Islam. The mosque is not just for prayer; it is also for scholarship. It has a sacredness and with its beautiful, spacious architecture of domes, columns, and minarets, it radiates the power of respect. During the holy month of Ramadan, my friends and I would always meet after *iftar* (the meal that breaks the fast at sunset) and go to the mosque. Afterwards, either we would go to my home or I would go to their homes, but in any case, we would study until dawn, and then we would go to pray. So the mosque was central to my life and to the lives of the townspeople. The mosque was like a glue to keep everyone working and living together in harmony.

Sidi Ibrahim was just a few meters from our house. There were many streets and alleys that branched out from it and our house was on one of these streets. As a result, we could hear the prayers five times a day. The

Friday prayer was special and my family encouraged our regular participation. The mosque had a positive effect on us and on our behavior. We never heard, or at least I don't remember hearing, of a boy smoking hashish or getting involved with drugs or drinking. Some were trying to learn how to smoke a cigarette, but never in front of their parents. We never heard of violence on the streets. The moral and ethical influence of the mosque created a simple and sheltered environment that was also exciting. I vividly recall the sunset during the month of Ramadan when people were hurrying home to the tranquil sound of prayer in the background, and all shops closed down for *iftar* just before the boom of the cannon signaled the time for us to eat.

All the shopkeepers around the mosque knew me by my first name; they knew my father and they knew my family. I could buy things from the grocery, for example, and I didn't have to pay. They got the money from my father. A sense of security and trust existed there and it set a standard for community behavior. I remember I used to sit on a wooden bench, with 'Amm ("Uncle") Hamouda, who owned a grocery store and who was the father of one of my friends, Mohammed. The store was across the street from the mosque, and I would welcome the opportunity to ask for advice from 'Amm Hamouda, but more importantly to listen to him and to his wisdom—I respected him and he liked me.

As youngsters we were attracted to, not repelled by, such an institution of faith, and the leaders of the mosque continually encouraged scholarship. We saw the simplicity and the enlightenment of the religion, but not the rigidity and dogma I sometimes see today. We saw scholarship in thinking and analyzing and repeatedly we were told of the fundamental role of science and knowledge in our lives. After all, we were told again and again, the first message revealed to the Prophet begins with the word *Iqra!* ("Read!"). My family supported this attitude and I do not recall incidents in which they imposed rigidity in thought or behavior.

Growing up in Desuq, I had no exotic desires to, for instance, go to Spain for summer vacation or drive to school in a BMW or have private lessons at home. When I see my own children taking classes in swimming, art, basketball, soccer, and violin, I feel that in my adolescence I must have been living on another planet. My soccer balls were made of used (but clean) socks, my hobbies were limited to reading, listening to music, and playing backgammon and cards, and my travel all took place within 100 or so kilometers. But the fundamental forces in life were abundantly present—the love of my parents, their confidence in me, and the peaceful home I had in a middle-class family, with all the expected family quarrels.

Growing up I do not recall being punished except on one occasion. I thought I knew how to drive a car because I had figured out how it worked—*theoretically*. When my uncle's car was parked near a canal, I tried the experiment without realizing that theory and experiment could be far apart. The car very nearly plunged into the canal and if it were not for my good fortune I would have died. I got what I deserved from my father, though. He had taught me many practical things, including bike riding, which I enjoy to this day, but I don't know why I didn't ask him for driving lessons, perhaps because I didn't anticipate owning a car.

My father was a dedicated person, and he combined two things that I hope I have followed in my life. He was very sincere about his work and his family, and he made us all laugh and have fun until the last day I saw him, just before he passed away; at that time I was living in America and had come to see him by way of Europe. He always believed that "Life is too short—enjoy it." He enjoyed his time with people and everyone who knew him, and I think they liked and admired him—'Amm Hassan. I admired his wisdom too; life is a journey that you have to learn to enjoy—and he did! Perhaps the most valuable thing he taught me was that there is no contradiction between devotion to work and enjoyment of life and people.

My mother is a devout person and always says her five daily prayers on time, including the one at dawn. Her name, Rawhia, comes from the word *ruh*, or "spirit," and she is indeed spiritual. Only 18 when she married my father, her official record of birth is February 2, 1922; because that date was registered after the fact, it is uncertain. My mother now is close to 80 years old. She is a kind and serious person and has devoted her life to her children. Even today, she worries about us and about me, with lots of tears. Such devotion from the age of 18 to 80 is surely heroic, especially by the standards of the modern world! My mother is intuitive and smart, but she wasn't educated formally. She saw her job as creating a stable family environment and taking care of the household and finances. She was central to the peace and contentment of the home and was certainly the driving force supporting my education.

I went to a state school, which was tuition-free in Egypt, and the family was supportive of whatever direction my achievements would permit. Throughout my schooling, I strived to achieve the best possible, though the drive came from within. Incidentally, the alphabet did help in pushing me to the front of things. When I was born, as I mentioned, my father named me Ahmed. In so doing, he did me a favor. With the *A* in Ahmed, I came at or near the top of listings in schools and elsewhere, since in Arabic we list people by their first names, not their last, as is the custom in most Western countries. In America I lost this privilege as the *Z* of Zewail took over and I now appear toward the end of alphabetical listings.

Education in Egypt was of excellent quality. It had the elements of healthy competition and was centered in a community environment. Moreover, the teachers were highly respected and the student–teacher relationship was genuine and supportive and not customized around moneymaking private lessons. The community as a whole respected and valued education—if you really excelled, the community would take notice of you. Desuq would know that So-and-so was an excellent student, and people would offer encouraging comments. Additionally, the educational achievements paid out social benefits. They conferred a unique high-status position for marriage into a well-off family. As people used to say, "they [the family] are investing in the future." It's clear that the positive memories of my education exceed any negative ones.

The worst thing I remember about school was the intense memorization that was required in some subjects, like the social sciences or languages. These subjects were taught strictly and formally. Emphasis was placed on the memorization of full names, for example, Mohammed ibn Rushdi ibn 'Ali ibn al-Khalif—but what did he really *do* that is exciting?

How did his work fit into the big picture? My interest has always been in analytical subjects, with the desire to ask why and how. It's ironic that one of my most enjoyable hobbies now is reading history. I have a library of diverse history books and I enjoy the subject immensely, but I didn't as a youth.

Another aspect I didn't like was the use of corporal punishment in primary schools. The punishments were never so severe that they were abusive, but the whole idea was an assault on my sense of what a school should be and what educators should do for their pupils. When the occasional disruptive incident occurred, sometimes the teachers would strike the students. I remember once, the children did not like one of the Arabic teachers, so we all decided (I don't remember how) to do something to tease him. He lost his temper and slapped me on the face. When my father learned about this incident, he was displeased, especially since he knew I was a good student. He came to the school and lodged a formal complaint in protest. He subsequently received an apology from the headmaster.

Those negative elements were counterbalanced by a certain degree of freedom to run and play and let off steam. I learned to play basketball, for example, while I was in preparatory school, and there was always the recess time, when I would get a morning snack. I vividly remember the taste of the fresh falafel sandwiches made by our local street vendor. His name was 'Amm Ibrahim, and I would run to his cart, which was parked just outside the perimeter of the school grounds near the train station, and say, "Please, I need a falafel sandwich." I would watch as he formed the dough, dropped it in the oil, and then took it out piping hot a few seconds later—what a sandwich! And he wouldn't take money, because he would get that from my father, and I would just run back to the school. I still enjoy falafel sandwiches and I always eat them in the first days of my arrival in Cairo.

The activities in preparatory school, which is between the primary and secondary schools in the Egyptian system, were memorable and enjoyable. For example, I took part in a play, and although I have forgotten the role I played, I remember having a lot of fun taking part in it. We didn't have a regular theater, but we made do with imagination and creativity. For example, we had to make our own curtain and we did it with a line of students, and I remember being part of this. We would stand side by side to form the curtain. Someone announcing "Ladies and Gentlemen!" would be our cue to quickly jump down on our haunches so the "curtain" could open. It was fun and taught us how to be together and how to enjoy ourselves socially. We also went on field trips to historic places and had picnics along the Nile.

During school vacations and when my father had his vacation from his government job, we would go to the Zewails' chalet on the beach in Alexandria. That was a big treat for me. The chalet was owned by some of the Zewails who were better off, but other members of the family were welcomed. We went in July or August, and we would be joined by relatives. We spent the time playing games like beachball or backgammon, chatting, swimming, and eating fish. At night we would either stay with relatives in Alexandria or go back to Desuq. Interestingly, I was more inclined to use the beach time for relaxation and general reading—the time for developing swimming skills must have been limited since I now know my real skill in this sport leaves a lot to be desired.

I also used to use the vacation to read ahead for the following year's subjects. I was inquisitive and eager to get back to my studies. Even as a young child, I dreamed of going to the university. For me, the university was something special, because of my passion for learning and because of its prestige. My father had what might be called a basic education, one sufficient to earn a post in the civil service. In his day, I was told, you couldn't get into the university unless your father owned land or was rich. It was also a matter of *wasta*, or "influence," for a select group. This was to change in 1952.

The Free Officers Revolution, which overthrew King Farouk, opened up opportunities for the youth in Egypt. At the time I was six years old, just going to the first grade. Gamal 'Abd al-Nasser, the charismatic leader of the revolution, said in his speeches: "We're all equal. We're all the same." That meant that *ibn al-fallah* (the son of the peasant) and *ibn ra'is al-gumhuriya* (the son of the president) could both go to the same university. This made us aware that this was a new era for all of us and it gave us hope. By 1956, when I was ten, I was so excited to see the first Egyptian-born president now in charge, with a new future ahead of us, that I decided to write to him. So I wrote to President Nasser and told him *Rabbina yiwaffaqak wa-yiwaffaq Misr* ("May the Lord give you and Egypt success").

I still have his reply to me, dated January 11, 1956, and remember the thrill of seeing where he wrote my name by hand and signed the letter. In retrospect, it was as if he was predicting my future in science. He wrote, from the Office of the President:

> My son Ahmed, I wish you the very best . . . . I received your letter, which expresses your thoughtful sentiments, and this letter has had a great effect on me. I pray to God to protect you to remain essential to Egypt's bright future. I ask you to continue with patience and passion in harvesting *al-'ilm* [knowledge, science], armed with good behavior and good thought so you can participate in the future of building the great Egypt.

It was about this time that I was introduced to Umm Kulthum's singing by a very special uncle, Uncle Rizq Dar, my mother's brother. He and my mother were close and she became like a mother to him, especially after their mother's death, when he was living in the same building with us. He was a self-taught person, meaning he didn't go to college, but he was a voracious reader. He was the one who introduced me to reading newspapers critically; he showed me how to read an editorial and how to grasp the impact of what I was reading. Like my father, he too was good with people.

With Uncle Rizq I spent a lot of time, especially in the summer. He had become a successful businessman in import–export, and he had a big workshop for cars. He was well-off and owned a three-story house in Desuq at a time when most people rented an apartment. At his place I learned backgammon and intermingled with many of his friends. I had a special relationship with him and he was pleased with my success in school. I still remember him as a wise and supportive uncle who wished to see me reach the highest goals. From my father and mother I learned about the present, day-to-day life; with my uncle I dreamed about the future.

For a treat, Uncle Rizq would take me to Cairo to hear Umm Kulthum, a lady who was to become an important part of my life. If there is one thing that has been consistent in enhancing my mood, it's Umm Kulthum. Umm Kulthum came from a village in Egypt and rose to become the "Pyramid of Arabic Song." She sang poetry in classical Arabic and sang passionately about love. My appreciation of her songs began when I was in preparatory school, about age 13. Throughout my study days in Egypt, the radio would be next to me, and I would go through all the channels to find her voice, because we didn't yet have LPs or tapes or CDs. I knew what time her songs would be broadcast on the different channels, Sawt al-'Arab, Cairo Broadcasting 1, Middle East channel, and so on. I would just keep turning the dial so I could have her songs in the background as often as possible while I was studying in my room.

Omar Sharif, the famous Egyptian actor, asked: "Why do we feel so connected to her?" Perhaps each of us hears our own story in her songs. And, I would add, her singing inspires in us what is called in Arabic *tarab*. There is no direct translation for this word into English, but perhaps "ecstasy" comes closest. I recall almost every one of her concerts and especially the one in 1964 when she sang "Inta 'Umri"—"You are My Life." I felt that all of Egypt and the Arab world were enjoying her *tarab* that evening. The words were powerful:

> O my love
> Come, enough, we've already missed so much
> O love of my soul
> What I saw, what I saw before my eyes saw you was a
> wasted life
> How can it even be counted? You are my life
> Which began its morning with your light
> You, you are my life

This was the first song composed for her by another famous Egyptian, Mohammed 'Abd al-Wahab. He was a modernist and she was a classicist, and in their collaboration the two joined to reach *al-qimma*—the summit—of Arabic song in "Inta 'Umri."

With the passion I developed for Umm Kulthum, it was a truly special thrill to go with Uncle Rizq to one of her live concerts—she appeared every first Thursday of the month in season. Her concerts were broadcast live and the streets were empty. She would give three *waslat* (performances), with extended songs, each one of which was like a concert in itself. I knew all the details of the songs of the season—the musical composition, the lyrics, and even some touches of her own that she introduced on different occasions. The quality was outstanding. To Egyptians and to the Arabs, Umm Kulthum was like Mozart and Beethoven are to Westerners who love classical music. When she died, I went into mourning, as did millions of like-minded lovers of her art. But the voice of Kawkab al-Sharq ("The Star of the East") never died; it remains, echoing love and passion. Classics such as "Ruba'iyat al-Khayyam," "al-Atlal," "Ana fi Intazarak," and many others are still part of the daily life of millions, not only in Egypt, but all over the world.

I have been listening to Umm Kulthum for forty years and derive real joy from her voice. It's amazing how she has stayed with me and contributed to the shaping of my sentimental feelings. At Caltech, I have a stereo in my office where I play her songs, and along with photos of my family, my wife, and my children, I have one of her near my desk. Even now, when I'm pressured, with work, with four secretaries, faxes, e-mails—the whole world—I turn on that CD player and I am relaxed by her voice in the background. It is enough to hear a classic like the one composed by the renowned Sayyid Mekawi, "Ya Msahharni." Recently, a Public Broadcasting Service (PBS) documentary featured her life and work, reflecting the immense reach of her voice beyond Egypt.

This background music did not distract me from learning. On the contrary, it enabled me to handle many hours of study with pleasure. I have a passion for learning, and as my mother used to say, I was always intrigued and excited about learning new things. The family predicted the future—a sign was posted on my door reading "Dr. Ahmed" when I was in preparatory school. I did not have a sense of guilt about having to study and this came from within, without any family prodding. My father used to come to my room and tell me I didn't have to kill myself over my studies. But then, if I got a score of, say, 98 out of 100, he would joke with me, "*Ya-bni*, my son, what happened to the other two?" It was all in good fun. I had a small room, which was highly organized, and at late hours during a break they would visit me and we would discuss family matters.

The *thanawiya* (secondary) school in Egypt was academically strong and had programs for disciplinary and extracurricular activities. In the morning, we would come into the courtyard where the flag was raised, and we would all sing the national anthem. We were proud to be Egyptians, proud of our country, and the morning anthem heightened our self-confidence and self-esteem. Besides the academic work, there was time to pursue hobbies. In my case, I took part in art and photography activities. There were two kinds of photography projects that I got involved in. One was just to learn how to take photographs of friends and to develop them. I still have a number of these. I was also involved in enlarging a famous person's portrait. For example, we would take a small portrait of Nasser, typical of the time, and learn how to magnify it by hand, dividing the photograph into twenty or thirty graphed blocks. We would use carbon pens to shadow it and do other things to manipulate the image. At the end, we had a big, impressive portrait.

But the academic competition was fierce, because at the end of three years there was a nationwide exam called the *thanawiya 'amma*. Each student competed with every other student in the country, not just the twenty or so in his or her local class, and the scores determined which students would enter which university and which department. It wasn't like in the United States, for example, where a student chooses whatever course of study he or she would prefer. In Egypt it was all determined by the scores, and the students with the highest scores were selected to study for the most prestigious professions. During my last year of secondary school, the pressure of the upcoming exam made life more intense, but I was comfortable with my progress. All through the previous years, I loved solving problems in mechanics, physics, and chemistry and other analytical challenges. I also enjoyed explaining things to others in the class.

Experimentally, I was interested in observing how things worked, so I built a little "instrument" in my bedroom using an Arabic coffee burner as the heater. I wondered how and why a substance like wood—a solid—changes from a solid into a gas when it burns. That transformation just intrigued me so much! So I put some wood in a test tube, connected with a cork to an L-shaped glass tube, and then I burned the wood to see how the gas would come out at the end of the tube. In the company of a friend, Fathy Gaweish, I then used a match to see a flame. I was observing the transformation of one substance to another—eureka! I came close to burning the room and my mother reminds me of this incident to this day.

The final exam of the *thanawiya 'amma* passed uneventfully for me. The scoring was done by subject, and I passed Arabic and history, but I scored very high in chemistry, physics, and mathematics—it was abundantly clear that it was the orientation to science that was driving me. To enter the university, one had to apply, and the student's score determined the admission to the different faculties. I knew that I had the chance of being admitted to either Cairo or Alexandria University. But the government—this was still under Nasser—established an institute *(ma 'had)* system, so there was an institute for agriculture and an institute for every kind of technical applied field. As it turns out, one of the institutes was in Kafr al-Sheikh, near to Desuq. After some consideration, my father thought I could go to this institute, get a B.S. from there, then go on in life as an agricultural engineer. But I wanted to go to the university; in Egypt universities are more prestigious than institutes. Fortunately, my mother and Uncle Rizq supported my decision, even if the expenses were higher.

I then applied to Maktab al-Tansiq (the placement office), which was in charge of assigning students to the various faculties and universities throughout Egypt based on their test scores. In those days the top disciplines were engineering and medicine, followed by pharmacy and science. After a few weeks, I got the note saying that I had been admitted to the Faculty of Science (equivalent to a US college of sciences) at Alexandria University. I was thrilled! I didn't think of how much money I would make as a graduate, but I *was* thinking of the great future ahead—the potential for learning at the highest level.

But the boy from Damanhur and Desuq had to make the transition to Alexandria, after a send-off party by my friends at Desuq's club on the Nile. There were some problems with this transition. Culturally, Desuq had a comfortable, sheltered environment. I didn't know much about the cosmopolitan city of Alexandria and its people. In Desuq, boys and girls were separated in two different schools, and I still recall waiting with my friends, Ahmed Barari, Nabeel al-Sanhoury, and Mohammed Hamouda, until we could see the girls coming out from their school—that was our biggest adventure! In Alexandria University, young men and women studied together. Studies in Desuq's schools were also very different from those at the university level—I didn't know what to expect. And there was the financial burden created by the need to live in Alexandria. Perhaps the most difficult part was leaving my family for the first time in my life.

2

The Gate to Science
The Alexandria Years

Some people think that Alexandria is nothing but a beach, and in fact, the city hugs the shoreline, making it one of the world's longest and narrowest cities. Egyptians flock to Alexandria's beaches in the summertime because, being on the sea, it's cool. There is a continuous breeze that freshens the air and soothes people's spirits. The natural harbor and the healthful *bahari* (north) breezes are said to have been prime considerations that Alexander the Great took into account in 331 BC when he founded the city bearing his name. We now know that he was taking the lead from his pharaonic predecessors, since marine archaeologists, working underwater beginning in the 1990s, have discovered remnants of harbor works that date to a time at least one thousand years earlier than Alexander. The modern Egyptians of Alexandria (with a population of more than 4 million) and of the whole country (near 70 million) consider *al-Iskandariya* the "Bride of the Mediterranean."

The ancient Greeks made themselves at home in Alexandria, and just like people today, they flocked to the beaches in summer to enjoy the sea and the air and, according to Strabo, an ancient Greek geographer who spent several years in Egypt, joyous merrymaking often lasted far into the night. This fun-filled sea-and-sand Alexandria was the Alexandria of my earliest childhood, as I've related, since my family spent time in the summer at the Zewails' chalet. But in my young adulthood, Alexandria was different. In Desuq we only had one *nadi* (club), located on the Nile side, but in Alexandria numerous clubs existed—Sporting, Yacht, Automobile, Smouha, and others. In Alex, as some Egyptians call it, the monuments and big towers make one feel the greatness of the city. These monuments reflect the rich Greco-Egyptian and Roman-Egyptian periods in the history of the city.

Remarkably, the architecture of the city is enough to tell the story of the continuous change of different civilizations: pharaonic, Greek, Roman, Coptic, and Islamic. The remains of the legendary Pharos lighthouse, one of the Seven Wonders of the ancient world, Pompey's Pillar, Qaitbay Fort, the Catacombs of Kom al-Shuqafa, Abu al-Abbas mosque, and the Antoniadis and Montazah palaces and gardens are shining examples of the greatness of Alexandria. For the boy from Desuq, the immediate impact of Alexandria came from its beautiful corniche, elegant cafés and patisseries, wide boulevards, and historic alleys and hotels.

In the famous Cecil Hotel on Midan Sa'd Zaghlul, the well-known author Lawrence Durrell, who lived extravagantly and colorfully for two and a half years in wartime Alexandria, told the story of Darley and Justine in *The Alexandria Quartet*. I read this masterpiece later—not in Alexandria but in Philadelphia! Many historians, novelists, and intellectuals visited nearby Pastroudis Café–Patisserie, Trianon Patisserie, and Venous Café–Patisserie as I did when I came to Alexandria. Sitting in Desuq's club I didn't hear the quiet flow of the Nile, while in Alexandria the crashing waves of the Mediterranean were loud but sounded like music.

I came to Alexandria not to study its history but to go through its gate of science, the university, to learn and acquire new knowledge. Since ancient times, Alexandria has had a tradition not only as the bride of the sea but also as a place of enlightenment. The Library of Alexandria—the Bibliotheca Alexandrina—stood as a beacon to all seekers of knowledge from around the world and especially those from the Mediterranean countries. In 1963, my first year in Alexandria, I was thinking only of the city's modern university and the exciting academic possibilities ahead, but of course there is a link between past and present. When I arrived in the United States and mentioned that I was a graduate of the University of Alexandria, I was asked: Who burned the Great Library of Alexandria? They also wondered: In the same place where that ancient repository of knowledge stood, could another now take its place for the modern world? Could the modern Egyptian scholars be as good as the ancient Alexandrian scholars?

Alexander of Macedonia intended to make Alexandria the most influential cultural and commercial center of the Western world and to replace Memphis as Egypt's capital. But for Alexandria to become the center of learning and knowledge for centuries, the leadership had to be visionary, and this was true for both Alexander and for his immediate successors, the first three Ptolemies. Aristotle was Alexander's tutor, and this intellectual linkage made Alexander interested not only in politics and war but also in science and art—throughout history, nations do not go forward without their leaders' appreciation of science and scholars.

The Museum and Library of Alexandria supported many of the best minds of the time, including the mathematician Euclid, the man of medicine Herophilus, the poets Theocritus and Zenodotus, and Archimedes, known for exclaiming "Eureka!" ("I found it!") while leaping from his bath when he had a sudden insight into the physics of floating bodies, a topic he studied in Alexandria and Syracuse in Sicily. Moreover, some of the most important scientific studies in history were made in Alexandria. These include the first measurement of the circumference of the Earth by the brilliant polymath Eratosthenes. The shores of wisdom, as they were described by Derek Flower, began to decline with the great fire that ravaged the library at the time of Caesar's naval war in 48 BC—Cleopatra's era—and its subsequent destruction occurred over time. Alexandria is about to inaugurate a new library, grand in structure. As a member of the board of trustees and a son of Alexandria, it is my hope that this new historic initiative will attract the best minds back to Alexandria, nationally and internationally, just as it did more than two millennia ago.

I was attracted to the University of Alexandria without knowing of all of these past achievements, not even knowing its detailed history prior to the 1952 revolution. The nucleus of the modern University of Alexandria had its beginning in 1938 in the form of two satellite faculties—Arts and Law—of King Fouad I University in Cairo. Alexandria's Faculty of Engineering was established in 1941. To meet the needs of the people of Alexandria, the University of Alexandria, formerly known as King Farouk I University, became a separate entity in August of 1942, with four additional faculties: Science, Commerce, Medicine, and Agriculture. In 1952, the name was changed to the University of Alexandria and since then other faculties have been added. The total number of students was about one thousand in 1942–43, whereas today there are more than 100,000, almost equally made up of male and female students.

The first time I visited the university's campus was with my uncle Rizq. I had to go to Kulliyat al-'Ulum, the Faculty of Science, which was in Muharram Bek in Alexandria, to register as a new student. As we walked along the street, the first thing we noticed was a large wrought-iron gate and a plaque with the words "University of Alexandria, Kulliyat al-'Ulum." There was a guard on the left as we entered the gates of the campus, and directly in front of us was an enormously inclined staircase on the campus grounds, totally open to the air. It was so steep, its slope so high, that when we reached the top, we felt like eagles, and we could view the whole campus from this lofty perch. The ten or so large buildings of the Muharram Bek campus are situated on a high plateau, and the stairs are common to all the different buildings.

That first day with my uncle, in late summer in 1963, I remember going up those stairs, and even before I reached the pinnacle, tears flowed from my eyes. Tears flowed because now, for the first time in my life, I was seeing with my own eyes the *haram*, the sacred precinct, of scholars: a hallowed slice of earth radiating the intellectual interests of its devotees, in the midst of quiet, serene trees and shrubs and grass-lined pathways. Each building was like a shrine to the individual sciences, one for geology, one for mathematics, one for physics, one for chemistry, and

so on. We had to climb up the stairs to see them—the buildings are bare-
ly visible from the street—but once up there, we had the view of the
whole campus. The view was invigorating and just simply beautiful!

We have a saying, *al-'ilm ka-l-ma' wa-hawa'*, which was first said
by the scholar Dr. Taha Hussein. It means "Knowledge—or science—is
like water and air." Without water and air you can't live as a human
being, and climbing up to this *haram* was like coming to the source of
all water and air. As we looked around, we saw university professors in
their trademark white coats, with suits and ties underneath, busily going
from one building to another or from office or classroom to laboratory.
There were special parking lots for the faculty and we saw imported
American and European cars that displayed the university insignia on
the windshield. We overheard professors and graduate students engaged
in serious discussions of their work. I guess tears flowed down my
cheeks from excitement and anxiety, too. Could I one day be one of
these scholars, spending my days in this exciting university *haram*?
That was the question.

Uncle Rizq must have been sympathetic, since he consoled me, but
I also think he was almost as excited as I was. The whole family shared
in my eagerness and happiness, but Uncle Rizq was particularly interested in sharing these moments with me. On this special day we went to
a fancy place on the corniche and we ate Alexandrian food at Darwish
Restaurant, still in existence today. Other members of my family were
also helping out. In order to attend the university and to minimize the
cost, it was decided that I would stay in Muharram Bek with my father's
relatives. I didn't like the situation, but I tried it out. I then moved to a
chalet in Sidi Bishr that had been built on the second floor of the house
of 'Abduh ('Abd al-Gawad), the son of my father's sister. It proved to
be too far from the university. Finally the decision was made for me to
live in Damanhur, where Uncle 'Ali had an apartment. Again, I had my
own room for study—and of course, Umm Kulthum was always in the
background.

Every day I would get up early to take the train to Alexandria. The
commuter trains were very good—fast, frequent, and reliable. There

were easily a hundred of us from the faculties of Engineering, Science, Literature, Law, and others, who regularly boarded the early trains between 6:00 and 9:00 A.M. for Alexandria. We usually returned between 5:00 and 8:00 P.M. Many train riders are well known today, such as Omar Batisha, who is now the head of Egyptian broadcasting.

One aspect that made living in Damanhur and having to take the train every morning and evening actually agreeable—desirable, even— was the fact that there was a high proportion of young women on the trains. On the train some of us were more assertive with these attractive girls from Damanhur. Omar tells me that I was always quiet, reading to myself and studying. He remembers it that way—it's his official version. But many of us—including me occasionally—kept going back and forth between our little gaggle of boys to the larger crowd of beautiful girls. We'd joke and laugh and before you knew it, we had arrived at Misr Station (the downtown station in Alexandria), from which some of us would go to Muharram Bek, walking a short distance, and others would board the tram for a few stations and then walk to the university's other faculties in Shatby and other nearby places. These train trips lasted for the following years of college, except for a short stint when I shared a villa in Alexandria with a student from Desuq, the son of our family's doctor. In Damanhur I got to know a few colleagues like Ragae El Gibaly, and with them I used to practice being a future *mu'id*.

In our freshman year at the Faculty of Science, we picked four subjects to study. I chose mathematics, chemistry, physics, and geology. In successive years we would drop a subject, one by one, until by the third year, we were down to two. This didn't mean just four courses—it meant four general areas of study. It wasn't like American universities, for example, with a core curriculum, where you might take history, a foreign language, or psychology in addition to your science and math courses. In Egypt you were supposed to have taken all of this general, broad educational curriculum in high school, and in the university you were to become serious about your major field. In my case this was science. In that sense, it was almost like embarking on graduate work in the United States.

The classes were exemplary. Many of the professors were worth emulating; they were role models for us. They had a professionalism about their responsibilities to their students that should be a goal for many university professors and lecturers today. They prepared their lessons in advance and were always prompt: if a lecture was at nine, it started exactly at nine. Students didn't arrive late and there was no foolishness or classroom distractions that took away from instruction time. Again this went along the lines of the *haiba*, or sacred awe and reverence, that one felt on entering the university campus. That first year, I took a mathematics (calculus) class with Professor Shehata Gouda. He was meticulous in his proofs and his problem solving; he would literally cover all three boards with the steps of his solution, integration, differentiation, writing all the equations clearly so everyone in the auditorium could see and understand—we took freshman classes in a new building in Shatby, and the lecture hall held nearly five hundred students.

I remember vividly that on many occasions Professor Shehata would write out a problem and ask for a volunteer to solve the problem or he would write out a solution and ask whether any step could be eliminated or whether a step had been overlooked. "Ahmed, come here!" I would go up on the stage in front of all those students and write out how to solve that equation. Even today, when I do mathematics or help my children with math, I use that same meticulousness in order to not be too quick and inadvertently make mistakes. I owe much to Dr. Shehata for being such a positive role model in precision and thoroughness. Equally meticulous was my professor of geology, Dr. al-Shinawy, an elegant and refined man. In geology we studied crystallography of rocks and minerals to get an image of the geological formation over time of the world and of Egypt.

The course lectures were mostly conducted in Arabic and the lecture notes and course books were in Arabic, except for the equations and formulas, which were done universally with the same characters; in later years, some of our notes were in English. In freshman year, there was no English per se, but we occasionally consulted textbooks written in English, such as those we borrowed from or used in the library.

Geology had a lot of Latin words in it, for example, the names of fossils and minerals, and we had to memorize these, making the subject less attractive to me.

In all of my classes, of course, I was striving to score the highest grade, what's called "excellent" —85% or higher. In my freshmen year, I scored excellent or very good in all my subjects, so I was considered a very good student, very promising. To be frank, this wasn't too much of a surprise to me, because I was taking nothing but science courses or courses related to science—no history, no social sciences, no languages. It was a perfect match to what I like to do. As a result of my high grades, there was a short notice about me in *al-Akhbar* newspaper, with a photograph, to let the country know about my success. That was actually my first mention in any newspaper and the first time my photo was published. People in Desuq were proud—they either got a copy or got to see a copy and everyone I knew was happy for me. Another result of my obtaining high grades was that I would be paid a monthly stipend of LE 13, a grand sum for such an achievement in those days, probably equivalent to almost thirty times that amount today; university graduates were getting LE 17.

During the summer of that first year, I was back in Desuq. I spent some time with my family and a lot of time reading. Reading was what excited me the most. I bought a number of books, including those for the second-year courses, to get a head start. I was eager to continue and I didn't want to lose any time. I was also convinced that in order to advance one had to learn from the masters. Isaac Newton put it well when he said: "If I have seen so far it is only because I have stood on the shoulders of giants." He had learned from Galileo and the other great scientists who preceded him and he was able to go on. I began to read about the work of famous scientists and found no limits to the ocean of knowledge.

Sometimes, however, I'd take a break to watch television. We were fortunate to get one in the early 1960s, as not everyone in our town was able to afford one. I'd go for a bike ride along the Nile just at sunset, when the air was beginning to cool down, and when I came back, I would watch the television for a little while. I especially enjoyed programs in which our most notable writers and scholars would speak. My family, like many others, watched when the country honored their achievements, with the president himself presenting the award. Egypt was rich with such people: in literature and languages, Taha Hussein, Tawfiq al-Hakim, Mahmoud al-'Aqqad, Naguib Mahfouz; in arts and music, Mohammed 'Abd al-Wahab, Umm Kulthum, 'Abd al-Halim Hafez, Farid al-Atrash, Faten Hamama; and in other areas—Mohammed Hassanein Heikal (journalism), Ahmed Riad Turk (science), Mustafa Musharafa (science), and many others. Again I would privately ask myself the same question that I asked on the first day of climbing the university staircase: would I ever be like one of those scholars? I wonder now how crazy I was at that age not to be thinking about making money or having the fanciest car, but I was possessed, I guess, by this idea of gaining knowledge and prestige—you are what you know!

In my second year of study, we were required to drop one of the four subjects of the first year. Reluctantly I dropped mathematics, and studied physics, chemistry, and geology. I took four courses in physics—sound, optics, properties of matter, and heat and thermodynamics—and I enjoyed these courses in part because of the mathematics involved in them. I scored distinction in physics. Although chemistry had less mathematics and more memorization, I liked the focus on the how and the why, how substances behave and why they interact. I scored very high grades overall, which was significant, since it was at the end of the second year when the faculty selected a small group for special study who were known by the English word "special." There were specials in chemistry, specials in physics, specials in geology, and so on, but you could be a special in only one subject.

The great advantage of being selected special was that in the third and fourth years I didn't have to take anything but my special subject, chemistry. I felt that my horizons were just beginning to expand, because it was known that specials would become mu 'ids ("demonstrators," equivalent to a graduate teaching/research assistant) and then, if you became a mu 'id, you would go on to become a university professor after obtaining a Ph.D. So making it to special was a big thing.

There were seven of us in the chemistry group, G-7, and there were similar numbers of specials in the other sciences of physics, math, and geology. That meant there was a total of perhaps thirty to fifty specials out of nearly five hundred students in the general class. The minute it became known that I belong to this special group, the students, friends, and even the nonuniversity people began to call me doctor, because they thought I was destined to go in this direction. I certainly felt special being one of this special group.

Making it to special was based on scholastic achievement and test scores. There was no *wasta* ("influence") from a well-connected relative or business contact; there wasn't anyone who could speak on your behalf without your meriting the place yourself. Many of the *mu'id*s came from small villages and their families didn't have a particularly high social status. It was all done in an honest, professional way. Once you became a special, the senior specials ahead of you who had already been appointed *mu'id* knew that in two years you might become one of their colleagues, so they began to treat you specially. They took us to their laboratories, they lent us books, and we even socialized with them. They were role models for us. There was also the respect and integrity that surrounds academia. It was a dream for all of us specials to be a part of this scholarly community and to join the faculty.

Women were also in the special groups, although in my year in chemistry there were none, but in the year ahead of me there were two or three. I recall well my collegial friendships with Shahira al-Shishini and Enas 'Izzat. Women were also well represented within the university as a whole and in the Faculty of Science. For example, out of the class of five hundred, I estimate that about one third were women. Also, there were many women on the faculty, such as Professor Tahany Salem, who became my official thesis supervisor after I became a *mu'id*. I didn't feel that there was major discrimination based on gender or religion either. I think the reason Egypt survived continuously for more than six thousand years is in part because of its national unity of many cultures and its tolerance. There were a few incidents of preferential treatment, and I even experienced its consequence first-hand in the fourth year, but these did not represent the normal state of no discrimination.

In the third year, as a special in chemistry, I studied only chemistry, but in many different areas: solid-state chemistry, electochemistry, physical chemistry, organic chemistry, inorganic chemistry, and I took several courses in each one. The friendly competition escalated among the specials—and I wished to be the first of this G-7. As a whole, the group concluded that the title of the first would probably fall to either me or Adel Naguib, who is now on the faculty in chemistry. During the second and third years I met and was influenced by Professor Rafat Issa, who taught inorganic chemistry and was keen on promoting special students to do research with him. Special students were special not only to the professors but also to industries in or near Alexandria. In the summer of 1966, I was invited as a special trainee at Shell Corporation, Misr, for Petroleum. The director was Mr. Sa'id Niazi, whom I later met in Philadelphia with his wife, Naglaa al-Nadouri, later a colleague of mine at the University of Pennsylvania.

During the academic year and in the summer, the university organized collegial and social events to give us a break from our studies. For the specials, it meant the university sponsored a two-week trip for the whole group to some place outside of Alexandria. During the summer between my third and fourth year, we went to Luxor and Aswan in Upper Egypt, where monumental remnants of the ancient civilization can still be seen. Two university professors accompanied us. There were seven of us, plus those who were in the fourth-year specials, maybe twenty altogether, who went on the long-distance train for the long journey to Luxor and Aswan.

We spent our days strolling through the Temple of Karnak, a magnificent example of pharaonic architecture, exploring the tombs of the New Kingdom pharaohs in the Valley of the Kings, and at Deir el-Bahari examining the walls of the Temple of Hatshepsut that tell of this female pharaoh's divine birth and reign. At night we took a *felucca* (Nile sailboat) ride to cool off and rest, taking in the spectacular scenery. We played together and even sang Umm Kulthum songs along the corniche as we walked to or from a restaurant. We all took lots of photos during our trip; I took about 300 and still have many of them. We stayed in fancy hotels like the Cataract in Aswan.

On another occasion (this time I was a *mu'id*), we went onto the *sahil al-shamali*, the northern coast, to the west of Alexandria, and to a place called Bagush. Again it was a small group of students, about twenty, plus several professors, and we pitched tents beside the sea and in the desert. It was an opportunity to get to know each other and to have fun. We listened to music on the beach or we sang; we also did a little acting and played different group games. On these trips and other gatherings, there were guidelines that one couldn't overstep. Female colleagues were treated like sisters and etiquette was part of the social protocol. Real romances started now and then and some students even got engaged through these university-sponsored trips. But the protocol and family traditions were followed.

The university had a policy that if one scored "excellent" in the final year and in all years received a minimum of "very good," then on graduation the title on the degree was "distinction of excellent with the rank of first-class honor." With a score of "excellent" in the final year and a minimum of "good" in all years one received a second-class honor. Below these levels, no class of honor was granted. Naturally, I wished to earn the highest title. After every exam I would evaluate myself to know roughly where I stood, so in the end I estimated that I had a good chance of earning this title of distinction.

In the summer of 1967, the university posted the results for all the students, and on that day, as on my first day, I went with Uncle Rizq to the campus. We came to the wall with the posting of all the names and the scores, and I nervously scanned the lists for my name. At last the two of us spotted the words "distinction of excellent with the rank of first-class honor." My score of 93% I heard about later. I was elated, and as a treat Uncle Rizq again took me to the place he liked, Darwish Restaurant, for a meal, and then on to a concert of Umm Kulthum. Of course, my mother and father in Desuq were waiting to welcome us with a big celebration—as were many of the people of the town.

Actually, I ranked first in the science class at the University of Alexandria. Adel Naguib and the other six in my special group were all appointed at the university as *mu'ids*. Maher al-Sheikh, a classmate and friend, now lives in the United States. My other four colleagues were Samir al-Sadani, 'Abd al-Motaleb Yousef, Othman al-Rais, and Kamal Kandil, who was the Dean of the Faculty at the time I received the Nobel prize. Since I'm not one to rest on my laurels by nature, I immediately set about considering what research I would do; this was called your research point, *nuqtat al-bahth*, and it's probably still so named.

But we also had to teach. Typically, we were asked to conduct the laboratory classes, and there were about thirty or forty students in each section. This was normally the extent of teaching required; a *mu 'id* was not expected to give lectures, only laboratory demonstrations, which was why the position was called "demonstrator." In my case, however, I was involved in some lecturing. After Professor Issa, who taught chemistry to the five hundred or so students of the general program, I was asked to repeat these lectures in the evening to the students and to explain to them details of the professor's lectures. Luckily, I used to gather in this recitation class a full lecture hall (the 'Ali Ibrahim Lecture Hall), because I had already acquired a reputation for simplicity and clarity as a lecturer. To this day, this is part of the enjoyment I experience in simplifying complicated concepts. I believe that behind every important and fundamental concept there must be simplicity and clarity of thought. If it's fuzzy and unclear, and one is making it complicated, then I'm not sure we have an understanding of it yet.

As far as the research was concerned, the most critical aspect was deciding with whom I would work. During the third and fourth years, as a special, one could monitor activities in all the labs in the department and see what projects everyone was working on. I knew that Professor Youssef Iskander had a project in physical organic chemistry, Professor Hassan al-Khadem was working on carbohydrates, Professor Hussein Sadek was doing physical chemistry, and there were others. They were all active professors, who taught us the basics in these different areas and who also did quality research.

Because of the high ranking I had achieved, professors were enticing me to join their group for the master's and Ph.D. work I was planning. I was attracted to and intrigued by the research that Dr. Rafat Issa and Dr.

Samir El-Ezaby were doing. With this in mind, I thought I would join both of these two young and energetic researchers to do research on the spectroscopy of some compounds. Dr. Samir, who was then in his thirties, had just come back from the University of Utah in the States as a fresh Ph.D. graduate and lecturer.

Dr. Samir didn't have an office, but he found a room in the building next to the cafeteria that was used, we'll say euphemistically, for storage. It was incredibly dirty and neglected and full of rodents' nests, old papers, and layers of dust. It was not spacious, of course, and it didn't have a nice view, but we could squeeze in a desk and a bench, and we liked the privacy, which allowed for intense discussions. The smallness of the room was actually a benefit for me, because I learned much from Dr. Samir, especially in his thorough and quantitative analysis of problems. We became good friends. We both used to go and eat fresh fish, especially *miyas*, or blue fish, and jumbo shrimp at different Alexandria restaurants. With Yehya El-Tantawy, we'd go to Abu Qir's most renowned restaurant—Zephirion—almost once a week.

Dr. Rafat Issa had more seniority than Dr. Samir and he was the one who proposed the research point. Dr. Rafat had done his Ph.D. work in Germany on infrared studies, and back in Egypt he used both infrared and visible-ultraviolet spectra to characterize many compounds and their complexes with metal ions. He was a prolific paper-writer. As a result, he had a large research group, because the graduate students knew that the research would result in publication. Aside from these guarantees, Dr. Rafat was a supportive and kind person. He interacted positively with us and gave us the time we needed—we even went to his apartment in Alexandria, where he would cook a meal while we were writing a paper. Dr. Rafat had a group that was interested in both science and soccer, the most popular sport in Egypt. I was a fan of one of the two top soccer teams, and every Friday afternoon in season we would watch games on the television with zealous attention. I even played soccer in Desuq, but at the university I did not have the time to be a part of Dr. Rafat's team.

At that time in Egypt, neither Dr. Rafat nor Dr. Samir could be my official research advisor, as this required the status of a full professor. I was not thrilled by this rule; neither were they. The Head of the Inorganic Chemistry Division, Professor Tahany Salem, became my official advisor, with Drs. Rafat and Samir as the two directly involved in my research. This was a sticky point, especially when the time came to put names on publications. In any case, I understood the system and made the best of it.

I was interested in learning and using spectroscopy in my research. Luckily, there was a new spectrophotometer in the department and Dr. Rafat allowed me to sign for a significant fraction of the time for its use. I worked very hard to get all my experimental work done, which I completed in a few months. There were two factors that helped me achieve my goals. The first one was the dedication of the faculty, the staff, and the people around us. I still recall the late hours of working, with 'Amm Ahmed's help in getting the tea, coffee, and the meals—*ful* (fava beans), falafel, and sometimes fish—to the laboratory. The second was the scholarly ambiance. *Mu'id*s were working on research in their laboratories until midnight or later, and afterwards we would sometimes meet up and go out for sandwiches near Ramleh Station and continue our discussions. I made this walk many times with Saber Sharaf, a decent colleague, and other *mu'id*s. We also met to go to the cinema together—the theaters were plush with red carpeting and crystal chandeliers, and we could see society ladies with their fancy ball gowns and jewelry and the men in formal attire.

The laboratories were modest, but there were facilities where one could learn how to do research and make a contribution. The material for us to work on was available, but the equipment wasn't very advanced, except for the new spectrophotometer. For example, I never saw a laser when I was in Alexandria, while in the late 1960s many researchers in the United States were already working with them (the laser was invented in 1960). Yet that type of equipment wasn't all that critical because our experimentation wasn't very advanced. For my spectroscopy work, the chemicals were there, and the instruments needed to measure the spectra were available.

The chemicals came from the British Drug House (BDH), among the finest in the world. If I needed a reference book, I'd just knock on the door of one of my professors and ask if I could I borrow it; I had some of my own, thanks to the LE 13 stipend I received as a student for my high grades. In some instances I traveled to Cairo to make copies *by hand* of some articles available in the National Research Council. The cooperation I received from the professors was exceptional. For example, when I wrote my papers and thesis, I got personal attention from my professors. My English was poor and Drs. Samir and Rafat would go through the reports patiently and carefully, teaching me as they went along.

As a *mu'id*, I received a modest increase in my stipend to LE 17 per month, only LE 4 more than I got from my student status! Even so, it was enough that I could live well. I didn't have a car, but I didn't need one. I shared a villa with two colleagues, Ahmed Gamal, a *mu'id* in the organic division, and Sami, a friend of his. I used to walk from campus to Ramleh Station to catch the tram to Sporting, where we shared our villa with the owners; I can still remember the address: 211 Port Sa'id Street in Sporting. I used part of my stipend for the rent, and the rest I could use for other things, like books, cinema, meals, or clothes. In addition, we were allowed to assist the students in private sections, for which we were given some extra money.

I had shared an apartment and a memorable time in Sidi Gaber with Maher al-Sheikh, also a *mu'id*, but the stay in Sporting exposed me to unique experiences, socially and politically. All things considered, I was living an enjoyable life, but with a real devotion to the goal of scientific achievements. Recently I saw Hani Hafez, a good friend and colleague who graduated at the same time (in 1967) with a B.S. in chemistry/geology and who is now well known in the petroleum industry in Egypt. Hani reminded me that my goals were clear even at that time—"You could find Ahmed Zewail in the classroom, in the lab, or in the library." Hani claims that I went to the cinema only when I became a *mu'id*! Maher al-Sheikh recently reminded me that I had said on occasions, *al-'ilm nur* ("Knowledge is light"), and that I was the only young *mu'id* who gave a lecture in the Chemical Society Lecture Series that was organized by Dr. El-Tantawy, and apparently did well.

The work for my master's degree was supposed to take between two and four years, and at least two. After eight months I had finished my thesis. Officially I couldn't graduate before the two years' time, but my supervisor of record, Professor Salem, gave the approval in a written document that stated that I had completed the experimental requirement for the thesis. Thus my thesis wasn't recorded in the university, but this approval made it possible for me to contact professors abroad for a Ph.D. program. Out of the thesis work, Drs. Samir and Rafat and I wrote a couple of papers together, which were my first published works and which appeared in print between 1969 and 1971.

I was doing my research in 1967 and 1968, a time of tremendous introspection for Egypt. It was wartime and spirits were low. Businesses were struck hard; spare parts could not be found for cars, buses, or other machinery; tourism was nonexistent. A good number of my friends had to go to the war front, and many of the university students were also involved. The news of the defeat left us in a state of shock and disbelief: in the first days of the June '67 war we were told that we were victorious and we went out in khaki army uniforms to aid the civilians—but these claims turned out to be false. I still recall the noted broadcaster Ahmed Sa'id exaggerating about the achievements of the army and victory.

The university had to interrupt the final year of graduation until the war ended. President Nasser announced his resignation to popular disapproval so strong he returned to his post. There was a wounded feeling among the youth. Many considered emigration, which was unprecedented, as Egyptians have a strong emotional bond to their homeland. In the past, people who emigrated were few in number and only a few of them were university graduates. But with the defeat and the gloomy economy, many university graduates felt compelled to leave.

I wanted to study in the United States, in large part because I liked the refreshing style I saw in the work of Dr. Samir El-Ezaby, who had spent some years in Salt Lake City, and Dr. Yehya El-Tantawy, who had been based in Philadelphia, the "City of Brotherly Love," as he used to tell us. Both men completed their Ph.D.s in the United States; Dr. Samir at the University of Utah and Dr. Yahya at the University of Pennsylvania.

Another teacher I admired, Dr. Ashraf El-Bayoumi, also studied in the United States, at Florida State University. All three encouraged me to do my Ph.D. work in the States and recommended me for the position. I also knew that the United States was leading the world in science—it was enough when I heard they were planning to send a man to the moon.

Of course, the United States wasn't a good friend of Egypt at that time, so most official scholarly missions were sent either to the Soviet Union or to Eastern Europe. I was determined, however, to go to the United States, because I knew that it was there that the best research in my area of interest was taking place and that I could be part of this new world of research. One can see this in the record number of Nobel prizes, about which I knew nothing at the time. Over the course of the twentieth century, since 1901, when they were first awarded, researchers affiliated with German institutions, then England and France, received the lion's share of prizes for roughly the first half of the century, but this shifted to the United States soon after World War II and the trend has continued.

So, in 1968, after completing the requirements for my M.Sc. degree, I began the process of collecting information on different universities. In early 1969 I applied to the three schools with which my colleagues had had experience: Utah, Penn, Florida State, and a few others including Caltech—I contacted specific professors based on the recommendations given to me by Drs. Samir, Yahya, and Ashraf. On a sunny spring day in April, I came back to our villa to find a letter, dated April 2, 1969, addressed to me from the United States. The embossed envelope indicated that it was from the University of Pennsylvania in Philadelphia, to which I had written on January 5 of that year. I unsealed it nervously, all the while hoping, praying—then reading the words, "The Graduate Committee of the Department of Chemistry has recommended that you be admitted . . . to begin on August 25, 1969." It was one of the most thrilling moments of my entire life! I knew very little about the United States from the point of view of tourist attractions, like the Grand Canyon, Disneyland, or even Broadway plays. All I knew was that I would have the best laboratories in the world and whole libraries of science books and journals.

I continued reading the letter from Dr. Donald Fitts, assistant chairman, and I learned that there was even more wonderful news: I would receive tuition remission, plus a stipend of $2,700 for the academic year and a scholarship for summer research of $900. If my work continued at a satisfactory level, the appointment would be renewed. I read and reread that letter more than a dozen times! I was ready to leave instantly, but there was a rule that master's students couldn't leave the country until the end of their two full years in their academic programs, meaning that I had to wait around for a while. As I've already noted, my thesis was completed and all my work was done. Moreover, the scholarship was fully paid by Penn, and the Egyptian Government was neither paying nor contributing to it—I had a "fellowship" from abroad, not a "mission" from Egypt. It was simply the bureaucratic requirement of physically remaining at the university that posed a logistical problem.

But there was another problem—that of the "Unknown Letter." It sounds like the Unknown Soldier, and in fact there is some similarity—both needed courage. The letter I received from Penn was addressed to me personally. The university's policies didn't allow for such a personal, direct offer. Instead, they asked that Penn offer the fellowship to the department of chemistry at Alexandria University, and the department would choose the person. This was impossible for Penn as they would have to write a letter inviting an "unknown" person. I wrote to the professor with whom I was planning to do my research, Dr. Robin Hochstrasser, pleading for his understanding about this bureaucratic problem. He graciously agreed to send the unknown letter, but explicitly stated that the final decision would be his—meaning that if our department in Alexandria came up with a name other than Zewail, he would veto the choice. I gave the letter to the head of the department and the process began. At the end I had to obtain the signature of all *mu 'id*s indicating that they had no interest in this scholarship—certifying that I was the only one interested—before the department would approve me for this privilege.

Then I took all the papers, including a request for permission for a leave of absence for the couple of months that I needed to bypass the exact two-year regulation, to the university administration in Alexandria, and ultimately to the Ministry of Higher Education in Cairo. I bought a train pass to Cairo to go every week, sometimes twice a week, to complete the paperwork and obtain the final approval. In Alexandria, I went to the administration building of the university, a multistory building of red brick and stone in Shatby on the corniche. I went to see the president of the university, because it was only with his approval that this strategy would be successful.

As I entered on the ground floor, I happened to see the man (if I remember his name correctly, it was 'Amm Mahmoud) who handled the mail for the university. When he caught sight of me, he stopped me. He knew that I was a *mu'id*, because I was in a suit and tie and because of the paperwork I carried. I found his stopping me a little surprising. I said, expecting him to be impressed, "I am Ahmed Zewail and I am a *mu'id* in chemistry," adding "It's urgent that I see the president." Amused by my courage, he asked, "Do you think it's that easy to see the president of the university?" I stumbled over my next words, taken aback by his question: "I will . . . I would just like to, uh . . . I have to say something to him." This garbled talk apparently met with his approval, because next he said, "Okay, carry this sack of mail and come with me." So I carried the mail as we climbed to the top floor, where he said, "Sit here while I see whether the president can see you." So the mail clerk went into the president's office on my behalf, while I sat outside the closed doors waiting for permission to enter.

As it turned out, the president was out of the country, but the acting president was in his office, Dr. 'Abd al-Rahman El-Sadr. After the mail clerk's caution and by the time I was admitted, I was shaking like a chicken. I said, "Dr. El-Sadr, I am Ahmed Zewail and I graduated having an excellent distinction with the rank of first-class honor, and I have been awarded a scholarship from the United States, from the University of Pennsylvania, paying full tuition and also a stipend for the years of my entire Ph.D. study. They will do all of this, but with one condition: I have to leave within a month or two in order to get there on time . . . with your signature."

Dr. El-Sadr, a medical doctor by training and a strikingly handsome man, considered my words and my letter for a brief few moments, nodded while looking at my file, and uttered these prophetic words: "I'm going to sign it, but you are not coming back." His statement was indeed prophetic, since I didn't return to join the faculty in Alexandria, but in another sense it was ironic, since he would later come to see *me* in the United States after I got the Caltech faculty position. Later we developed a close personal friendship despite the age difference, and went on to co-chair a conference in Alexandria more than ten years after our first encounter. It was in the walks of life that thirty years after my first visit, I went back to the same university building to meet the new president on the occasion of receiving the university's first honorary doctoral degree after the Nobel prize was announced. This time, as I mentioned in my address in Alexandria in December of 1999, the president received me downstairs, not upstairs with the mail!

With the signature of Dr. El-Sadr in the summer of 1969, I was able to receive the final approval from the Ministry of Higher Education, though not easily, and I began to see light at the end of the tunnel. I was now in a position to think about the prospect of a new life in Philadelphia. I naturally then wondered, should I go alone or should I marry before leaving? For my generation, it was normal to marry in the early twenties, and many *mu'id*s married and their wives accompanied them on their research missions abroad. This practice usually led to a romantic story between a *mu'id* and a student or a colleague. If you were going to America your stock was high. As a young man at age twenty-three, I felt that I was attracted to and admired by a few girls. But because of my background and my traditional and conservative nature, I was looking for someone who was serious and professional and, of course, attractive. At that age, experiencing the naiveté of youth, one has no concept of the real meaning of love and I'm not sure that I knew my desires well.

Alexandria had a social side to it—it wasn't all intellectual—and we used to meet, usually male friends, at cafés, restaurants, and a few times at the famous Sporting Club (I wasn't a member then, because I could not afford the membership fees, but I now have an honorary membership). I recall Mohammed Ahmed's delicious *ful* dishes, the special roasted blend at the Brazilian Coffee Store, the gateau at Aino, the sandwiches and pastries at Élite, Athineos, and St. Lucia—all were in the Ramleh Station area where the Sa'd Zaghlul statue and like-named street defined the center of the busy district. Throughout these social encounters, my relationships with young ladies were innocent and professional. Young men and women would look at each other, perhaps write a note or say a few words, but then, if serious, men would meet the woman's parents.

As a *mu'id*, especially during laboratory sessions, I got to know the intelligent and beautiful young women, so naturally I thought about becoming engaged to one of them, which I did. Mervat was my student in her third year in the laboratory class, and also when lecturing; a year later she graduated from the faculty with a B.S. in chemistry/physics. I saw easy-going girls who talked and laughed merrily, but Mervat was a very serious and professional woman. I admired that, and so I asked her father for her hand in marriage. My mother, father, and uncle came to Alexandria and both families met to bless the engagement.

We actually raced into marriage, even though the courtship had proceeded along conventional lines. I knew that the fellowship at Penn was becoming a reality, and I hoped that my wife would be able to join me— I didn't want to wait until I had finished my doctorate, and it seemed romantic to fly off with a new bride to a new country and a new experience. We got married literally days before we left for the United States. It was sometime in July that we agreed to get married and we left in August for the United States, so we never had a real Egyptian wedding. (Most Egyptian couples are engaged for a year or two and a big wedding is celebrated with a large number of members of the two families and their friends.) I was twenty-three, and she was a year younger—we were both very young. And in retrospect, this was fast. There was too much pressure and we didn't really have a chance to get to know each other before we made the commitment. We admired each other, and this kept the respect in our relationship even when we discovered we weren't as compatible over the long term as our romantic dreams initially promised. Mervat is a fine and refined person, but we are different.

I now had all the needed documents for departure: my passport, the first one I ever had, issued on July 17, 1969; my international certificate of vaccination; my medical test result for trachoma; and my approval forms from all the government agencies—the University of Alexandria for a leave of absence (signed and stamped on June 28); the Ministry of Higher Education to leave a few months before the completion of the regulation two years (signed and stamped on July 12); and the Ministry again to go abroad to study for a Ph.D. (signed and stamped on July 29)—all done weeks before the departure. This was bureaucracy at its best, and I do hope that young people in Egypt today don't have to go through this unnecessary waste of time and energy.

I managed to purchase our tickets and we secured exit visas, which weren't easy to get in those days. Stamped on our passports was the amount of money each of us could take out of the country. When we left, our small "fortune" for getting established in the United States was the maximum permitted $40. Mervat was much better in English than I was, because she had graduated from an American school before she entered the university. We had a lot of time on the plane and in airports on our way from Cairo to Philadelphia, with stops in Rome, Paris, and London, and she took notes on the journey.

We didn't know quite what to expect on our arrival in Philadelphia, and we had very little money, and we didn't have an apartment. The school hadn't paid me for anything yet, so it was difficult to imagine what to do. And on top of that, neither she nor I had family in the United States to help us out. I whispered to her while we were still over the Atlantic, "We're going solo!" which is what Egyptians say in such situations. But then I added that "the land of opportunity" would soon be within reach.

3

The American Encounter

Independence in Philadelphia

On August 23, 1969, we were at Cairo Airport at 7:30 A.M., ready for our departure for the United States. Our families came to the airport to say goodbye. For me, those were unforgettable moments, full of mixed emotions—the excitement of going to America, the sadness of leaving the motherland for the first time, and my departure from my family, with my mother's tears still fresh in my mind as I walked through the airport. I was the only son, and in the Egyptian family tradition I was the one who could take on the responsibilities as the head of the household after my father's death. (In fact, the reason I never served in the Egyptian Armed Forces was a law exempting only sons from military service.) We said goodbye, paid LE 27.45 for our excess baggage, and at exactly 9:00 A.M. we left Cairo for London, by way of Rome and Paris, and then on to Philadelphia. The flight to Europe was on Egypt Air and to the United States, TWA.

The dream was becoming a reality. With my optimism and excitement, I didn't understand the huge responsibility that was now ahead of me—a new country, a new culture, and a new education system. Moreover, my marriage was only three days old, with one night in

Alexandria at my in-laws' home, one night in Cairo at the Semiramis Hotel, and one night in London at a hotel near the airport. The three nights of August 21 to 23 were our real honeymoon. On the plane to Philadelphia we saw a Western—a story about going west to search for gold, with lots of shooting and hard living on the way to the promised fortune. It was as though TWA had scheduled this movie to show me that going after the gold in the West wasn't without a price! We arrived in Philadelphia at 4:25 P.M. on August 24, 1969.

Landing in the United States was almost like being thrown into an ocean, a vast sea where one could float this way or that. It was big and overwhelming, but beautiful, stretching as far as the eye could see. As a boy in Egypt, I saw America as a land of skyscrapers and sleek new buildings, neatly manicured lawns of vivid green grass. It seemed huge. The brochure (sent to me after I accepted the fellowship) described the 262-acre campus of the University of Pennsylvania in West Philadelphia and made it look like heaven on earth.

Upon arriving at the Philadelphia airport I was struck by its enormity and efficient organization, and by the friendliness of the Americans. To see a smile on the customs officer's face and to know that people were respecting my rights was an experience that immediately defined the core of the American society for me. Once we left the airport, based on the brochure, I was expecting the Garden of Eden, but the first thing I saw was a junkyard for wrecked cars. Now that I've been to many countries around the world, I realize that those first impressions were relative and were biased by irrational expectations.

In Philadelphia—the City of Brotherly Love—we were met by two helpful fellow graduate students sent by the foreign student office to assist us in our settling in. They were Fahd Shoreih and Shoukri Shakhsheri. Both were from the Middle East, but not Egypt. They met our flight promptly and welcomed us heartily. We stepped out of the air-conditioned airport into the hot, humid August air—our first breath of "fresh" American air. It was uncomfortable, even though the temperature was mild compared to some of our hot Egyptian days. I thought of the pretty green lawns and lush trees I had seen in the brochures and wondered whether Paradise had to be so muggy to be so pretty. Fahd and Shoukri brought a car to take us and our luggage directly to the university campus.

The University of Pennsylvania (Penn) was America's first university, founded in 1779 as the University of the State of Pennsylvania, guided by the dreams of Benjamin Franklin, the founder and one of America's most celebrated personalities. In a revolutionary concept at the time, Franklin created a secular university to educate students in contemporary subjects in a nonsectarian setting. He believed that "students should learn everything that is useful and everything that is ornamental." Today Penn remains a leader in higher education with more than 20,000 students enrolled in its undergraduate, graduate, and professional schools. It is also known as one of the prestigious Ivy League schools, with peers like Harvard, Yale, and Princeton.

My first moments on campus were spent in a churchlike building, which served as an office to direct new students. It was a little unusual, to say the least, to anticipate spending a night in a building that looked like a church, especially for someone coming from the town of Sidi Ibrahim al-Desuqi, where the mosque was the center of life and scholarship. We didn't have money to go to a hotel and felt that any room provided by the school was adequate. As it turned out, Fouad Agami, another colleague at Penn, was kind enough to have us at his apartment for the first few nights, and we were finally able to stretch out and sleep after the long journey with all its stopovers. On the first morning we had important new things to worry about.

Our first order of business was finding a suitable apartment within our limited budget. We were given a map of the area and some apartment listings—this was our first taste of the American independence, the do-it-yourself approach to daily life and self-reliance, which is a national characteristic. I don't mean to suggest that we were just cast adrift into the ocean. By no means. If a newly arrived student needed advance money from the first stipend check, there was a system to get that money right away—and I made use of that option, to be sure. I took out a loan since the money we had brought with us was not sufficient for a security deposit or rent on any apartment.

We trekked around the area adjacent to the campus on our first days in the United States. The neighborhood where we finally found a furnished one-bedroom apartment on the third floor of an old building was actually in a somewhat rough and run-down neighborhood. The landlady, Mrs. Hurley, did something as she was showing us the apartment that it is not easy to forget. I guess she had never met an Egyptian before and didn't know much about Egypt. I was speaking in broken English, which must have further dimmed her appreciation for things Egyptian.

Mrs. Hurley said, "Here is the refrigerator—re-FRIG-er-a-tor. It's a place to keep food cold, so it doesn't go bad. This is how you use it." Then she opened it and pointed to the shelves and the freezer compartment and the vegetable tray and went on to describe other features of the appliance. I felt she must have taken me for an idiot. So I said, "Mrs. Hurley, we are from Egypt!" And she continued, "Oh, yes, yes, and you will need to de-FROST the refrigerator once a week or so, and—" Still in my broken English, I cut her off: "We have refrigerators in Egypt!!!" My face was flushed, but that passed, and we moved in without further incident.

The staff at the student center and the students who welcomed us encouraged us to order a phone right away and told us it would be easy to get one. I called the phone company on Friday to place my order—in my totally broken English I gave the address and told them that I was a new graduate student. The representative said, "Monday the phone will come." Well, as scheduled on Monday the technician showed up with a phone and phone book—and he installed it right away! We were totally amazed—it was as though we were in a dream, because in Egypt at that time, people waited for a couple of years to even get the information that their name was coming close to the top of the waiting list for a new phone, and then they would have to put down a deposit and wait still longer.

I was very eager to meet my advisor, Professor Robin M. Hochstrasser. I had come all the way from Egypt specifically to do my Ph.D. work under his supervision, and I was excited about starting research on spectroscopy. Dr. Hochstrasser is originally from Scotland and had come to the States in the early 1960s after a few years in Canada.

He had spent two years (1955–57) in the Royal Air Force and had, ironically, taught electronics to navigators during the bombing raids on the Suez Canal. Later, in 1996 when I was involved with Bill Eaton in organizing a festschrift (a special issue of *Journal of Physical Chemistry*) honoring Robin's scientific achievements, I was pleased to learn that Robin's students had missed their Egyptian targets badly!

At thirty-eight when I met him in 1969, he was full of energy and ideas—and still is! Because I had corresponded with him prior to our move to America, I knew that he was the professor that I would be working with, and I knew that he would be my advisor—after all, he saved me with the "unknown letter" and made it possible for me to come to America! As I said, I didn't speak English well, just a few words to communicate with, and I couldn't understand spoken English too well either, because I had mostly read science books and journals, and I didn't converse in English much.

It was either the second or third day that I had been in the country, when I rushed into his office to introduce myself. I couldn't express myself well, but he has since told me that my enthusiasm came through loud and clear through the garbled English. He then said, "Well, you know, Ahmed, I'm going to be leaving this office"—apparently he was moving his office to another room—but I understood him to mean that he was leaving *Penn*! Flabbergasted at the news, I said, "But Dr. Hochstrasser, I came here to work with you!" In retrospect, it was remarkable that he could advise me in those first few days and weeks even though I couldn't understand him and he couldn't understand me.

During one of our first meetings, he described several research topics. He felt that I should just wait until I was a little better acclimated— "It's too early to decide, just find out more about the subject generally." But I pressed him for something to investigate, because I was eager to get to work, and he recognized this driving need on my part, so he said, "Well, I think that you should work on the Stark effect on large biological molecules." I knew nothing whatsoever about the Stark (electric-field) effect and I knew nothing about biology, so I said, "All right, fine, thank you." I then went to think about what all this meant.

Even though I had graduated from Egypt with distinction, the graduate-level science in the United States was new to me. Quantum mechanics, lasers, and electricity and magnetism were all to be a part of the new research I would be doing. I thought about Dr. Hochstrasser's suggestion, and I went back to him and said, "Professor Hochstrasser, this is really not what I want to work on." I had to choose my words carefully and add the word "please." I think he was shocked that here was a guy coming from nowhere in modern science saying that he didn't like what his advisor suggested as a research problem. "Why don't you want to work on this problem?" he asked. Intuitively, without any knowledge of the Stark effect, I felt that the problem was simply too qualitative. All along I had preferred more quantitative science, and this incident made me fully aware of this trait in me. But I instinctively felt that the molecules were too big, the effect was too small to measure, and the problem was a bit ill defined, at least in my mind.

So I said to him, "I really would rather work on something that is quantitative," and so he gave me a research problem on a smaller system, and that got me excited. In a few months' time, I was doing experiments. In September of 1970, we submitted our first paper on the Zeeman effect of the triplet state of sodium nitrite. By June of 1971 we submitted our second paper, on benzene, and by July of 1971 our third paper, on triazene. An important paper on Zeeman effect studies of the triplet states of benzene was submitted and published a few months later. By that time I was couched in the language of quantum mechanics and group theory so that I presented the interpretation for this significant piece of work. My work continued to go well, and I completed my Ph.D. work with twelve publications.

This journey from Alexandria to Philadelphia was a walk of life that led me along a particular path that ultimately determined the course of my scientific career. But life has other dimensions. To follow my father's advice to enjoy both the science and the people, I needed to appreciate living in the United States. Immediately ahead of me, I recognized three barriers that stood between me and the people around me. There was a barrier in science, another in politics, and the last one in culture. It might seem strange to talk about a barrier in science, since I had scored so high-ly in the Faculty of Science at Alexandria and I had graduated with a very high cumulative grade. What obstacle could stand in my way, when I had already taken organic chemistry, physical organic chemistry, and all kinds of chemistry classes? For one, I wasn't aware of the latest developments in modern chemistry and modern physics, as I mentioned earlier, and this posed a barrier. Yet this was an easy hurdle to overcome.

The real scientific barrier was the ability to handle complex instrumentation. The laboratory facilities I was accustomed to were modest and now I was working with state-of-the-art instruments, and this handling required special training. In fact, one night, while doing some experiments alone, I had to wake up Professor Hochstrasser from his sleep at 4:00 A.M. with a serious problem I had encountered with a new superconducting magnet. He didn't mind, but until this day he has not forgotten that late-night phone call.

There was yet another dimension to this science barrier beyond my unfamiliarity with the subject matter or the instrumentation. In Egypt we were used to the British system of writing essays, even in science courses. A question on an exam might have been "Write an essay on what you know about vitamin B_{12}." I would write maybe six pages, with an introduction, methods of synthesis of the vitamin, its various chemical properties, and its effects in the human body. My first exam in the United States was a so-called multiple-choice exam, and it had about 100 questions, which required the students to choose the correct answer from a list. It had to be completed in an hour or so. Generally speaking, my initial impression of this type of exam was that it was too much to read and I just didn't have time to think or organize my thoughts. I just wasn't used to this and so the result didn't match the honor of my B.Sc. degree grade. Luckily, this exam wasn't for credit, but rather was a placement exam to determine which classes I would need to take.

It was nonetheless quite an eye opener. I was determined to overcome this barrier by educating myself. I decided to audit courses in physics and chemistry and I read many library books. I bought many books that I have to this day, in order to supplement the required coursework. At first, the lectures were hard to follow because of the speed at which the professors talked, but the equations and the scientific expressions, since those are universal, helped me to comprehend. Within a few months' time, the language was no longer a real problem.

At the end of the first semester, I took my first course in quantum mechanics and was one of two students in the class who got an A. The university also had a wonderful system to help students with incomplete backgrounds such as mine with a series of courses on the fundamentals. These were known by their course numbers: 501, 502, and 503. The required coursework, spread out over two years, totaled about six courses. This is what was wonderful about a program like Penn's—they took someone like me who knew nothing about these modern topics and taught me the foundation, and let me audit a total of about fifteen courses. It was a well-rounded science education. Similarly, the barriers for American-style exams and modern instrumentation were disappearing or at least diminishing in height.

I did my research in a place called the Laboratory for Research on the Structure of Matter (LRSM), which was housed in a multistory building where different disciplines, such as chemistry, physics, materials science, and engineering, were part of the structure. Its location at 3231 Walnut Street was central to interactions with the rest of the campus, and it was across the street from the physics and electrical engineering buildings where I attended classes and other functions. At three o'clock in the afternoon, the professors and students would go to the first floor for tea and coffee with cookies at the LRSM. We'd meet the big-name professors and other graduate students and postdoctoral fellows, and we'd talk about our respective projects. At the time physicists and chemists were working on conductivity and superconductivity of organic materials. Two of the physicists later received Nobel prizes for their work on superconductivity (Bob Schrieffer, who shared the 1972 prize) and on conducting polymers (Alan Heeger in 2000); the chemist Alan McDiarmid, who shared the prize with Heeger (and Hideki Shirakawa), was not at LRSM, but worked in the older chemistry building at Penn.

Shrieffer, who was an incredibly inspiring teacher, taught me mathematical physics, and I learned about group theory and its applications with Dr. Hochstrasser and from his book on the subject. Dr. Hochstrasser had the habit of introducing topics with the words, "It's obvious that . . . ." In fact, it took a lot of work to understand what was apparently so obvious to Professor Hochstrasser. While taking these and other courses, I was studying for one of the most difficult requirements—the cumulative exams—which I successfully completed in a relatively short time.

In the LRSM, the ratio of faculty to students was about one to ten, with a total of maybe ten professors and probably 100 people working with them, on average. There might have been between thirty and fifty people at this tea time, all discussing different topics. There were about twelve of us in Robin's group, each from a different place—myself from Egypt, Douwe Wiersma from the Netherlands, Paras Parasad from India, several Americans (John Michaluk, John Whiteman, and Joel Friedman), and students and postdoctoral fellows from other countries. It was a multicultural group and many became my friends. I also met Dr. Hochstrasser's former students and postdoctoral fellows who visited the lab on several occasions, including Bill Eaton and Gerry Small, who also became friends.

I worked on three to four different research problems at the same time, because I was so hungry for learning and because of the lure of possible collaborations. These problems involved the spectroscopy of solids, the magnetic- and electric-field effect on crystals, behavior of molecules in an electric field, optical detection of magnetic resonance, and others. The work was done in collaboration with Dr. Hochstrasser, but I also worked with others in the group. For example, I benefited from collaboration with at least two American postdoctoral fellows, John E. Wessel and Gary W. Scott, with whom I published some papers, and we became personal friends.

Likewise, I remember profitable collegial encounters and friendship with Douwe Wiersma, my officemate (who is now a professor at the University of Gröningen in the Netherlands), although we never published a paper together. I also appreciated the time with Bob Bray, Paras Parasad, Sally Dym, and John Michaluk. We talked science, even while socializing. We used to go to Gino's, a pizza parlor on campus, and Nick's in South Philly for roast beef sandwiches, and then go back for late-night work.

The atmosphere was friendly, but I felt from the beginning that some weren't that confident in my abilities. I was treated well by intellectual people and, even if they had views different from mine, they respected me as a human being and as a young scientist. One senior graduate student, however, seemed anti-Arab and at times mixed politics with science. Although he was occasionally helpful to me in the lab and we even coauthored a paper together in 1971, I don't think he expected an Egyptian to excel. He was a very conservative person who firmly believed in the power of technology; since Egypt had been devastated by the 1967 war, in his mind Egyptians weren't prepared for great experiments in the laboratory. This sort of prejudice hurt me. In other words, it was as though genetically I wouldn't be able to be up to the level of the Western European or the Israeli or the American. On the other hand, this experience and others like it provided me with a strong motivation: one day, you'll see what I may be able to do! And indeed, in the case mentioned above, I changed the opinion of my colleague—later I met him at a conference where I received the prestigious Peter Debye Award and he sat in the front row, sharing in the celebration with the Egyptian from Penn.

The political barrier was something I found relatively easy to overcome, but at first the cultural and living barriers presented themselves as insurmountable problems. There were everyday differences that I could take in stride—the weather, for instance. We didn't know how to turn on the heat in our first fall season in Philadelphia. The temperature dropped considerably, almost near freezing, and Mrs. Hurley had to show us how to use the heater. We had to buy heavy winter coats and get used to snow. I remember one night being wrapped in coats and blankets, just like a mummy. We were on our own in America, and I had this thumped into me when I was still wearing the slick-soled dress shoes I had brought from Egypt in the snow. Walking to the lab, I slipped and landed flat on my behind while cars and other pedestrians passed me by. No one stopped! If I had fallen in downtown Cairo, on Tahrir Square, someone would have brought a chair, someone else would have brought tea with mint or put water on my face to help me recuperate. Of course, it was my fault—those shoes and clothes weren't meant for this climate and we were supposed to know that.

We were also supposed to know about supermarkets—everything in one place and so much variety. In Egypt we had traditional markets, vegetables from one shop, bread from a second, meat from a third. For some other items, you waited for someone to come around peddling it from a cart. In Philly, we would go from aisle to aisle in amazement, and we could fill up our refrigerator on just $20. We especially liked the baked Idaho potatoes, which we'd garnish with butter and sour cream, because we had never seen such a colossal size before. Ice cream and steak were other treats on the top of our list when we were getting adjusted. We went to a steak house occasionally, and I remember once, soon after we arrived, we decided to have a sweet after dinner, and ice cream was on the menu. I said to the waiter, "I would like to have one desert," pronouncing it as if I was really thinking of the Sahara back home. He was patient in explaining the difference between *desert* and *dessert*.

There were also differences in dress and behavior that were striking. I arrived with a suitcase full of dress shirts, suits, and ties, since as a *mu'id* in Alexandria, that's what I wore and I expected the same in America—in Alexandria I even had my own special tailors for suits, shirts, and shoes. But this was in the late sixties, when students would come to Penn in jeans, with holes in them, and big boots and colorful shirts—I didn't understand why they'd walk around in public with holes in their clothes, while at the same time they were amazed when they saw an Egyptian in a gallabiya on the street! I kept wearing my suit and tie with a pressed white shirt every day, until John Michaluk asked me, "Are you coming here to meet the president of the university?" I got the message and I started to wear slacks and to dress a little more casually, although I don't think I tried a pair of jeans until after I had been in the States for many years, but even then, it was certainly without the holes.

My behavior also stuck out, and in some ways I refused to change the culture and customs I valued in life. There was a truck, Frank's, that used to park outside the lab building at 12:00 noon to sell sandwiches—roast beef, cheese, and so on. If I went down to Frank's, I would ask Dr. Hochstrasser if he would like to have a sandwich, because I didn't think he should leave his office, and I'd bring him whatever he ordered. And I always had a pot of coffee in my office, and after lunch and at midafternoon, three or four o'clock, I'd say, "Dr. Hochstrasser, would you like a cup of coffee?" I would put it in a clean cup and take it to his office. The American students didn't understand this; they thought maybe I was trying to get some kind of favor from him.

This is what we Egyptians did to show respect for our professors. We have a saying in Egypt, *man 'allamani harfan, sirtu lahu 'abdan* ("You become a slave to anyone who teaches you even a letter"). When a professor was giving me such a valuable education and supervising my Ph.D., I felt I should be grateful and if I could do even something small in return, such as making coffee and bringing a sandwich, that was my way of saying thank you. I also brought him a small gift from Egypt, and again this seemed strange to my fellow students. I now see these traditions being followed by my Asian and European students, who bring symbolic gifts to me, and I perfectly understand that their motive is a polite gesture of appreciation.

Some Egyptian habits had to change, such as the verbatim translation of jokes from one culture that would be offensive in another. For instance, in Egypt, when you know someone well and are really close, you might threaten him by saying *ha 'tilak!* ("I'm going to kill you!"), and everybody knows it's just a joke, an affectionate way of talking. The first—and last—time I said this to an American friend, I got a look that said it all. I was drinking coffee with a friend, and after I said "I'm going to kill you!" (thinking this was the American equivalent), I could see what he was thinking: "This guy is serious—whoa, he's from the Middle East—he might do it!" In the emotional climate of the late sixties and early seventies, I realized that it was best to avoid jokes that might be misinterpreted and to adjust to the language of this new culture.

Some American traits also surprised me. In my first year, as a teaching assistant, I had an unforgettably shocking experience. In Alexandria, students called me Dr. Ahmed, even though I hadn't completed my Ph.D. I was always treated with respect. In contrast, in my first American class—a freshman chemistry class during the 1969–70 academic year—they looked at me as though I was supposed to be their nurse because they were paying a stiff tuition. That's another concept I had to learn—in American private schools we worked for them because they paid the tuition, but in Egypt we were educating them.

During one of the laboratory sessions, a young woman whose lab table was next to a young man's table began working with him and while they were waiting for the titration of the solution, they began kissing each other in front of me and everyone else. I couldn't believe my eyes. In Egypt this scene in the lab would be impossible. And here these two were kissing with passion while they were waiting, oblivious to the other people around them. I was supposed to oversee the class and I had absolutely no idea what to do! Should I kick them out? Should I break them up? What should I do? So I slipped out to get my supervisor's advice and he said, "Well, Ahmed, you know . . . they . . . they, you know, they do this here. . . ." So I learned immediately that things were more relaxed—free—culturally, and very different from my conservative background.

Another surprise occurred in my teaching experience when a premed student came to my office to complain about the points I had taken off for an answer he gave. In group theory, there is something called point group symmetry, which is notated as C_{2v}, and in this question you either get it right or not—there is no half-credit reply. But this premed student said, "I wrote C_{2h}, so it's half right, but you took off for the whole thing." I was astonished that this student had the effrontery to complain, especially about something that was either right or wrong with no in-betweens. So I learned another cultural difference—that American students can question the establishment, but still do so professionally. In spite of these differences in our backgrounds, I had fairly decent communication with my students. Frankly, I don't know how we communicated, but I guess I was clear enough in my explanation.

These scientific, political, and cultural differences were counterbalanced by the ease of American life and by the friendliness of the American people. On the first day of registration in the fall of 1969–70, after standing in line, I reached the window where I gave the clerk a check. I had waited in a long line for my turn, and she was surprised to see me still waiting after handing her the check. Finally, I asked, "Where is the rubber stamp?" She didn't understand me, but smiled and gave me a polite gesture to move on. I left the window and understood the ease and trust the people have in the system. By contrast, my certificate of graduation from Egypt has so many rubber stamps that you can scarcely see my photo.

This ease and trust were evident in our everyday campus life, especially in the system of borrowing books from the library, purchasing items on credit from the bookstore, or checking out equipment for laboratory research needs. One incident was particularly telling. Dr. Hochstrasser had given me a desk to work on in the group and I bought a lock as was the custom in the faculty of science in Alexandria—we obtained chemicals, tools, etc., for our own use and locked them up when we weren't using them. I realized after a week that no one was doing this at Penn, and they would borrow from each other by simply writing a note, so I threw out the lock—I laugh now when I think of this incident!

The friendliness of the people made me and my wife feel accepted. Even with my broken English, some Americans would say that they loved my accent, giving me confidence in trying to speak. Mervat adjusted to the new culture rapidly. She knew English well and, because of her experience at an American school in Cairo, she was familiar with various aspects of the culture. I felt that in many ways she liked the American culture even better than the Egyptian culture. I bought a tape recorder on the installment plan from the university bookstore so I could listen to Umm Kulthum—I missed Egypt so much—but I don't think she related to it as much.

Given the stress of the first years in the United States and the culture shock that I felt, I wanted to have a little corner of my life just for things Egyptian. We sought out a couple of friends from Egypt, Sameh Sa'id, from the engineering school, and Hussein Shaheen, in computer science. We also had contact with Naglaa al-Nadouri, who was from Alexandria and was doing her Ph.D. at Penn, and with 'Omar Khalil, who was from Damanhur and had completed his master's degree in our department at Alexandria. To broaden the circle we socialized with foreign and American students and went to some of the free open-air movies that were organized on campus. I began to integrate the Egyptian and American cultures. I attended one meeting of the Arab Student Association at Penn in Houston Hall, but it was the last meeting I attended because I felt that the politics the members espoused were far from a rational way of thinking about the subjects they examined; they were just letting off steam.

We had to find a position for Mervat so that she could complete her education, and to accommodate Mrs. Hurley's wish for Mervat to not stay at home. Mervat enrolled in the chemistry department of Temple University, also in Philadelphia, but at the other end of town. In the evenings, since we didn't have a car, I took the bus to Temple to pick her up for safety and we came back together. This was tiring for both of us, and we decided that I would ask whether she could transfer to Penn. I spoke with the chairman of the department, Professor David White, who was on my Ph.D. exam committee and who already believed I was going to be a good student, and he granted my request. (In 1997, on the occasion of my receiving an honorary degree from Penn, he told me that my performance had convinced him to do everything possible to transfer Mervat to Penn.) This transfer made our lives much easier, as did the purchase in August 1970 of our first car.

It was a white MG with a stick shift. I didn't really know how to drive, since my only driving experience, back in Desuq, had been somewhat traumatic. However, I still thought it would be easy to drive and in the process I damaged one door of the car and Mr. Longstaff, the seller, hurt his elbow. We paid $200 to Mr. Longstaff for the car, fixed the door for $60, and with the payment for the title and a few other things, the total cost of the car was $390. It was in good shape. With the help of Paras Parasad we visited Independence Hall, the Liberty Bell, and the museums in Philadelphia. We went with friends to New York City and

Washington D.C., and on our own visited friends like Naglaa and her husband Sa'id Niazi. We regularly made visits to our first and second host families, the Mertins and the Blooms, especially on occasions such as Thanksgiving, a holiday on which family and friends gather together in thanks for the bounties of life.

There are a large number of very interesting museums and historic places in Philadelphia, in part because the city was the unofficial capital of the pre-Independence nation when the United States was still just thirteen colonies of England. The city is part of the Independence (or Freedom) Trail, so called because it was the place where the Declaration of Independence was signed. It was also the meeting place for the Second Continental Congress, where the Constitution was drafted, and holds the building where George Washington was made the Commander-in-Chief in 1775 (he was elected the first President of the United States in 1789). I especially enjoyed Franklin Court, named for Benjamin Franklin, where I learned about this great savant, a founding father of the United States and an outstanding scientist of the late eighteenth century.

With our new car, we went even further afield. We later upgraded to a brand new car, a Nova, and we went on some long trips. One incident still in my memory is of a trip to New York City on the turnpike. Egyptians don't use maps; we prefer to ask someone how to get to a place, and we might ask five or six different people for directions along a route from one city to another. So naturally, I didn't bother with a map before we got on the road, and then I lost the way. I asked someone and we continued for a while, but I missed the road sign. I rolled down the window at the next toll, and explained I needed directions to New York. I couldn't understand the long list of directions he recited, because he was talking so fast, but in the end he said, "Follow me." I tried, but he drove as fast as he spoke and I couldn't keep up. We finally made it to New York and were impressed by the Empire State Building, the Statue of Liberty, the high-rises, and the culture of New York. On a trip to Canada, Sameh and Hussein accompanied us and we learned how to camp. In the summer we made several trips to the beachfront of Atlantic City, just as I had to Alexandria when I was a boy.

On the weekends we often socialized with food and music. One day we needed to buy *ful*, an Egyptian staple that is as common in Egypt as hamburger in America. We went to a store outside of Philadelphia where they sold it in large quantities, ten kilograms, in a sealed package. The owner brought the bag to the car and said to us, "I hope your horse will do fine"—to him it seemed impossible that humans could eat these beans in such a huge quantity. Hussein had a sense of humor, even when the situation was serious. Once he had a severe headache and Sameh and I accompanied him to the hospital. The doctor thought his headache was possibly due to a brain tumor, with a real threat to his life. It turned out that without being aware of it, he had worn down the heels of his shoes, making him experience a pressure that may have caused the headache; we never stopped laughing about this episode. Across from our Graduate Towers there was the International House where I met people from different cultures over a cup of tea or a snack, and Hussein and Sameh were present at many such breaks.

While our scientific and cultural lives were prospering, we had our first daughter, Maha, on January 28, 1972, on a snowy day in Philadelphia. It was so snowy that I had to stop a policeman to take me to the University of Pennsylvania Hospital. But we had a real problem. Upon enrolling, we were sent a letter about medical insurance. I hadn't read it carefully, and I hadn't understood all of the "options," the medical coverage that one could choose for a little extra money. So I hadn't signed up for the maternity option, and by good accident my wife had gotten pregnant. This was some months after we had moved, in August of 1970, into the new Graduate Towers located at 3650 Chestnut Street on campus. The new apartment, B-305, was a much better place for us, since there were other graduate students there and many were couples like us and some even had infants as well.

I didn't know what to do, because it cost one or two thousand dollars to cover the entire birth in the hospital, and we had no money beyond the $300 per month that I was making with roughly the same amount coming in for Mervat. That money went for rent, telephone, food, loan payments, and daily expenses. So I asked Dr. Hochstrasser whether there was any way the hospital could help us. My grades and my performance helped at this point, because he had the chairman explain the situation to the hospital billing department and they made a generous arrangement where everything for the birth of Maha was covered, and I would pay in installments every month.

The installment plan offered us a great relief, because we would have had to pay for the delivery anywhere in the United States. By contrast, in Egypt, there were two kinds of hospitals: public ones, which were free, and private ones, where the whole bill had to be paid in advance or service would not be provided. And then there was the midwife who came to the house for a small fee. The hospital of the University of Pennsylvania was on campus, and it happened that Mervat was working on an experiment in the laboratory the day she delivered. We had our first baby, a beautiful and healthy daughter, and payment for the delivery was now fully arranged for.

By the summer of 1973, I finished my Ph.D. work and had already coauthored more than ten publications. My thesis was on "optical and magnetic resonance spectra of triplet excitons and localized states in molecular crystals." *Exciton* is the name given to a particle of excitation, a molecule that has been excited by light. I studied how this particle of excitation moves in crystals and what its properties are when it becomes trapped on a single molecule. I completed the dissertation on December 20, 1973. During this period of my thesis work I attended two scientific meetings, the Ohio State conference on molecular spectroscopy and the molecular crystals symposium held at LRSM in 1970, where I had the nerve to be in the conference photo standing right beside the famous A.S. Davydov from the USSR. I also interacted with scientists at the experimental station of DuPont, and made my first train trip to the South for a collaborative experiment on magnetic circular dichroism at the University of Virginia in Charlottesville.

In the introduction to my thesis, I thanked those who helped me achieve my goal, most of whom I have already mentioned. When I looked at it recently, I was surprised by the eloquence of the quotations I had used introducing each chapter:

To myself I seem to have been only like a boy playing
on the seashore, and diverting myself in now and then
finding a smoother pebble, or a prettier shell than ordinary, whilst the great ocean of truth lay all undiscovered
before me. —Sir Isaac Newton

Science creates more science, like a fire; and the conditions for nursing it and keeping it burning are much the
same. —John R. Platt

Happiness is at once the best, the noblest and the pleas-
antest of things. —Aristotle

I never think of the future. It comes soon enough.
—Albert Einstein

Eureka! —Archimedes

These quotations reflected some of my views on science and life
then, and still do today. I was also surprised by what I used as the opening quotation by R. Landau:

There is no reason to assume that Arabs have lost any of
those gifts of faith, intellect and imagination that, at one
time, enabled them to serve as the intellectual yeast for
the West.

This last quotation must have been written to reflect my concerns
about the state of the nation and its image in the West. The image of
Egypt and the morale of the Egyptian and Arab people had hit rock bottom shortly after the defeat of the 1967 war. President Nasser had
brought optimism to the people of Egypt—through socialism there was
going to be prosperity and progress in modernization and industrialization. As a leader of the July 23, 1952, revolution he made people feel that

Egypt was on a new course and now belonged to the ordinary Egyptians, like himself; he had come from a modest family—his father was a postman and not a king or high official. After sixteen years of his leading Egypt, all of these hopes ended with his death of a heart attack in September of 1970. Despite all the mistakes of 1967, I mourned the loss of this charismatic and giant leader in the history of Egypt and the Arab world. I wore a black tie for the mourning period, and my colleagues at Penn, including Dr. Hochstrasser, paid their respects.

On October 6, 1973, I woke up in Philadelphia to hear that the Egyptian Armed Forces had crossed the Suez Canal and were in the process of destroying the Bar-Lev Line—this wasn't a simple line in the sand, but a "mountain" built by Israel as a barrier to prevent an Egyptian crossing of the canal toward Egyptian Sinai. Similarly, the Syrian Armed Forces were advancing on the Golan Heights. This event more than anything else helped the recovery of national pride, and President Sadat's vision of peace began after this October War. Regrettably, as of today, we haven't achieved real regional peace in the Middle East, even though Egypt and Israel did later sign a peace treaty on March 26, 1979, in Washington, D.C., witnessed by President Jimmy Carter.

Living in the United States, I was proud that Egypt had restored its pride and that there was no need to assume that the Egyptians and Arabs had lost their will and abilities. I was, and still am, hopeful about the future and desire for a just and comprehensive peace. The opening quotation in my thesis reflected these feelings. But there was another message in it. As a scientist I was aware of the Arabs' contributions to science and to the West, and yet I was frustrated to see the lack of appreciation for these contributions, even among educated people in the West. The history of science in the Arab world is largely connected to the history of science in Islam, which flourished during the golden age from the eighth century AD to the eleventh. During this period, Arab science was crucial for the subsequent intellectual movement that led finally to the Renaissance in Europe; Arab intellectuals were active, especially throughout Spain, and they gave the world outstanding scientists.

With my Ph.D. thesis completed, the time came for us to decide what we were going to do after Penn. Because my Ph.D. work was essentially completed by August of 1973, my advisor, Dr. Hochstrasser, gave me a three- to five-month postdoctoral-type fellowship, so that I could write the unpublished work as papers during this time. Also I obtained a raise in my salary. I still had my position in Egypt as a *mu 'id* to go back to as a professor, or more accurately as a lecturer. But I decided that I wanted to pursue a postdoctoral position in the West for two reasons: One, my research was going well and my advisor was eager to recommend me to top laboratories, so I thought why not take the chance for two years as a postdoctoral fellow. I could learn about being a professor and then go back to the University of Alexandria. The second reason for pursuing a postdoctoral fellowship was to improve our status so that when we would go back to Egypt, we could have at least a good American car— like Samir's Impala, which used to take us to the Zephirion Restaurant in Abu Qir, or maybe a big Ford—but in any case, we wanted an impressive car, the trademark of those returning from the United States!

I wrote inquiries to five places, looking for a position as a postdoctoral fellow. I wrote to Professors H. C. Wolf of the University of Stuttgart in Germany, J. H. van der Waals at the University of Leiden in Holland, Charles Harris at the University of California at Berkeley, Gus Maki at the University of California at Irvine, and Mostafa El-Sayed, an Egyptian American and Professor at the University of California at Los Angeles (UCLA). I received five offers. They were all attractive, each one for a different reason. I now know all of these scientists well, and they are accomplished and preeminent in their fields. One of them, Mostafa, is special, and we both have enjoyed attending conferences together all over the world.

In the end, I decided to remain in the United States because I wanted to go to one of the high-power places. If I was going to be in the United States, Berkeley was just such a place for big science. So the decision was made—I had to go west. Dr. Hochstrasser and his lovely wife, Carol, had a farewell party in their home; I still can taste the fresh lemonade made for us with lemons bought from the nearby Italian market, although all the food at the party was superb. At this party, we said

California Gold

From Berkeley to Pasadena

The 1848 Gold Rush made California a prime destination for thousands who sought its fabled wonders. The Spaniards named the state because they saw in its serene vistas something totally fabulous—which reminded them of a legendary island, California. It is still blessed with gold—golden sunshine and shimmering beaches that stretch all along the coast. For the scientist, it provides what gold can buy: big science with world-class research laboratories and the instrumentation and budgets to attract top-notch talent—the Gold Rush has never really ended. With renowned scientific institutions such as Stanford and Berkeley in Northern California and Caltech and Scripps in Southern California, it's a paradise for scientists.

There's another connection with the Gold Rush, because back in those days, wild though they may have been, there was a group of visionaries who wrote into the state constitution of 1849 that the legislature must "encourage by all suitable means the promotion of intellectual, scientific, moral and agricultural improvement" among the people of California. It was through this legal decree that the University of California ultimately came into existence, being chartered to "contribute even more than California's gold to the glory and happiness of advancing generations."

My small family moved to Berkeley, California, in early 1974, around Maha's second birthday, January 28. We took a plane to San Francisco and then a helicopter to Berkeley on the same ticket. Seeing the Bay Area from above was like going up into heaven, and the contrast with east-coast cities was clear. Moreover, the Pacific coast reminded me of Alexandria. We stayed at the Durant Hotel while we searched for a suitable two-bedroom apartment. We found a nice one at 1836 Hearst Street, from which we could see the Berkeley Hills. It was better than any of our earlier residences in Philadelphia, and we could now afford it. We quickly settled into our daily routine—Maha attended a Montessori School, Mervat plunged into her work on her thesis at home, and I was totally involved in my research.

Strange as it sounds, after four years of being in the United States, I encountered the same three barriers in Berkeley—cultural, scientific, and political—as I did on arriving in Philadelphia. The transition from Philadelphia to Berkeley was as dramatic as the one from Alexandria to Philadelphia. Arriving in Berkeley, I first set my eyes on Telegraph Avenue and that said it all! Telegraph Avenue was widely known for its unique, loose culture. There were hippies strolling around, wearing colorful T-shirts and jeans with much bigger holes than I had ever seen before. People were conversing in colorful language and dressed like gypsies with billowing blouses, loosely flowing hair, and lots of bangles and beads. I saw children sitting with their parents in small shelters right in the street, and that was quite a culture shock! It was different from what I had become accustomed to, the clean-cut conservative crowd at the University of Pennsylvania. Many of the undergraduates at Penn came from wealthy families and they at least owned suits and ties for special occasions and always wore clothes that were clean. It was just a different world.

There was another difference that characterized the two universities. Penn is an Ivy League school with its own endowment—it is a private institution—whereas the University of California at Berkeley (UCB) is a public school that is part of the UC system. The University of California was founded in 1868 in a merger of the College of California (a private institution) and the Agricultural, Mining and Mechanical Arts College (a land grant institution). The Board of Trustees of the College of California had purchased 160 acres of land four miles north of their location in Oakland on a site they named Berkeley. In September of 1873 the combined college, with an enrollment of 191 students, moved to Berkeley. UCB became renowned for the size and quality of its laboratories and facilities, the scope of its research and publications, and the distinction of its faculty and students. The student body was, and still is, diverse and culturally very liberal; in the 1960s it was the base of the free speech movement, and this spirit of free expression of political views and lifestyle continued well into the 1970s while I was there.

I would probably have encountered the same experiences in teaching at Berkeley that I did at Penn, only more of them—but I didn't have to teach, because in the first year I was a regular postdoctoral fellow and then I became a full-time IBM fellow: I didn't have any other responsibilities than my research. I did get a taste of some of the Berkeley students' habits and jokes, though. One was particularly shocking. In my first week of research I was conducting experiments on the fifth floor of the Latimer Building and, as usual, I stayed late. Around 2:00 A.M., a student by the name of Mark ran past my door, naked and wearing a face mask. Of course, I was scared and I didn't understand what was going on. Later I learned that this was called "streaking." When I told my new colleagues at Berkeley about the incident, they said, "Welcome to Berkeley—anything is possible!"

I grew more comfortable with American culture and this was reflected in the relationships I made with many American colleagues. I also met a Lebanese postdoctoral fellow, Stephan Isied, who was in the same department in chemistry, and we became good friends. He had completed his Ph.D. at Stanford with Henry Taube, a Nobel laureate, and was doing his postdoctoral work with Ken Raymond. We used to go out to an Italian café on campus for an hour's break to talk about work, the Middle East, and the future.

I began to develop a close relationship with the university, and with the professor with whom I was working, Professor Charles Harris, known as Chuck. Chuck was a graduate of the Massachusetts Institute of Technology and was newly tenured at Berkeley. He described his roots as Lebanese, pronouncing his name "Harees." We would have lunch together in neighborhood restaurants and on many occasions we would discuss science into the late hours. He often loaned me his Jeep when he traveled to Holland and I would pick him up at the airport on his return. It was my first experience with Jeeps, which cost him some money. Sometimes we would go to the faculty club and there I got to know another young and energetic professor, Alex Pines.

Chuck's labs moved to a new space in the D-level of the Hildebrand Building. My desk was close to three students, Bob Shelby, Bill Breiland, and Mark Lewellyn (not the streaking Mark). I had good interactions with all three and collaborated on research with two of them. I had significant discussions with them and also with John Brock, who was in another office. We had lively discussions on phenomena and techniques, which turned out to be useful for later research. John was a typical Berkeley student in his appearance and discussions, but when he invited my family and me to Thanksgiving at his parents' home, located on the Seventeen-Mile Drive in Monterey, a very exclusive area, I wasn't sure that he was the same John that I knew!

Politically, I encountered another new experience. I met a number of students with very strong views on the Middle East. Of course, I had my own views on the Middle East, and they too were strong. So we ended up having heated debates about those issues. What was impressive was that we didn't mix politics with science. Now we often talk about the good old days when we were immature in the way we became emotionally involved in our political discussions. With time, I became more sophisticated about politics in the United States, especially after watching the Watergate story unfold while I was in Philadelphia and Berkeley. The break-in at the heart of the scandal occurred on June 17, 1972; the hearings began the following year; and President Nixon resigned on August 9, 1974. The hearings were often rebroadcast late at night, and I would listen to them after a long evening in the lab as I was eating a sandwich for a late dinner—I was in awe of how the American political system worked.

By then I thought that there was no scientific barrier left, and actually there wasn't, but the style of science at Berkeley was different from what I was used to at Penn. It was like coming from Desuq and visiting the big capital city of Cairo for the first time. Penn earned its high reputation from the distinction of individual research groups, headed by distinguished professors such as Dr. Hochstrasser, who was highly regarded in his field in national and international communities. There were quite a few such outstanding groups at Penn, especially in our department. The same was true of the students and postdoctoral fellows. Of course, it was modern science that was being conducted by very good researchers. But Berkeley showed me a new world of big science with big funding. Many of Berkeley's groups were the so-called "high powered" groups. And the quality of the students was superb—graduate students came from all over the country and the world, and the university selected from the best.

The science was big because more money was spent on instruments, and researchers could dream of more big-ticket items. Money was obtained from a variety of sources. First of all, the professors were known for their achievements, so they were able to raise money from the Federal Government through the peer-review system of the National Science Foundation. Secondly, the Department of Chemistry wasn't just a department, but a college in its own right, and there was a lot of funding from the state. Thirdly, UCB has the Lawrence Berkeley Laboratory (LBL), an establishment supported by the US Department of Energy. Many professors in chemistry were associated with and received funds from LBL.

This high-tech LBL was the research home of several Nobel laureates, including Ernest O. Lawrence, who developed the first cyclotron and received the Nobel Prize in Physics in 1939. Also, Edwin McMillan and Glenn Seaborg shared the 1951 chemistry prize for their discoveries in the chemistry of the transuranium elements. Element 106 is now named after Seaborg, seaborgium (Sg). LBL was located in an idyllic spot in the hills of Berkeley. When I visited LBL, I saw immediately that it was a big-science organization, and I had the good fortune of being associated with it as a postdoctoral fellow working with Chuck. But I now had to learn how to do science in this new environment.

This feeling of big science was also evident in the departmental seminars that were attended by around two hundred people. Every Tuesday, we had a speaker in the general area of physical chemistry / chemical physics who was invited from outside UCB or, occasionally, from the UCB faculty. These speakers came from all over the world, not just California or the United States. The seminars were attended by the students, postdoctoral fellows, faculty, everybody. It was a unique experience. The late George C. Pimentel, for example, in a typical California style—high boots and a scarf around his neck—would ask probing questions. He was good with people, he was thoughtful, and he was a distinguished chemist. Ken Pitzer, another distinguished chemist, was also easily spotted in the crowd. He had a habit of sitting in the front row where he appeared to be asleep for most of the seminar. Suddenly at the very end he would wake up and ask very deep, insightful questions. Chuck and Alex also always asked questions, some of which were over my head.

Chuck cared about the "big picture" and used language from different fields that sometimes appeared too complex or unclear to the specialists. I recall a few of these incidents and one of them in particular. When Bob Shelby and I were working on the setting of a picosecond glass laser, we had many problems. Almost every time I spoke with Chuck about the problems, he would say, "It's due to the fluctuations of the vacuum state." Nobody understood what he meant, or the relevance to our problem. So one day before dawn, after being in the lab for fifteen hours, I found a blackboard in the hallway. I wrote on it in big letters: "Dear vacuum state—would you please stop fluctuating!" and signed my name. This reflected my near-dawn frustration with the problems of the laser.

The board was kept and when I returned to Berkeley on February 18, 1997, to give the George Pimentel Memorial Lecture in the same departmental seminar hall, they told me that they had kept it for a good reason—I guess they were anticipating the Nobel prize. It was during this recent visit that my daughter Amani, who accompanied me, made the decision to attend Berkeley for her undergraduate education—she was impressed by the warm reception at Alex's home, by the faculty, and by the beauty of the campus, despite my hesitation about Telegraph Avenue, whose culture was still thriving! Amani graduated from UCB in the summer of 2001, and the family stayed at the Durant Hotel, just as we did when we arrived in Berkeley in 1974.

The exceptional facilities and the scientific environment at Berkeley opened my eyes to another concept in American science: What keeps American science on the forefront of new frontiers is in reality a handful of outstanding institutions—not every university in America had costly facilities and a distinguished faculty. Later, when I started to reflect on what could be done in Egypt to improve the science base, I was convinced that centers of excellence had to be built to attract the best researchers, both young and senior, and to provide the scholarly ambiance for the exchange of ideas. It would be possible to build unique facilities and install a sound infrastructure in such centers. After going to Caltech, I began to have the Caltech model in mind because of its small size and its unusually high level of excellence.

That first year at UCB stimulated me immensely; I set to work right after my arrival. I completed three papers with Chuck and two authored by myself alone; we submitted the first paper in May 1974, a few months after my arrival. I published a total of eight papers while at Berkeley. This was an important transition in my scientific career, because it set me on a course of research that in retrospect shaped a direction in my walks of scientific life. We were investigating electron-spin transitions in crystals and Chuck's group was advancing techniques for studying particle-type excitons, the excitation that moved in crystals.

With my Ph.D. in the background, I introduced to the group at Berkeley my interest in the studies of pairs of molecules (dimers), so we could begin to understand the physics of excitation transfer between two molecules. I was intensely working on the theory of dimer excitation and the physics of the phenomena associated with it. The experience with coherence in these spin systems made me think about the implications of this work for how atoms and molecules behave, coherently or incoherently. I studied the theory of coherence and learned everything I could about it, and I also studied the fundamentals of new fields such as quantum optics, quantum electronics, and theories for ensemble coherence. In my last year at Berkeley, I was absorbed in learning about new lasers, then called picoseond lasers, and their applications to the new directions I was thinking about for the future.

At Berkeley, I felt I was unknown and unnoticed by most of the faculty, with the exception of a few. I spoke occasionally with George Pimentel, Brad Moore, and Alex Pines, with whom I had lively and long discussions on spin coherence. Another professor I was introduced to was Fritz Schaefer, who was then at Berkeley and is now at the University of Georgia. Recently, during a visit to Caltech, he told me that he kept track of me in the Tuesday seminars at Berkeley and noticed that I had always participated in them and asked penetrating questions. Fritz was apparently sure of the trajectory! The department began to notice my presence toward the end of my stay. Some of the faculty read my publications, and more importantly they were hearing that I was receiving job interviews from several well-known universities. However, the job search didn't get serious until toward the end of my second year at Berkeley.

Our social life in Berkeley was limited because we were very busy. We had an old white VW, which we used for local transportation. On some weekends, we went to nearby San Francisco or Sausalito, and we went many times to the marina restaurants in Berkeley to have a meal overlooking the water. The students, postdoctoral fellows, and I went to the famous International House of Pancakes on University Avenue, usually at very late hours after we had finished our experiments. We invited a number of our friends to our home, including Stephan and Chuck. Our two years at Berkeley were a "transition state" and we didn't have time for long trips, except one.

In August of 1975 I was invited with my family to visit Iraq. Our hosts paid for the airfare, and the accommodations were first class. A

Laser and Optics Research Center, under the leadership of Dr. Marwan Nakshbandi, was being built in Baghdad to be named after the great Arab scientist, Ibn al-Haytham (Alhazen). Five of us from the United States were invited to teach at a workshop, and I gave lectures at the center on the banks of the Euphrates. The vice-president at that time, Mr. Saddam Hussein, met us on arrival, and the Iraqi officials tried to convince me to accept an offer to stay. We enjoyed our visit for its cultural opportunities and for the interactions we had with the students—many of whom are now in tenured positions in the United States.

We stopped in Philadelphia on our way to Iraq so that Mervat could finalize her Ph.D. exam. On our return, the two of us and Maha, who was only three and a half years old, went to Beirut and Paris. We enjoyed seeing both places—Beirut with its lofty mountains, sparkling seaside, and rich Arabic culture in Hamra and other streets, and Paris with its cafés, monuments, and famous districts including the Champs-Élysées, the Place de la Concorde, and the Latin Quarter—for a postdoctoral fellow this sightseeing was a real treat. The trip was timely because it gave me a break from all the hard work of the past six years and provided a visit to the Middle East, which allowed for consideration of future research opportunities.

Earlier in that same year, on February 4, 1975, the Egyptian radio interrupted its normal schedule and broadcast verses from the Quran, signaling that a person of great importance had died. It was Umm Kulthum, and four million people poured into the streets of Cairo to mourn this tremendous loss. Throughout the Arab world, tens of millions mourned her passing. The "Pyramid of Arabic Song" had died and I was deeply saddened. I played and replayed her song "al-Atlal" ("The Ruins"), which she sang in classical Arabic with such perfect articulation and soulful emotion that the song was heard in cafés, taxis, boats, and even in the streets. I would hear the following repeatedly:

> We were drunk with love
> We sheltered ourselves in dreams
> We walked down a moonlit road

> Ah, we walked down a moonlit road
> Joy danced ahead of us
> We laughed like two children
> And we outran our own shadows

Indeed only her shadow is now with us, yet her legacy will continue to shelter our joy.

We returned to Berkeley. Life had to go on. After a year at Berkeley I had begun to think about the future—whether to stay in the West or go back to Egypt or some other place in the Middle East. I wanted to go back, but the research was going well, and I was worried about the lack of modern equipment at Alexandria University. I considered the American University in Beirut, which we had visited, because of its good reputation, but something happened that once again defined one of the walks of my life. Chuck told me that he felt that I should really be applying to top universities in the United States. There's an old American expression, "Just try it," and another, "It doesn't hurt to ask." And these expressions seem to sum up his feelings. He said, "Why not give it a chance? Just try and apply to good universities." At the time, Chuck was clearly very supportive and I was grateful.

My American friends pointed out the benefits of "checking it out" and investigating the possibilities. After all, if I received any offer, I would get interviews with the travel paid for—this was a good way to see science in different places *and* to see America! I still had my University of Alexandria leave of absence renewed annually, which meant I had the right to return as a faculty member and I could collect the salary that had been accumulating over the years. At the time, my salary was slightly above LE 20 a month, and although they wouldn't send it to the United States, it was kept in an account for me in Alexandria.

That first year, I applied to a few places, including Caltech. But the following year, in the fall of 1975, my search began in earnest. I applied to about ten institutions and I got interviews all over the place: Chicago, Rice, Harvard, Princeton, Caltech, Northwestern, and a few others; as my American friends had promised, I saw a lot of the country. It was also good in another way—I met first-rate scientists and got to know them and their work first-hand. There was only one negative incident, and it was at Princeton, where one of the faculty members was emotional and unkind to me. I was looking for a job two years after the 1973 war between Egypt and Israel and the oil crisis in the United States was on everyone's mind. So this man said to me—I remember it as if it happened yesterday—"For heaven's sake, why don't you go back to your country? You people have the oil resources." What he said wasn't appropriate, certainly in the United States, the land of immigrants. In fact, he wasn't correct either—Egypt doesn't have much oil, not on the scale of Saudi Arabia or Kuwait. Don McClure, a colleague of his and a well-respected scientist, apologized on behalf of the department, and in any case Princeton didn't make me an offer. Of course, I did remind them of this no-offer decision when they recently invited me to give a lecture in a prestigious series.

Interestingly, this was the only incident of blatant prejudice that I can remember. But I am aware that such opinions exist in human beings, and it's not a question of being Egyptian or being an Arab or being a Muslim. One could be a Christian against a Jew or a Jew against a Christian, or a white against a black, or a man against a woman. My philosophy is not to let such attitudes stop me from what I want to do. I don't take it very seriously, although as you can see, I remember the incident very well. The point was I had to get on with my work and had to behave properly, and in the process perhaps even change the opinion of these people. But on the other hand, if I did nothing but complain and feel sorry for myself, then I wouldn't get anywhere.

My interview at Caltech went well despite the fact that I had an exhausting two days, visiting for a half hour with each faculty member in the chemistry and chemical engineering division. The visit was exciting, surprising, and memorable. It is remarkable that during this visit I developed a rapport with some faculty members who continue to be friends until today. One of those was Peter B. Dervan, who had been hired as an assistant professor three years earlier. At the time of my visit, I recall having been exhausted by 3:30 P.M. My talk was at 4:00 P.M. and

Peter was kind enough to offer me a glass of water, two aspirins, and some rest in his office. Vince McKoy and Harry B. Gray, the personable chairman of the staffing committee at the time, took me to lunches at Burger Continental, a Middle Eastern restaurant, and dinners at the top-rated Chronicle, and they gave me the feeling that I was the person for the job. Vince became a special friend and an office neighbor and until today we spend time together discussing science and life.

During my interview at Caltech, an incident took place that helped me score on style. I was discussing an important theory that related to the description of coherence. It was called the FVH theory and I mentioned that it was named for three scientists—one of them, the late Richard P. Feynman, a physics professor at Caltech and a Nobel laureate. For some reason, I thought I needed to write the names on the board: Feynman, Vernon, and Hellwarth. As I started to spell Feynman, my mind went blank and I couldn't spell it. I wrote F-E-Y—and I just couldn't contin-ue. So I faced my audience and said, "Well, I guess you know how to spell Feynman here." A big laugh followed, and the audience thought I was joking—I wasn't!

After completing all my interviews, I received offers from Rice, Chicago, Harvard, and Northwestern. But I didn't receive a call from Caltech and I began to get anxious. By sheer coincidence—again, the walks of life—Dr. McKoy came to Berkeley shortly after my talk at Caltech to give a lecture in the Berkeley seminar series. Chuck intro-duced me to him, and then asked pointedly, "How did Ahmed do on his interview?" Vince said, "Well, I really liked what he presented to us and I hope we will see him again." I had the feeling that, because of the way the interview and the talk went, Caltech was interested in me—and I was interested in Caltech. So I called Professor Aron Kuppermann, the chair-man of the search committee, who told me that the committee hadn't yet made its decision, and if I was pushed for a decision, I should go ahead with my plans. I was puzzled to say the least.

Finally I called Dr. McKoy: "I now have several offers, and I'm about to make a decision. Professor Kuppermann informed me that no decision has been made, but I thought from what I knew from you and how the

At the age of twelve

My mother, Rawhia Dar,
at the age of twenty-five

My father and I (age 10) on the beach in Alexandria

My father, Hassan Zewail, on
the balcony of the Zewails'
chalet in Alexandria in 1949

My sisters Seham (left) and Nana
and I in Desuq's club, with one of
our cousins, in 1980; Hanem was
not present on this occasion

My mother and I on a visit to the Pyramids in 1988

Uncle Rizq

بسم الله الرحمن الرحيم

رياسة مجلس الوزراء

مكتب الرئيس

ولدى العزيز أحمد

تحية أبوية ربعد

تلقيت رسالتك الرقيقة المعبرة عن شعورك النبيل تجاه لها الجمل الأمر في
نفسي وأوصى الله بأن يحفظكم لتكونوا عماد الوطن في مستقبله الزاهر ، وأوصيكم
بالمثابرة على تحصيل العلم مسلحين بالأضداد وه الكريمة ، لتساهموا في بناء مصر
لتخلد وفي ظل الحرية والمجد .

والله آبد والعزة لمصر

القاهرة في ١١ / ... / ١٩٦

رئيس مجلس الوزراء

My letter from
President Nasser

Umm Kulthum

Downtown
Damanhur, the city
of my birth, in a
photo from 2001

A vegetable
market in
Damanhur today

Sidi Ibrahim mosque in Desuq in 1998

My art and painting group at preparatory school; I am in the front row, at left

Outside our secondary school in 1961, with several
of my friends; I am second from left

The G-7 specials in chemistry in 1966; I am in the front row in the center; the photograph was taken on the Luxor/Aswan trip

The staircase of the Faculty of Science of the Muharram Bek campus of the University of Alexandria, in December 1999

During a university trip to Upper Egypt in 1966; Shahira al-Shishini
(seated) and Enas 'Izzat are to my left

As a *mu'id* in 1968 with
students of the Faculty of
Science; I am fifth from left
in the back row

Dr. Yehia El-Tantawy, who gave me
this photograph in 1969 as a
memento; he wrote on the back
"To a very special friend, to Ahmed"

Dr. Samir El-Ezaby, my
M.Sc. thesis advisor and friend

A group of *mu'ids* and students with professor Rafat Issa (third from
right, standing), my M.Sc. thesis advisor, in 1968

My landlady and I on the balcony of the Sporting villa in Alexandria, before I left for the United States in 1969

Letter of admission from the University of Pennsylvania

UNIVERSITY of PENNSYLVANIA
PHILADELPHIA, PENNSYLVANIA 19104

Department of Chemistry   April 2, 1969

Mr. Ahmed H. Zewail
211. Port Said St.
Sporting, Alexandria
United Arab Republic

Dear Mr. Zewail:

The Graduate Committee of the Department of Chemistry has recommended that you be admitted to the Graduate School of Arts and Sciences. You will be notified of your acceptance by the Graduate School of Arts and Sciences.

I am glad to offer you a Teaching Fellowship in Chemistry at the University of Pennsylvania for the period August 25, 1969 to Commencement Day, May 18, 1970. These appointments are made on a yearly basis with continuation and renewal subject to satisfactory performance in your teaching duties and in your academic work.

The duties of a Teaching Fellow include the supervision of laboratory sections in undergraduate courses, the conduct of recitation sections, and paper and report grading, all of which involve a total of about twelve hours per week. You will register for three courses of graduate work each term, which is considered a full-time program. The stipend is $2,700 for two terms, plus remission of tuition and charges for supplies and apparatus used in connection with graduate research. A general fee of $60 per term is charged to each student in the Graduate School. This fee provides for non-academic services not covered by tuition.

A Summer Research Scholarship of $900, plus remission of tuition and charges for supplies, will be offered to you for the Summer, 1970, subject, of course, to a satisfactory academic record. Thus, the yearly stipend is $3,600.

I note that you have also applied for a Research Fellowship. The Chemistry Department has no Research Fellowships to offer you; these Fellowships are available only from a student's research supervisor.

I shall appreciate it if you would let me know as soon as possible whether you will accept this offer of a Teaching Fellowship.

Sincerely yours,

Donald D. Pitts
Assistant Chairman

pjb

With Dr. 'Abd al-Rahman El-Sadr (far right), Nico Bloembergen (second from right), and George Porter at the 1983 conference, held in Alexandria

The participants in the International Conference on Photochemistry and Photobiology at the Giza Plateau, January 4, 1983; in the background are the Sphinx and the pyramids of Khufu (Cheops, right) and Khafre (Chephren)

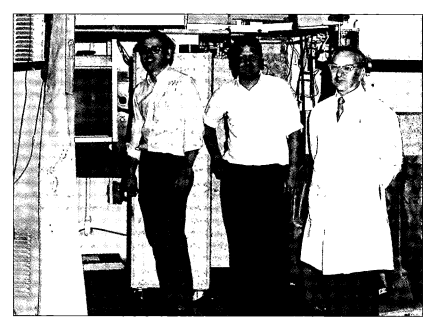

In the laboratory at Penn with
John Wessel (at my right) in 1970

Robin Hochstrasser
at the blackboard

At the wedding of John Wessel, with Douwe Wiersma (second from left)
and his wife (extreme right), and Carol Hochstrasser (third from left);
Robin Hochstrasser is in the background; Mervat is on the left

Graduation day at Penn, 1973; the photograph
was taken by Sameh Sa'id

In the hall where I received the
Franklin award in 1998; above me
is a model of the medal

Charles Harris and
Amani at UCB in 1997

On the occasion of receiving an honorary doctoral degree from
the University of Pennsylvania; Bill Cosby stands at the extreme
left; the president of the university is seated beside a statue of
Benjamin Franklin

faculty position Decision — 1/13/76

was added later 2/16/76

Criteria	Harvard	Chicago	Caltech	N.Western	Rice
1. Graduate students	10	8	10	6	6
2. Research money	10	10	10	10	5
3. School reputation	10	10	10	7	7
4. Stimulation	9	10	7	8	6
5. Lab space	8	10	10	7	7
6. Tenure	3	8	8	7	10
7. my position in the dept.					
* Speciality	10	7	10	7	10
* field as attractive to G.Students	~~9~~	~~4~~	~~10~~	~~10~~	~~10~~
1. family living	10	5	10	8	8
2. Mervat job	10	10	10	10	10
3. Safety of campus	9	5	10	8	8
4. Salary					
	89 ~~60~~	83	95	78	77

My "faculty position decision" table

The faculty of Caltech's Division of Chemistry and Chemical Engineering at the birthday celebration for Linus Pauling (front row, sixth from left), 1986

Our first laser laboratory, 036 Noyes, at Caltech, with Tom Orlowski (1976)

The first lab for a picosecond laser at Caltech, 048 Noyes,
with Dan Dawson (left) and Rajiv Shah

interview went that I should contact you." Vince couldn't understand the delay, so he immediately called Harry Gray, who's still a professor at Caltech. Harry, in turn, called the chairman of the division, John D. Baldeschwieler, who called the chemical physicists and everybody else involved, and Harry said (as he told me later), "You guys have got to have a meeting right now—this man has offers from Harvard, Chicago, and other places—we've got to find out what you want to do. Make up your minds!"

Caltech made me an offer and Harry called me the next day with the news, saying in his characteristic style, "Ahmed, we badly need you! We love you!" I started to laugh with joy: "Harry, it's going to cost you a lot of money!" He then interjected, "Come visit us again." Now with an offer, we had a room at the Hilton Hotel, instead of the faculty club as on my first visit, for my wife, Maha, and myself and we were treated very well. We had an open account at the hotel so that the faculty could come for dinner and talk with me. They even arranged for a babysitter for Maha, so we could look around for housing in the area.

It was a class act and it's something I value about Caltech. They talked to me about my laboratory space and even about my parking spot, which, once I accepted, was labeled with my name. Years later, Tina Wood, my secretary from 1978 to 1990 who at the time was working for Professor Sunney Chan, told me that after she saw me in the elevator she said to Sunney, "This is the guy to hire." I told her that if that was true, from now on we should put her on the search committee!

It was a hard to make a decision, especially as far as Chicago was concerned, because of the strong chemical physics program they had and, I should add, because they were also extremely nice to me. The chairman of the department, Stuart Rice, and his wife threw a party for me at their house. The other universities were also professional and friendly. The people at Rice were warm and hospitable and reminded me of people back home. The faculty had brought their wives to the dinner given for me and we enjoyed ourselves—culturally I felt I was in sync with these warm Southern manners. At Northwestern, Professor Mark Ratner and his wife gave a wonderful dinner for me in their home, and at Harvard Martin Karplus had me to his house for snacks, before we went out to dinner.

At Harvard, after my seminar, I met with Professor E. Bright Wilson, who had been Pauling's student at Caltech. He took me on a tour of the campus and explained in his gentle manner the attractions of Harvard. Later, when I received the first E. Bright Wilson Award in 1997 from the American Chemical Society I told the story of my interview at Harvard to members of his family, remembering his kindness and the favorable impression he had made on me.

Earlier, the University of Illinois had expressed interest and invited me to give a seminar. I was one of the applicants chosen for interview, but they hired another person. This situation was doubly ironic. The person chosen wasn't given tenure later. And the head of the search committee at Illinois was Rudy Marcus, who wrote me the no-offer letter; I was so impressed with my visit with him that later, when I was tenured at Caltech, I was instrumental in moving him to Caltech, where he was when he was awarded the 1992 Nobel prize—he is still at Caltech and we remain friends.

One of the things I learned about this American system of hiring is that young scientists are treated well. I was treated as a somebody even though I was still a nobody in science. Richard Smalley, like me, was searching for a position in that same year. Rick shared the 1996 Nobel prize with Robert Curl and Harry Kroto for their discovery of fullerenes. It is a tradition in US universities to look for promising young people and it is this promise that the faculty evaluate prior to the interview. By then, I had published twenty papers and they must have received supportive letters of recommendation on my behalf. It is truly remarkable how the system works—it identifies promising young scientists, gives them opportunities and independence, and then in a relatively short time they can become world leaders in their fields of research. As an assistant professor I didn't work for another professor and I was treated as a faculty member with all due rights and privileges. Students could work directly with me for their Ph.D., unlike the seniority system prevalent in Alexandria and in many European and Japanese universities.

To help reach a final decision, I tabulated scores, evaluating the universities that made me offers, and in the table I tried to compare the prestige of the university, the quality of the students, everything that was important. I still have that table today, which I had scratched out on a piece of loose-leaf yellow paper. To me, the most important thing for achieving really high-quality science was having good graduate students. That was number one on my table, and I listed seven points in order of importance for my career and my family. Research money was no. 2, because I had to have support for my scientific research or I wouldn't have research. I also included the school's reputation and something I called stimulation, which would be determined by the colleagues I would work with. I didn't want to be the only king or the big fish in a small pond—I wanted to be among people who could challenge and stimulate me.

I also thought about the possibility of staying on long-term, positioning this factor in a row I called tenure, no. 6. Another row, "My position in the department," involved weighing the specialty and whether the field would be attractive to graduate students. I also had a section in the table for family matters, and one of the most important issues was the accommodations for my family ("family living"). And of course, there were my concerns about my wife's job and about the overall safety of the campus. I initially wrote *salary* as an element to consider, but I scratched it out! I didn't count it! This was done in 1975, when I was twenty-eight years old, and I think I would do the same today, I hope with the same clarity.

Caltech scored 95 out of a possible 100 on my list and was unique for several reasons. Experimental chemical physics needed help, especially after the departure of major figures like Linus Pauling, Harden McConnell, and G. Wilse Robinson. I felt that there was an ocean to swim in and I could find my own way. The situation at Chicago was different as many well-known scientists were already there. Also, the class act at Caltech was unique and evident—the laboratories, the offices, and the support staff are of the highest quality. And its smallness was attractive to me as I enjoyed the interactions with first-rate colleagues from different areas of science and engineering. Finally, the California weather reminded me of Egypt and it felt like home.

There were a few drawbacks. One was the concern that there weren't enough experimentalists to interact with. There were also rumors that the chairman wasn't a real fan of chemical physics, but instead preferred bioresearch. On the personal level, I sensed that there was a lack of enthusiasm by some members of the faculty about my field of interest, since it wasn't *really* chemistry. Some members were lukewarm about my appointment and some were again displaying a "wait and see" attitude. My optimistic nature wouldn't let me consider the drawbacks, though, and I pushed forward. The decision to go to Caltech was the best career move I made, and I have never regretted the outcome of my table of scores!

The California Institute of Technology—Caltech—is a small, independent university that carries on instruction in science and engineering for a student body of 900 undergraduates and 1,100 graduate students. With an outstanding faculty, and such on- and off-campus facilities as the Jet Propulsion Laboratory (JPL), Palomar Observatory, and the W. M. Keck Observatory, Caltech has become one of the world's major research universities, focusing on those areas in which it has the faculty and facilities to excel. Twenty-nine Nobel prizes have been awarded to Caltech faculty and alumni. On the Caltech faculty, of about 280 members, one out of four is a member of the National Academy of Sciences— an incredible ratio considering that most universities in the nation aspire to have one or two members. Caltech's endowment is $1.5 billion, one of the highest per capita in the United States.

Caltech's 124-acre campus is situated in Pasadena, a city of 135,000 at the foot of the San Gabriel Mountains, some 25 miles inland from the Pacific Ocean, and 10 miles from the Los Angeles city center. Pasadena is in one of the most attractive areas of Southern California and it is the home of the famous annual Rose Parade, which welcomes a million or more visitors every year to the city on January 1. In the area around Pasadena, other cities such as San Marino boast wide boulevards, palm trees, and, of course, sunshine for most of the year. Many of the buildings on the Caltech campus have a Spanish–Arabic architecture, which makes for a refreshing landscape and which has won the admiration of the city of Pasadena for many years.

The California Institute of Technology traces its origins to a local school of arts and crafts that was founded in 1891 by the Honorable Amos G. Throop. For almost two decades, Throop University served the Pasadena community, offering training leading to a bachelor's degree, as well as providing an elementary school and an academy whose emphasis was on vocational training. Astronomer George Ellery Hale, the first director of the Mount Wilson Observatory, became a member of Throop's board of trustees in 1907, and envisioned a totally different future for the school. He saw it becoming an institution of engineering and scientific research of the highest rank, and, under his leadership, its transformation began. By 1921, Hale was joined by physicist Robert A. Millikan and chemist Arthur A. Noyes.

These three men, Hale, Millikan, and Noyes, set the school—the renamed California Institute of Technology—firmly on its new course. They were dedicated to the development at Caltech of exceptional research and instruction in engineering and the fundamental sciences of mathematics, physics, and chemistry, and to the enrichment of that curriculum with course work in the humanities. Millikan and his successors, Lee DuBridge, Harold Brown, Marvin Goldberger, and Thomas E. Everhart led the institute to achieve the highest levels of scientific education and research. Over time, new disciplines were added in geology, biology, aeronautics, astronomy, astrophysics, the social sciences, computer science, and computation and neural systems. Now serving as president is David Baltimore, a distinguished biologist and Nobel laureate.

My appointment officially began on May 26, 1976. I had brought the old white VW that we had bought in Berkeley, and this car didn't fit in on the prestigious campus. The car was the butt of countless jokes—it was rusty, yet I had the privilege to park it in a named spot next to the Arthur Amos Noyes Laboratory of Chemical Physics, where my new office and lab were situated. Across from my parking spot, there was Dervan's old Porsche and McKoy's old Volvo. The chairman, John

Baldeschwieler, used to give me a subtle hint: "I'm sure you'll get a new car soon," and I would reply, "I'll get it sooner if you increase my salary." Then we would both laugh. We bought a car soon after our arrival in Pasadena, where we moved into a two-bedroom apartment at 550 East California Boulevard, which was close to the lab—in fact, only about five blocks away.

Caltech's reputation was intimidating to any young assistant professor. By any standards one had to be humble. In the first few weeks I felt that I was now on an "Island of Giants"—I heard the names of some of the greatest scientists in the world. In physics, there was Richard Feynman, a 1965 Nobel prize winner for his fundamental work on quantum electrodynamics. Murray Gell-Mann was a 1969 Nobel prize winner for showing that protons and neutrons are made up of even smaller particles, quarks. Carl Anderson won the Nobel prize in 1936 for his discovery of antimatter—the antielectron or positron. Willy Fowler won the Nobel prize in 1983 for studies made at Caltech's Kellogg Laboratory that showed that nearly all the elements in the universe were originally cooked up inside stars. Earlier, the chairman of Caltech's Executive Council, Robert Millikan, had won the prize in 1923 for his famous experiment with an oil droplet, which accurately determined the magnitude of the charge of an electron.

The list goes on, with many similar exceptional contributions in chemistry, biology, astronomy, geology, and engineering. Linus Pauling won the Nobel prize twice: first for chemistry in 1954 and then for peace in 1962. Roger Sperry won the Nobel prize in 1981 for his discovery that the left and right hemispheres of the brain were specialized for different capacities, and Max Delbrück won one in 1969 for his fundamental discoveries concerning the nature of viruses and viral disease. In engineering, Theodore von Kármán led the world during the 1930s in the studies of the principles of modern aviation and jet flight and turned Southern California into the aircraft capital of the world. Caltech's JPL was established in 1944 as an outgrowth of the pioneering work of von Kármán and his associates.

In geology, everyone knows of physicist Charles Richter and mathematician Beno Gutenberg who in the 1930s invented the Richter scale for measuring the severity of earthquakes. Also in geology, the age of the Earth was first estimated to be 4.6 billion years by Clair Patterson in 1953; in astronomy, Maarten Schmidt established in 1964 that quasars were the most powerful and distant objects in the universe. It was overwhelming to hear about these discoveries, to see many of these distinguished scientists and engineers on campus, and to know that scientists like Albert Einstein visited Caltech and that J. Robert Oppenheimer, the leader of the atom bomb project, was on the faculty—and this is only an abbreviated list.

It was clear to me that I was in the mecca of science and that Caltech was the right place. I also realized that I might not be going back to Egypt. Still, I thought it a good idea to wait a little bit on the Alexandria decision since it wasn't clear that I could make it at this prestigious institution. This decision helped me because it gave me the freedom to design new experiments and to pursue new science—I wasn't hobbled by the pressure for tenure. In the tenure system in the United States, one could work for six years and then be asked to leave with a civilized handshake of "no tenure." Ironically, soon after I decided to postpone the decision, the University of Alexandria gave me an ultimatum to come back or lose my position. It was clear to me by then I wasn't going back. I had probably accumulated about LE 2,000 in salary there, which I had to pay back to the university along with a token penalty. It turns out that they had already terminated my services as of August 23, 1974, file no. 869.

At Caltech, they gave me a laboratory (036 Noyes) and an office next to it, and another lab down the hall (018). The laboratories were in the subbasement of the Noyes building, and the chairman, John Baldeschwieler, made sure that they were ready with electrical and water connections on my arrival—everything he promised was delivered. I also felt the moral support of the department and the desire by many for my success. My research budget was $50,000, and I had $15,000 of free service in different shops. I had secretarial help, free of charge, and all the shops in the division were ready to assist the new assistant professor in building his new laboratories.

Adding to my luck, when I had given my interview talk in January of 1976, two able graduate students, Duane D. Smith and Dan Dawson, who hadn't yet decided on a research advisor, had come to me, saying, "If you accept the Caltech offer, we would like to work with you." I arrived in May, and already had two graduate students interested in working and doing their Ph.D. work under my supervision. Shortly thereafter, Tom Orlowski, a capable experimentalist, joined the group, and I also had in the group a brilliant undergraduate, Kevin E. Jones.

In 1976, my research budget was good, but to do the planned experiments I would need more than $50,000—I needed lasers, new electronics, and other equipment, so I made an arrangement with new laser companies to give me some of their lasers at a discount. I also rented much of the electronic equipment. This was a big risk, because they could take the equipment back before I had completed my work, or the experiments might not have worked and we would have put all of our eggs in one basket. But I had some exciting ideas to pursue and felt it was very important to do new things rather than continue along strictly safe lines. Why not try something new?

The new area for me was coherence, but not of spin. It was the coherence of molecules that interested me. I wanted to understand this phenomenon using lasers and to build a new direction of research. While still at Berkeley, I was in contact with the students Duane, Dan, and Tom, and we ordered some equipment, so even before my arrival, we were able to work at getting the laboratory structured—I still have my notebook full of to-do items and checkmarks! The focus was on probing coherence of molecular systems.

The concept of coherence is general and you can get a sense of what it means by thinking of people walking on the street. Imagine that there are 10,000 people walking on the street at the same time, but there is no relationship whatsoever between how person A walks, how B walks, how C walks, and so on. So A could go east, west, north, or south, and likewise B could go east, west, north, or south. Multiply this random movement 10,000 times—scientists call this motion *incoherent*. It is usually slow and diffusive. One person bumps into somebody else and so do all the others; it's a process that's not very efficient because it is inco-herent—slow and random.

On the other hand, imagine that in the motion, each of the 10,000 people knows exactly what everybody else's motions will be; everyone marches in harmony. They create a coherent motion, which is very effi-cient. They know what's called the *phase* of every other person, so if one person moves an arm one way, the next person can move the same arm in the same direction. The phases are all controlled together. Coherent motion is ubiquitous in many phenomena in this universe. For example, in lasers, the reason that the atoms or molecules in a light beam come out intensely in one unique direction is that the atoms or molecules are mov-ing coherently. This is not too different from the situation with soci-eties—coherent or partly coherent societies are efficient, while incoher-ent ones are inefficient and seem chaotic.

The idea of using lasers to probe the coherence of molecules proved successful and we made experimental observations in gases and solids. We submitted our first paper from Caltech in August of 1976, two months after my arrival in May. This was followed by other publications and the group's work generated a great deal of interest. Our research was branching into different areas: optical coherence of molecules; disorder in solids; and the development of a new device, based on molecular ener-gy transfer, known as a Luminescent Solar Concentrator (LSC). This device could concentrate solar energy and convert it to electricity—it resulted in a patent and in several publications. A fourth area of research was focused on the development of new techniques of time-resolved spectroscopy. The research group grew in number and space and more laboratories were allocated.

My duties were now professorial, so in addition to my research, I had to teach. My colleagues, however, helped by decreasing my teaching load in the first year. I taught mostly graduate-level classes in the gener-al fields of lasers and spectroscopy, but the classes at Caltech were unique. The number in each class was relatively small, typically ten to forty students, so I got to know them all by first name. Both undergrad-uate and graduate students at Caltech are among the very best in the country and the world, and teaching them was a rewarding experience, but still with some cultural novelties. For example, while lecturing in one class in 1977, I faced a pair of bare feet instead of a face, because the undergraduate student had propped his feet up on the chair in front of him. Quite in keeping with the character of the institution, he was academically brilliant, but I let him know privately that the feet in my face were not necessary! For lay audiences, Caltech sponsors a series of Earnest C. Watson lectures, where a thousand or more attend. I gave several of these lectures throughout the years. Such public interface is also rewarding, as it allows me to indulge in my passion for explaining science in simple language.

Research, teaching, and lecturing weren't a problem—getting money to support the research was, however, especially for somebody who wasn't yet known in the scientific establishment. I had to start writing proposals for grant funding. My first one was to the National Science Foundation (NSF), a major adventure for a beginner. I wrote it my first year in Pasadena, before I received tenure. I had written other, smaller proposals tailored for young scholars and successfully secured funds. But once I was a professor, the real challenge was to be funded by the NSF or the Department of Energy (DOE), or by the Department of Defense divisions such as the Air Force Office of Scientific Research (AFOSR) or the Office of Naval Research (ONR).

Our research was funded by the NSF. The program director at NSF, Fred Stafford, now at the University of Chicago, was told by one of the referees at the time that he was unable to evaluate the proposal because of the newness of the science involved. In the United States, peer review by experts in the field is required by the NSF and, typically, five to eight reviewers rank the proposal from excellent to poor. The referee apparently had suggested that "even if only 10% of what Zewail proposes works, he should get the Nobel prize," obviously doubting that I could achieve what I had claimed was possible. Fred was a visionary who decided it was right to support a young person to embark on work in an uncharted area. I didn't learn about the Nobel comment until after I had won the prize, when Fred referred to it in his congratulatory letter. Since that first proposal, over the years I have been supported by the NSF, AFOSR, and ONR.

The thrill of science, the success with funding, and the opportunity to do truly new things were absorbing me completely. I was working around the clock, with short naps stolen here and there. With our apartment nearby and because the campus was safe, I felt I could go to the lab at any time—my poor students had to follow suit! In those days I was less tolerant of the lack of scientific commitment by students. The pressure was high, not because of anyone else, but because I was so excited about what we were doing. The world was taking note, too—I was invited to conferences and seminars all over, and after one year at Caltech I was invited to give plenary and keynote lectures, which weren't usually reserved for a beginning assistant professor. It was difficult to find free time for myself and my family.

Once, I remember my wife and I were going to UCLA for an event and, rather than taking the freeway, we decided to take the famous Sunset Boulevard, which runs through Hollywood. This was the first time on Sunset that I had seen a Middle Eastern restaurant, called Ali Baba's. The façade and the interior decor were made to resemble a cave, Ali Baba's cave. I asked, "Do you mind if we stop?" So we had dinner there, with taboulah and shish kebab, and there was a Middle Eastern *firqa* ("band") that provided light music in the background.

For me it was just like finding Ali Baba's cave, where he says *Iftah, ya-simsim!* ("Open, sesame!") and a world of wonder, enchantment, and wealth opened up before him. I don't think my wife was as excited about it as I was, so I went there later by myself, just to go and listen to the music, since some of the band members were Egyptian and happy to chat with someone from home. After the show they would come and sit with me and we'd exchange Egyptian jokes and laugh. They also played the songs of Umm Kulthum especially for me. I took people there who had come to give seminars at Caltech, and many relished the food and the atmosphere. Occasionally, Vince McKoy and I went in the evening, and I met several times with Mostafa El-Sayed from UCLA there, since Ali Baba was halfway between UCLA and Caltech. Ali Baba is no longer in business, but since then I have become aware of other Middle Eastern places. Lately, I don't have the time for even a few hours at such places.

In early 1978, after eighteen months at Caltech, the chairman, John Baldeschwieler, came to discuss the possibility of tenure. The work of my group had made an impact, and scientists were excited about what we were doing. John informed me that my colleagues in the Division of Chemistry and Chemical Engineering were pleased with the progress I was making and they would like to consider my case for tenure, with the risk of granting or not granting it depending on letters from experts outside Caltech. At the time, UCLA and Chicago had contacted me about an appointment with tenure, and this made Caltech's response a prompt one. The division sent out my "package" —the list of publications and curriculum vitae—and the response of outside experts must have been positive. I was granted tenure in less than two years, compared to the usual five to six years.

About the same time that I gained tenure, my wife and I began to go through a difficult time, and things weren't working out. Mervat, who had finished her Ph.D. while we were still at Berkeley, had gotten a teaching job at the nearby Ambassador College, and when we arrived in Pasadena she had the pressure of the new job as well as the care of four-year-old Maha. On March 11, 1979, good news arrived in the person of our second daughter, Amani, who was born at the Huntington Hospital in Pasadena. Even so, Mervat and I had developed our own worlds, and with the respective pressures that we each faced, communication had broken down. She was always proper, honest, and respectful, but we were different, even in our culture. So we decided on a separation, and finally on divorce. It was hard on me, because of my background—as I mentioned, my parents remained true to each other for more than fifty years. What broke my heart the most was having to leave my two daughters, although I would have them on weekends and holidays.

I decided from then on that my life was going to be totally devoted to science. I wouldn't think about getting married again, just science, full time, 24-7. I took out a loan and, with Caltech's help through David Morrisroe, our Vice-President for Business and Finance, bought a condominium one block from my lab—the condo was at 1000 East California Boulevard, practically on campus; Caltech's mailing address is 1200 East California Boulevard. Mervat and the girls stayed at the townhouse at 260 Cordova Street that we had bought in January of 1979, two months before Amani was born. It seemed as though we liked to move around the time of Maha's birthday in January: we moved to Berkeley in January and also to our first house in January.

The condo's location couldn't have been better—I had my graduate students and postdoctoral fellows over to write papers. In fact, the first two papers I wrote on the development of femtochemistry were completely written at the condo. I had a quiet office there, overlooking trees and flowers. I also had some of my colleagues and friends over to the condo. Sometimes I would finish my work at midnight, and then I'd drive to some Middle Eastern places on Beverly or Santa Monica Boulevard, where I would eat something light and then come back and read until four or five in the morning. It was a special time, reminding me of the Alexandria years of total devotion to research.

In this condo I experienced my first major earthquake, the Whittier Quake on October 1, 1987, at 7:42 A.M., the same year that we made the discovery that led to the Nobel prize! This quake, approximately 6.0 on the Richter scale, was frightening. I ran out of the condo in a hurry in my pajamas and Clarence Allen, also a professor at Caltech and a world expert on quakes, who owned another condo in the same building, saw me and said, "Go back to your condo—this quake's a small one." Small for him maybe, but not for me!

Clarence is one of many professors with whom I interacted at Caltech. He and I with a number of other Caltech professors regularly have lunch at 12:00 noon in our faculty club, the Athenaeum. At our "round table" sessions, faculty from different disciplines join us for discussions on science, politics, society, and other topics raised by round table members. It's an enlightening experience and I have been a regular attendee at these sessions for all the years I've been at Caltech. One table group in particular is unique, with eight to ten regulars: Francis Clauser, Bob Christy, Ned Munger, Jack Roberts, Maarten Schmidt, Lee Silver,

Ed Stolper, and I. We've tackled diverse issues from the Middle East problem to the Big Bang origin of the universe, and we all get an opportunity to play devil's advocate at one time or another. Lately, I have had less time to join this special group.

In 1982, I had become a full professor of chemical physics. Our research was continuing successfully and we were publishing papers from each of our four different research areas. I also received some awards, including the Alexander von Humboldt Award for senior US scientists in 1983, which gave me a stay of six months, over two periods, in Munich, where Professor Ed Schlag and his wife, Angela, received me with warm hospitality. In 1984, the NSF gave me an award of extended funding for especially creative research and in 1985 I received the Buck–Whitney Medal, the first national recognition of our work. In 1987 through a John Simon Guggenheim Foundation fellowship, I was able to spend some time at nearby UCLA.

By that time I had already embarked on a new direction of research, which opened up new vistas for science at Caltech.

5

The Invisible Atom
Close-up at Caltech

hen you travel just a little way outside my hometown of Desuq, you find groves of oranges and tangerines, along with green fields broken by irrigation canals that tap the waters of the Nile's Rosetta branch on its way to the sea. In some of these fields you may find short stands of cotton shrubs, waist-high or a little higher, and just before the plants are harvested, you can see the lustrous, white fibers bursting out of their bolls. You can even take a boll in hand, and pull out a length of the fiber for which the country is so famous— Egyptian cotton.

The two-inch long fiber that you hold in your hand may eventually be spun into thread and woven into cloth that can then be cut and sewn into a multitude of products—but what you are looking at in the field is just the basic fiber from which the finished cloth is made. Even so (and this is perhaps the most important aspect of making fine cotton clothing) you have to start with the best cotton, with long fibers that retain a slight twist so they can latch securely onto other cotton fibers when they are spun. For a physicist or a chemist, looking at atoms up close is a lot like inspecting fibers inside cotton bolls. But how small is the atom? And how difficult is the task of looking at the "fibers" of the chemist's "boll"?

Imagine that you are observing an opened cotton boll, about 10 cm across, from a distance of one meter. If we enlarged an atom (with its actual size on the order of 0.000 000 01 cm) to the size of the boll (10 cm), to keep the proportion you would be looking at it from beyond the moon, which is about 385,000 kilometers from the Earth. In other words, the size of the atom to the cotton boll is like one is to a billion, that is 10^9 times smaller. With this general proportion in mind, it is easy to understand why atoms, something like a tenth of a billionth of a meter in size (or even smaller), were for so long considered imaginary.

The idea of the atom is in fact not at all modern; it dates back to the time of the ancient Greeks. The word *atom* in Greek means indivisible (*a-tomos* or "not cuttable"), since the term was originally used to describe the most elementary particles of nature that could not be cut into constituent parts. Many of the earliest Greek philosophers weren't what we would call philosophers today so much as they were scientists—they were looking at the natural world and trying to explain what they saw. They searched for the source of all matter, for what constituted the universe and what we were made of. Some said that since the Earth and its life all needed water, then water was the primary element of all nature. Others believed in fire as the first principle, and still others said everything was change—that nothing stayed the same. While all these concepts had a philosophical bent, they were also early attempts at a scientific understanding of the universe.

Democritus, whose portrait is now on the Greek 10-drachma coin, fully developed the concept of the atom, which was first conceived by his teacher Leucippus: everything that is material is made up of tiny indestructible particles—particles that cannot be seen by the naked eye. These first atomists said that the world was made of innumerable individual atoms and that complexity resided in the infinite multiplicity of their arrangements. But these atoms had weight (mass) and "vibration," that is, they moved and interacted, and the "collisions" created new materials. This was quite an astonishing breakthrough, since they had very little experimental data on the subject, two and a half millennia ago. It was a thought problem for them, which yielded a new hypothesis about oneness in the complexity of matter.

Democritus' atomic theory was dismissed as time went on and even Aristotle rejected it. To some, atomism hinted at a totally materialistic world, one without the divine; as Democritus explained, "There are only atoms and the void." Because the early atomists combined their scientific views with an ethical and philosophical outlook, their choice of the words "pleasure" and "happiness" in their writings as supreme goals in life later convinced many religious leaders that they were pure hedonists, people who lived only for wine, women, and song, as the saying goes. This wasn't the case, since they also said that happiness could not be found in material possessions and money, but only through doing what was morally right and through the pursuit of truth. Yet as a consequence of the misunderstanding, atomism's views on the natural world vanished from scholarly discourse.

The atomic theory wasn't seriously revived until modern times, around AD 1600. In retrospect, Democritus had managed, through rational thinking, to "lift a corner of the great veil," as Albert Einstein said of Louis de Broglie when he provided the hypothesis for the duality of matter in 1924. As Hans Christian von Baeyer wrote in his book *Taming the Atom*, "No empire can rival this idea of atomism in power and longevity." After twenty-five centuries, we still celebrate this fundamental idea. In June of 2001, when I gave the Onassis Public Lecture in Crete, Greece, I spoke about atomism, from Democritus' days to the twenty-first century, and I was pleased to see that the Greek people are still proud and remain interested in the science they inspired.

Even when "atom" reentered the scientific vocabulary, there were problems of conception—what exactly does an atom look like, does it have internal components, how many types of atoms are there, how does one join with others, and are there rules for such joining? A myriad of experimental data led to certain conclusions about atoms. Today we know a lot about how molecules are formed from atoms and how they interact. This is basic chemistry now—if you take this and that and combine them in certain amounts you get such-and-such reaction products. These were among the first concepts that modern chemists could investigate, and these reactions helped them to better understand the atom.

By the late nineteenth century, there was a basic periodic table, developed by a notable Russian, Dmitry Mendeleyev, to group elements of nature, some sixty elements at the time, nearly half of what we know today. It was agreed that atoms came in a finite number of types, distinguished, for one thing, by their unique atomic weight. Around 1800, the work on the chemical atom by the Englishman John Dalton and others laid the groundwork for thinking about atoms in combination and how they formed compounds. Interestingly, for centuries, our vision of atoms continued to be largely imaginary and speculative. It wasn't based on photographs or other direct images, because the technology wasn't there. Scientists had learned about chemical composition, but their visualization of the resultant structures often seemed to borrow too much from the macroscopic world or from another kind of "other world," such as that of witches, wild spirits, or vital forces.

An eminent scientist (with a background in architecture) of the mid-nineteenth century, Friedrich August Kekulé, was known for his studies on chemical structures. He struggled to envision how carbon atoms arranged themselves to form the benzene molecule, an organic compound common both in and out of the laboratory. As the story goes, frustrated, he finally dozed off beside a blazing fire and had a vision in his sleep of the flames turning into a snake that coiled itself in the air and took its own tail in its mouth. This was apparently the first vision of the benzene ring!

In 1895, x-rays were discovered by Röntgen in Würzburg, Germany, and in the 1910s, William H. and W. Lawrence Bragg established x-rays of crystals as a new experimental technique for studying the structure of molecules. Just as it is possible to take images of our bones with x-rays, the new technique makes it possible to see molecules at the atomic scale. For these contributions, Röntgen received the first Nobel Prize in Physics in 1901, and the Braggs, father and son, shared the 1915 Nobel prize, also in physics.

Early in the twentieth century, there was consensus on the constituents of the atom: proton, neutrons, and electrons. The electron was actually discovered in 1897 before the turn of the century. J.J. Thomson was in Cambridge, and set up an apparatus to study the nature of "cathode rays." These rays form when electrodes, cathode and anode, are placed in a low-pressure gas tube at a given electric field. Thomson noted that when the rays from the cathode passed through a hole in the anode, a green glow on the glass window of the tube was observed, and that this glowing point was then deflected downward by a magnet. The movement of the glowing point, together with the fact that the behavior was independent of the cathode material and of the gas, convinced Thomson that the rays (current) were made up of electrically charged particles. He was able to calculate that these individual particles had a mass that was almost two thousand times smaller than the then known mass of the hydrogen atom.

Thomson's discovery of the "corpuscle" (electron) as a constituent of all matter and with a specific charge (the well-known charge-to-mass ratio, e/m) was an advancement of knowledge that had great utility. He received the 1906 Nobel prize for discovering the electron and its particle character (e/m)—his son, G.P. Thomson, received the 1937 prize in physics, with C. J. Davisson, for discovering the *wave* character of the electron. I had the honor of giving a Centennial Lecture in 1997 celebrating this great discovery by J.J. Thomson at Cambridge, and I overviewed the impact of this discovery on chemistry.

From the work of Ernst Rutherford, for which he received the 1908 Nobel Prize in Chemistry, we now know that protons and neutrons form the nucleus of the atom. Furthermore, we know from particle physics that quarks are the components of these two larger atomic constituents. Despite this "cutting" of the atom into subparticles, atomism remains a profound concept. As Feynman once asked, "If you had only one sentence to describe the most important scientific knowledge we possess, what would that sentence be? The answer is, everything is made of atoms!"

The landscape of the atom emerged only with the development of quantum mechanics, beginning in 1900. Many have contributed to this development, and among the leaders were some of the twentieth century's most illustrious physicists: Niels Bohr, who came to work in England before returning to build a renowned school in Copenhagen, Werner Heisenberg of Germany, and Erwin Schrödinger, an Austrian who did his initial work at the University of Zurich. Bohr developed a model in which electrons orbit their nuclear core of protons and neutrons in discrete shells, or orbitals, in much the same way that the planets in the solar system orbit the sun. But these orbitals cannot be defined in the same way that the path of the Earth around the sun is, since the electron orbital represents not a clear-cut pathway for movement but a region of probability in which the electrons might exist. Still, Bohr's model, with its quantization hypothesis, was so powerful that it allows for the description of the orbiting of electrons around a nucleus—stable atoms—and for an understanding of their observed spectra. Bohr received the 1922 Nobel Prize in Physics.

The planetary atom's picture is incomplete because the atomic landscape is different from that of the macroscopic world. In the microscopic world of atoms (and molecules), matter has a duality—it can behave as a particle or a wave. What a strange idea, since we think of objects in our everyday life simply as masses at rest or in motion—we don't think of our wave character! Another strange concept of the microscopic world deals with uncertainty in knowledge. In our everyday life, we know, I hope, our position in space, where we are, and our speed to where we are going. With Newton's equations we can predict with precision our trajectory of motion.

In the microscopic world, such precision is lacking and we speak of the Heisenberg uncertainty principle. We do understand why such uncertainty is insignificant to heavy bodies like ours, and we know how to calculate such uncertainties. We will consider this point later. Despite these uncertainties in the microscopic world, we know how to apply quantum mechanics and make the connection between the wave character and the probability of finding the electron. When atoms combine to make molecules we also apply the same quantum rules.

In the pre-quantum era, the bonding of atoms in molecules was described "classically" as if the electrons were shared (indicated in chemists' notation as dots) between atoms, or were moved toward some of the atoms involved, as ions, carrying positive or negative charges. This description was helpful to explain chemical structures and properties. Early in the twentieth century, G.N. Lewis at Berkeley made a major contribution to this area. In the post–quantum mechanics era, Linus Pauling at Caltech gave us a simplified picture of how atoms arrange in space, based on the hybridization of atomic orbitals and using quantum mechanical descriptions. His 1954 Nobel prize was for this work on the nature of the chemical bond.

Pauling and all of the modern theorists in this field have built on Schrödinger's work on wave mechanics, which was introduced in 1926, and for which he shared the 1933 Nobel prize with Paul A.M. Dirac, another renowned physicist. In 2001, I gave the Schrödinger lecture at the University of Zurich, celebrating the seventy-fifth anniversary of his first equation, and I spoke about the status of chemical bonding and dynamics and of the impact of this equation, which has applications in all areas of the physical sciences—it is surely one of the most important equations of the century.

We didn't get our first *stationary* photograph of an atom, whether free or bonded, until the 1980s, more than ten years after Neil Armstrong took the first human steps on the moon on July 20, 1969. The electron, the charged atom (ion), and the neutral atom have since been isolated and studied using electric and magnetic fields and using lasers. Several Nobel prizes have been awarded for these contributions to single-electron and ion trapping and spectroscopy (in 1989 to H.G. Dehmelt and W. Pauli), to laser trapping and cooling (in 1997 to S. Chu, C. Cohen-Tannoudji, and W.D. Phillips), and to scanning tunneling microscopy (STM).

STM provides images of stationary atoms bonded in molecules and on surfaces, and the contribution earned Gerd Binnig and Heinrich Rohrer, of the IBM Zurich Laboratory, the 1986 Nobel Prize in Physics. By applying current between the tip of a needle and a near-touching metallic surface, the tunneling of electrons diminishes so rapidly around the tip that the resolution of substances on the surface approaches the atomic scale—much smaller than any manufactured needle. This way a contour map of the surface can be displayed, as was done for the first time in 1988, showing what the benzene molecule looks like on a metal surface—Kekulé would have been thrilled!

In spite of these major advances in visualizing the stationary atom and its components, modern scientists had never seen atoms *in motion* and had only the faintest idea of what chemical interactions would do to the motion in "real time" and on the atomic and molecular level. My group's research in 1976–78 had led me to think about coherence in molecular systems and this was crucial to the later work on the atomic-scale dynamics of chemical bonding. Going back to the example, given in the preceding chapter, of people marching on the street, if one person put his left foot forward, then there would be an expectation that every-one else would put their left foot forward in a similar fashion in order to keep the pattern coherent. That is, people in the twentieth row would be moving "in phase" with people in the first row. For molecules, even bil-lions of them, we can make them coherent if we can probe and control them by a coherent means.

I was captivated by this idea of coherence and the possibilities it offered for looking closely at molecules, large and small, in action. Several Caltech colleagues—and many outside of Caltech—were less than thrilled with my coherence studies. At a conference where I was giving a public lecture I remember a well-known chemist expressing the general sentiment that coherence was *not relevant* to chemistry! But the concept is fundamental to many physical processes, and not surprisingly I was frequently invited to *physics* conferences to report on our latest results on coherence of molecules. My confidence in the initial idea about the importance of coherence remained unshaken. Indeed, the con-cept of coherence turned out to be fundamental to femtochemistry, and it is now well accepted that coherence is a key element in the probing and controlling of molecular dynamics on the atomic scale.

In May of 1980, Rick Smalley came to Caltech and gave a talk enti-tled "Vibrational Relaxation in Jet-Cooled Polyatomics." He spoke about his exciting work on the spectra of a large polyatomic molecule named naphthalene. From the spectra, he inferred the "relaxation time." As I listened to Rick, biased about my ideas on coherence, I became convinced that the way to monitor the dynamics wasn't through the apparent spectral feature but by using coherent laser techniques. This conviction was further kindled by the need for direct measurement of energy redistribution rates, that is, how fast did the energy within an isolated large molecule like naphthalene redistribute among all the atomic motions?

To test these ideas, we had to build a new apparatus with a vacuum chamber for molecules coming out of the source as a collimated beam at supersonic speed. Our first supersonic molecular beam apparatus was huge. We did not know much about this kind of technology, although the methodology was known to some physicists and chemists. Our challenge was to build an ultrafast laser to be used with the new molecular beam. It was designed in a relatively short time and built from scratch, thanks to the efforts of two graduate students (one of whom must have consumed hundreds of kilos of coffee!). The molecular beam and picosecond laser system were interfaced, and this was a critical step for much of our later work.

In the beginning, our goal was to directly measure the rate of vibrational-energy redistribution for an isolated molecule, using our picosecond laser. The laser deposits energy in one type of atomic (nuclear) vibrational motion and we wanted to see the evolution to all other motions. We expected to see a decrease with time (the so-called exponential decay, or dying away) in the population of molecules in the initially excited, vibrational state and to possibly see a rise, or build-up, in the population of the new state of motion after the redistribution, thus seeing the entire process from birth to death in real time.

What we saw in these large systems, in this case the isolated anthracene molecule, was unexpected and was contrary to popular wisdom. During the redistribution, the population was oscillating *coherently* back and forth with well-defined period(s) and phases, that is, there was no decay, but instead we saw rebirth and all molecules, like the people on the street, moving coherently in phase. When Galileo saw the swinging of a lamp in Pisa's cathedral, as the story goes, he came up with the sixteenth-century concept of the pendulum with its periodic and coherent motion. Likewise, in a large molecule, each vibrational motion is like a pendulum, but there are myriad such motions because the molecule has many atoms. If these motions had no coherence, we wouldn't have seen anything like the observed behavior.

We were excited about the results because they revealed the significance of coherence and its existence in even complex molecular systems. I knew this finding would receive considerable attention and skepticism. We had to be thorough in our experimental tests of the observation and my students and I went to the laboratory to see how robust the observation was. Then in 1981 we published a "Communication" in *Journal of Chemical Physics*. There had been earlier attempts by another group to observe such a "quantum coherence effect" in *large* molecules, but the observation turned out to arise from an artifact. Some scientists in the field were skeptical of our new observation, and theorists argued that the (anthracene) molecule was too big to see such quantum coherence effects among the vibrational states. It was also argued that molecules could rotate and that the rotational and vibrational motions would couple, resulting in the washout of such observations.

We followed the initial publication with several others, and the effect became even more pronounced with a shorter time resolution. Physicists appreciated the new results and we published an article in *Physical Review Letters* on the nature of this nonchaotic motion in isolated systems. Nico Bloembergen, a 1981 Nobel laureate, was visiting Caltech at the time, and one of the products of our interaction was a review, published in 1984, on the relevance of these new results to laser-selective chemistry. Our group and others in the United States and Canada subsequently showed the prevalence of this phenomenon in many other large molecules. In retrospect, as is often the case in science, after the facts have been established, the phenomenon seems clear, or even obvious to some, and is soon accepted. Looking back, our novel and unexpected observation resulted in a paradigm shift.

For future developments, these findings on coherence were significant for several reasons, in particular because they showed that out of the expected chaotic motion in molecules, ordered and coherent motion can be found, despite the presence of what was called a "heat sink," which could drain energy and destroy coherence. Now I knew why coherence hadn't been detected previously in complex systems—not because it didn't exist, but simply because of the inability to design a proper probe. In our anthracene experiments, both time and energy resolutions were introduced and correlated—a key element to our success and to the ultimate development of femtochemistry.

We continued to pursue a variety of studies on vibrational-energy redistributions, but we also began new studies at shorter time resolutions for molecules exhibiting different chemical processes and for molecules undergoing rotational motions. Our success with the anthracene experiment made us ask a similar question, but now one concerned with the coherent rotational motion of isolated, complex molecules. Some theories suggested that such motion was not possible because of the general belief that complex molecular interactions would destroy coherence.

We worked out the theory, and the implications were surprising: if we could align the molecules with a polarized ultrafast laser, and probe the rotating molecules with another, we would be able to observe the coherent rotational motion (called recurrences), which would then yield the full period of the rotations. Classically, it was as though the molecule rotated back into its initial configuration. This rotation period gives the moment of inertia of the molecule and, since the masses of the atoms are known, we could deduce distances and hence obtain information on the molecular structure of very large molecules.

These recurrences were indeed observed with high precision and the molecular structures were deduced. The observations changed a long-held dogma. Coherence in rotational motion of a complex molecule was clearly evident and could be probed in a manner similar to that in which we had studied vibrational coherence. The approach was again met with some skepticism regarding its applicability to molecular structures. However, it is now accepted as a powerful technique; more than 120 structures have been studied this way. The method is termed "rotational coherence spectroscopy" (RCS) and it has been successfully used in many laboratories.

In the meantime, something interesting happened in the early 1980s that brought me back to Egypt for the first time since leaving in 1969. I received a call from Dr. El-Sadr, the M.D. whose signature I had acquired on my leave papers at the University of Alexandria. While visiting Los Angeles he heard about the success we were having at Caltech and he wondered whether I would be willing to meet with him about a project he was developing. I was shaken to see Dr. El-Sadr again, not from fear, as in my first encounter, but from surprise. The moment I entered the meeting room, where many had already gathered to welcome him to Los Angeles, I recognized him and he recognized me. Clearly he hadn't forgotten signing the letter that gave me permission for a leave of absence so that I could attend the University of Pennsylvania—*I* certainly hadn't forgotten it. We reminisced about our first encounter and both had a good laugh. He said, "But now I need *your* help!"

Dr. El-Sadr actually had several projects that he wanted to discuss. The first was for me to give a series of lectures to the students at a university center he was directing in Alexandria, an invitation I gladly accepted. Secondly, he wanted my help in planning a science program at the center, and finally, he thought I could actively participate in directing research at the center's newly built facility, which was to be called the United Nations Alexandria Research Center (UNARC). UNARC was intended as a new institution for state-of-the-art research in modern sciences that would operate free from normal bureaucracy. I promised that I would make a visit to UNARC.

In December of 1980, I went to Egypt eager to see my family and my homeland after eleven years of living abroad. I went to Alexandria, Damanhur, and Desuq in succession and spent some time with my family. I saw the effect of aging on my parents and I felt guilty about not returning for a visit earlier. I devoted all possible time to my parents and sisters, and I also took them with me to Cairo, partly in an attempt to stop my mother from crying, which intensified the closer we came to the date of my departure.

I returned to Alexandria to give a series of three lectures at UNARC and I also met some old friends and revisited places I had enjoyed in Alexandria, including Zephirion at Abu Qir. Mostafa El-Sayed and I stayed at the Cecil Hotel and we had a great time together. My stay at the Cecil brought back memories of the "good old days" in Alexandria. There was an incident that reminded me of the relaxed culture, even among academics. A professor had invited me to give a lecture at the university and arranged for me to be picked up at 9:00 A.M. The time to give the lecture was set for 11:00 A.M. With the American obsession of being prompt, I was in the lobby by 8:30 A.M. I waited and waited, until he finally showed up at 11:30 A.M. I was nervous and immediately asked, after we greeted each other, "What about the lecture at 11:00?" He said, "Don't you worry, we will go have a good lunch today and tomorrow you can give the lecture." I asked myself, could this incident happen at Caltech? Of course not. But I must say, we had a delightful lunch and I gave the lecture the next day—*and* the world didn't end!

In the course of these various projects with Dr. El-Sadr, I organized an international scientific conference in Alexandria, which was to be held from January 5–10 in 1983. I returned to Egypt in December of 1982, and Tina Wood, my secretary at the time, went with me to help with the organization of the conference. We began in Cairo, then went to Alexandria, where the conference was held at UNARC, and stayed at the Palestine Hotel, which overlooks the Mediterranean Sea. After the conference, we went to Upper Egypt and saw the remnants of 5,000 years of civilization in Luxor and Aswan, refreshing my memories of my first visit to these places when I was a student in Alexandria.

The conference was a total success. It brought people to Egypt from all over the world; more than 200 people attended, many of whom were to later become Nobel prize winners; Yuan Lee, Rudy Marcus, and John Polanyi were there. We also had at the conference two Nobel laureates, Nico Bloembergen and George Porter. Attendees still remind me of that historic event, and I received numerous letters of congratulations after the close of the conference. Throughout the conference, I had to worry about all the fine details, from the lamp in the slide projector, to the security of the guests, to requests for aspirin at midnight. The organization had to be carefully and meticulously planned, a feat that prompted George Porter to write in the published proceedings of the conference:

> As everyone knows very well by now, this meeting was conceived and, to a considerable extent, nurtured by Ahmed Zewail, last of the pharaohs, now in exile in California. He has made it his business to see that, in this timeless city, not a minute was wasted and every lecture was programmed as precisely as if it were a discourse at the Royal Institution. I have been given five minutes tonight. This means, I am afraid, that there will be no time for lecture demonstrations—such as the belly dance that I had planned for you. But this is the sacrifice you have to pay for efficiency and the otherwise perfect organization for which we are greatly indebted to Ahmed and the others on his hard-working committee.

Tina and people at UNARC, and of course Dr. El-Sadr, were of immense help!

After my first unusual "reunion" with Dr. El-Sadr, we became good friends, a friendship that continued until he passed away. Looking back, it is ironic that he was the person who signed my official papers giving me permission to go to the United States, while saying to my face that I wouldn't be coming back. At a glance I knew then that he was a visionary man, and his work with UNARC surely proved it. This man was unique in many ways, especially in terms of his eloquence—his address published in the proceedings of the conference reflects that eloquence quite strikingly. In his honor, and on behalf of the International Conference on Photochemistry and Photobiology (PAP), I established a prize in his name at the University of Alexandria. A few years before his death, he asked me about returning to Egypt to become UNARC's director, but I declined with respect.

Back at Caltech, my research was going strong, and we had four different laboratories busy with experiments and people. In one of these laboratories, we were continuing with our work on coherence; in others, advancing techniques for shorter time resolution and for developing an optical analog for nuclear magnetic resonance (NMR). In NMR, the spin of nuclei with their transitions at radio frequencies is used for a variety of applications, ranging from the studies of molecular structure to magnetic resonance imaging (MRI), which is now commonly used in hospitals throughout the world.

Doing such NMR experiments in the optical domain with lasers was not trivial, as the control of phases was extremely difficult when optical pulses of light were used instead of the radio frequency pulses used in NMR. With Warren Warren, a postdoctoral fellow in my group who had come from Alex Pines' group at Berkeley and is now on the Princeton faculty, we conducted the first of these experiments and published the work in 1981, right next to the anthracene "Communication" we published in the same journal, with Bill Lambert and Peter Felker. In a year's time, we had further advanced this work, with a number of applications. With this latest development, not only could we excite and probe molecules coherently, but we could also control with pulsed lasers the phase at optical frequencies.

My thoughts were now directed toward better resolution in time. We had picosecond (10^{-12} second) lasers at Caltech, but I wanted to cross the barrier into the subpicosecond domain. A new technological development, the pulse compressor, helped us move in the right direction. I was very eager to buy one as soon as I heard about them, but the pulse compressor I wanted, one from Spectra Physics that could reduce the laser's pulse width to a subpicosecond, wasn't available immediately. A company sales representative told me that it would take "only a few months" to build one, which seemed like an eternity to me. He also mentioned that there was already one in existence that belonged to Professor Duane Smith at Purdue University. This was fabulous news, because Duane happened to have been one of my very first graduate students and I was sure that he would be willing to lend it to us until the new one arrived.

So I called Duane, excitedly outlining how we intended to directly monitor the elementary bond breakage in a molecule with this new pulsed compressor, which would be a part of our already-built laser setup. He was delighted to ship the compressor to Pasadena, and he even joined us in our experiments for a couple of weeks. With this pulsed-laser setup, we observed the bond breakage in a molecule with three atoms at the subpicosecond time scale, and we wrote about our observations, publishing them in December of 1985 in *Journal of Physical Chemistry*. The paper was coauthored with Norbert Scherer, a graduate student at the time and now professor at the University of Chicago, Joe Knee, a postdoctoral fellow and now a professor at Wesleyan University, and Duane.

We didn't yet resolve the transition states—the structures between reactants and products—of this reaction, but we did detect the rise of the product, so I knew we were close. I knew that we *could* resolve the transition states, if we only had pulses of a laser with just another single order of magnitude improvement in time resolution! I wrote about this in the last paragraph of the 1985 paper. Put in everyday terms, our "picture" was still blurry, still slightly out of focus, but we had caught the motion, in a close-up at Caltech.

The running horse caught in the act by stop-motion photography offers a neat parallel to our work. Horses were the subject of the first clear macroscopic stop-motion photographs, made in the late nineteenth century not far up the coast from Caltech, at Palo Alto, and then later at my alma mater, the University of Pennsylvania. Back in the spring of 1872, a heated discussion between Leland Stanford, a railroad magnate, and several of his friends took place. A long-standing argument centered on whether all four horses' hooves were off the ground at the same time at any point when a horse is trotting.

In fact, ancient Egyptians depicted pharaohs in chariots drawn by "running" horses with one, or usually two, feet touching the ground. The story goes that Mr. Stanford, who owned a stable of thoroughbreds, laid out a bet of $25,000, quite a hefty sum in those days, that the horses' hooves were all airborne at some point in the gait. To prove his point, he commissioned the photographer Eadweard Muybridge to develop a means of getting action photographs of his horses.

After a couple of sample trials, he set out to obtain the sharpest, most scientifically accurate series of photographs possible with the equipment then available. To reduce dust, which might blur the legs of the horse, he constructed a special rubberized track with a white backdrop to provide the best contrast against the dark, moving horses. Opposite the backdrop, on the other side of the track, he set up a forty-foot-long shed—first for the twelve, and then for the twenty-four dual-lensed cameras he had placed one foot apart from each other.

Each camera had a trip wire attached to it that ran across the track. The horse would break the wire as it moved forward along the course, triggering a snapshot. The shutter speed was the fastest possible for the experiment, about one thousandth of a second, and he also used the fastest film he could find. Moreover, he ran the horses at times when the sunlight would provide the most distinct image. A few years later, he published prints (which had already been circulating privately in the interim) with the general title of "The Horse in Motion," in several journals, including *Scientific American*, the oldest scientific magazine in the United States.

Muybridge went on to record the motion of a great number of domestic and wild animals as well as human beings. What he clearly showed with those first series was the individual "transition states" between the starting gate and the finish line—in clear enough detail that there could be no further doubt: at certain points in time, horses on the run *are* airborne. The impact of his work was felt worldwide, and the findings have had an influence on wide-ranging studies of animals and humans in motion.

To capture the transition states of molecules, the time resolution is vastly different. But however short it is, we need stop-motion photography, as I will explain in the next chapter. With our time resolution improved in the mid-1980s by 10^{10}, or 10,000,000,000 times that of Muybridge, we were able to see atoms in motion. We were able to observe the transition states, frame by frame, of chemical bonding between atoms and to make a motion picture, which in our case takes at most a few picoseconds—or a millionth of a millionth of a second. Almost a century after Muybridge's work with the horse, I published our findings, also in *Scientific American,* with the title "The Birth of Molecules." As the Nobel citation later stated, "We can now see the movements of individual atoms as we imagine them. They are no longer invisible."

The arrival of Dick Bernstein, a well-known chemical physicist, as a Sherman Fairchild Distinguished Scholar at Caltech, from his home institution at nearby UCLA, was a real boost for us. Dick was a man of integrity and had no problem in appreciating new developments. He had been in the field of reaction dynamics for thirty years and knew the significance of the, as he called it, breakthrough. He came to Caltech specifically to work with us and I was encouraged by his enthusiastic support for the new field. Dick was indeed magnanimous. It was at his house in Santa Monica that the word *femtochemistry* was coined, helped by a discussion in the company of his wife, Norma, and brother, Ken.

The coining of this word was appropriate as it captured the interconnection between the time scale and the chemistry, the marriage between time and matter in studies of the dynamics of the chemical bond. A femtosecond (abbreviated fs) is a millionth of a billionth of a second or a quadrillionth of a second, 0.000 000 000 000 001 second or 10^{-15} second. Prior to the femtosecond we had the scale of picosecond, 10^{-12} second; the nanosecond, 10^{-9} second; the microsecond, 10^{-6} second; and the millisecond, 10^{-3} second. The prefix *milli* comes from Latin (and French for "thousandth"), *micro* and *nano* from Greek (for "small" and "dwarf" respectively), and *pico* from Spanish (for "small"). *Femto* is Scandinavian, the root of the word for "fifteen" *(femten)*—nuclear physicists call a femtometer, the unit for the dimensions of atomic nuclei, a *fermi. Atto*second, the next smaller unit, 10^{-18} second, uses a prefix also derived from Scandinavian, from the word for "eighteen."

Dick came to Caltech as a Fairchild scholar in 1986, and in 1988 we wrote a feature article together (published in *Chemical & Engineering News*). Over pots of coffee we had great fun writing this article and we learned an enormous amount about molecular dynamics. We also had a genuine collaboration out of which came a few more papers. Dick returned to Caltech in 1990, but sadly died before ending his sabbatical. He was editor of the prestigious *Chemical Physics Letters*, and I took over as acting editor to help his wife Norma with the remaining manuscripts. I was then asked to be editor, and I accepted the position, which I hold to this day.

By that time we were convinced that the new field of femtochemistry would open up the world of atoms and molecules for a new era in dynamics and all my labs were busy with new experiments and applications. But how did we reach this femtosecond world, and what were the stations in this race against time?

The Race against Time
Six Millennia to Femtotime

I n the history of human civilization, the measurement of time and the recording of the order and duration of events in the natural world have been among the earliest endeavors that might be classified as science. The development of calendars, which permitted the tracking of the yearly flooding of the Nile Valley in ancient Egypt and of the seasons for planting and harvesting in Mesopotamia, can be traced to the dawn of written language. Ever since, time has been an important concept and it is now recognized as one of the two fundamental dimensions in science, the other being space. The concept of time encapsulates an awareness of its duration and of the passage from past to present to future and surely must have existed from the very beginning as humans searched for the meaning of birth, life, and death and, in some cultures, rebirth or reincarnation.

My ancestors contributed to the beginning of the science of time, developing what Otto Neugebauer has described as "the only intelligent calendar that ever existed in human history." When humans began to arrive in Egypt's Nile Valley, more than 10,000 years ago, the rich black soil provided the nutrients for the growth of large quantities of fruit and grain that were sufficient for both the people and their livestock. Egypt was like the Garden of Eden—agriculture was made easy for the first Egyptians because the Nile regularly flooded and then retreated, leaving behind a layer of fertilizing silt. Even to this day rain clouds rarely darken the skies and the climate is almost always gentle and easy to tolerate. And much like the original Garden of Eden, there was something miraculous—in Egypt's case, the regularity of the flooding in the almost complete absence of rain. Year after year the summer would be hot, there would be no rain, and then in mid-June or so, the flooding would start. The "Nile calendar" was an essential part of life, as it divided the year into three seasons: flooding (inundation), followed by planting, and then harvesting, each four months long. A civil year lasting 365 days was ascertained by about 3000 BC or before. This was based on the average time between the arrival of the flood at Heliopolis, just north of Cairo.

By the time of the First Dynasty of a united Egypt under Menes (in ca. 3100 BC), the scientists of the land had introduced the concept of the "astronomical calendar" by observing the heliacal rising of the brilliant star Sothis, or Sirius. Inscribed on an ivory tablet (now at the University Museum in Philadelphia), which dates from the First Dynasty, were the words "Sothis, Bringer of the Year and of the Inundation." On the Palermo Stone, the annals of the kings and a time-line of each year's chief events were documented from predynastic times to the middle of the Fifth Dynasty. Thus, as early as 3100 BC, the Egyptians recognized a definite natural phenomenon that allowed for accurate prediction of the timing of the coming flood and they recounted the observed reappearance of the star as the New Year's Day—real-time observation of daily and yearly events with the zero-point of time being well defined!

Most cultures measured time with reference to the phases of the moon. But for the Egyptians, the yearly flooding marked the beginning of their civil year and it didn't occur in sync with the moon; instead, it was the sun that provided the key to the cycle. The civil calendar was therefore 365 days per year and differed from the astronomical calendar of Sothis by approximately one quarter of a day every year. The two calendars coincided at intervals of 365 x 4 = 1,460 years, and historians, based on recorded dates of the reappearance of Sothis in dynastic periods, gave dates for the coincidence of both calendars: AD 139, 1317 BC, 2773 BC. Using the AD 139 date, one can determine (+139 – (3 x 1,460) = 4241 BC) an earlier coincidence occurred at 4241 BC, a date that many historians regard as the beginning of history; anything earlier is prehistory.

Even though Egyptians discovered the astronomical calendar of 365.25 days, they decided, presumably for bookkeeping, to use the civil calendar of 365 without leap years. They also divided the day into two periods of twelve hours each for day and nighttime. This remarkable calendar of years, months, and days was adapted throughout history and formed the basis for the 365.25-day Julian calendar (adopted 46 BC) and the 365.2422-day Gregorian calendar (adopted in AD 1582, on the edict of Pope Gregory XIII). In the words of the notable Egyptologist James Henry Breasted, "It has thus been in use uninterruptedly over six thousand years."

At about 1500 BC, another major contribution to this science was made, the development of sun-clocks, or sundials, using moving shadows. Now in Berlin, the sun-clock bearing the name of Thutmose III (named for Thoth, the Egyptian god of wisdom and enlightenment), who ruled at Thebes from 1501 to 1447 BC, showed the graduation of hours for daytime measurements. This clock with uneven periods for hours was manmade and transportable. The water-clock was invented for nighttime, and the device provided even periods for timing. With these developments, the resolution of time into periods of year, month, day, and hour became established and they have been in use for more than three millennia. The division of hours and minutes into units of sixty each, according to Neugebauer, "is the result of a Hellenistic modification of an Egyptian practice combined with Babylonian numerical procedures."

Around AD 1000, Islamic civilization made contributions to the advancement of the engineering of clocks. Water clocks were constructed in 1085 on the banks of the river Tagus at Toledo, Spain, and some are still to be seen; the remains of two large water clocks still exist in Fez, Morocco. Hydraulic timekeeping flourished and books were written on the subject of water clocks and other time-keeping devices, for example, the treatise by Ridwan ibn al-Sa'ati, dated 1203, titled *Kitab 'amal al-sa'at wa-l-'amal biha* ("Book on the Construction of Clocks and Their Use"). Contemporaneous clock designs by al-Jazari have such precise details that it was possible to construct a reproduction of one at the World of Islam Festival in the London Science Museum in 1976.

In Europe, about AD 1300, the mechanical clock was advanced, ushering in a revolution in precision and miniaturization. The precision has continued to improve since then, culminating in the use of our present time standard, the cesium atomic clock. Since 1967, one second has been defined as the time during which the cesium atom makes exactly 9,192,631,770 oscillations. A precision of about $1:10^{13}$ can be obtained—the clock loses or gains one second nearly every million years. For this work, Norman Ramsey shared the 1989 Nobel Prize in Physics.

In our universe, time scales vary vastly among the myriad of natural phenomena of the very big to the very small. To observe and clock such phenomena, we depend on revolutions in scientific instruments and in concepts. History is rich with contributions made to both, and here I discuss only the relevant works of Alhazen in optics and sight and of Galileo in time and motion, both of whom gave us a new vision of the invisible world through their developments of new concepts and new instruments.

Abu 'Ali al-Hassan ibn al-Haytham, known in the West as Alhazen (ca. 965–1038), was the greatest scientist of the Middle Ages (as pointed out by John Gribbin), and his many achievements weren't surpassed until the time of Galileo, Kepler, and Newton, more than five hundred years later. Alhazen was born in the Basra region now in Iraq and lived in Cairo until his death. It is reported that, in a foolhardy attempt to impress al-Hakim, the caliph of Egypt at the time, Alhazen claimed he could devise a method of controlling the flooding of the River Nile. To escape the inevitable wrath of the caliph for nonfulfillment of the promise, he pretended to be insane, but had to maintain the charade for years until the death of al-Hakim in 1021. Despite his problem with the caliph, Alhazen wrote on numerous subjects, with his greatest work contained in a seven-volume treatise on optics, written around the year 1000. This work was translated into Latin at the end of the twelfth century and was published in Europe as *Opticae Thesaurus* ("The Treasury of Optics") in 1572. It was studied widely, and became a major influence on the thinkers who started the scientific revolution in Europe in the seventeenth century.

Alhazen fundamentally changed the dogma about vision. His contention, against the prevailing wisdom at the time, was that sight was not a result of some inner light reaching outward from the eye to probe the world around it, but was solely a result of light entering the eye from the world outside. One of his arguments concerned the familiar phenomenon of after-images and the time of their persistence in the eye. But his greatest influence on the scientific development of an understanding of the behavior of light was his discussion of the way images were formed in a *camera obscura*, meaning literally "darkened room."

To see this phenomenon at work, stand in a darkened room on a bright, sunny day, and place a heavy cloth over the window. Make a tiny hole in the cloth, about the size of the tip of a ballpoint pen, to allow some light into the room. You will see something striking—a full-color image of the world outside projected upside-down on the wall opposite the curtained window. The idea of *camera obscura* eventually led to and gave its name to the photographic camera. Recently I went with my family to see an original design of this camera in Santa Monica, California, and we were all impressed by the phenomenon. But how does it work?

The key point, as Alhazen realized, is that light travels in straight lines. Imagine that someone is standing on the street some distance away from the window that a *camera obscura* faces onto. A straight line from the top of that person's head through the hole in the curtain will travel down to a point near the ground on the opposite wall. But a straight line starting from the feet of the person will go upward through the hole to strike the wall at a higher point. Lines from every point in between from top to bottom and left to right strike the wall in a corresponding manner, resulting in an upside-down image of the individual and of everything else in the street.

Alhazen's thoughts about light and vision were revolutionary—light, he said, was made up of a stream of tiny particles produced by the sun and by flames on Earth and travels in straight lines. Light bounces off objects that it strikes, eventually reaching the eyes. That is how we can see and how the image in a *camera obscura* is seen. He realized that light couldn't travel at an infinite speed, even though it has to travel very fast. He realized that refraction, the effect observed when a straight stick looks as if it is bent when one end is placed in water, is a result of light traveling at different speeds through water and through air. With his knowledge of refraction, he also worked out the curvature of a lens, which enables it to focus light. But Europe wasn't ready for all of this in the eleventh century, as Gribbin noted. The first European to take up Alhazen's work was Johannes Kepler (1571–1630), today remembered primarily for his discovery of the laws describing the motion of planets around the sun.

The relevance of Alhazen's seminal work to my own is evident. Only with light were we able to capture images of atoms in motion. Only now can we address his millennium-old theory of vision on the molecular level and on the femtosecond time scale. While Alhazen was interested in light and its associated phenomena, another great scientist, Galileo Galilei, was concerned with the motion of bodies and planets, and with his instruments, based on concepts in optics and light propagation, he opened up the new world of the heavens for observation. Like that of Alhazen, his work is also relevant to our observations and study of motion in the world of molecules.

Galileo was born in Pisa, Italy, on February 15, 1564, the same year that William Shakespeare was born; he died in 1642, the same year that Isaac Newton was born. As detailed in many biographies and in the Galileo Project at Rice University, his life as a scientist was unique for many reasons, including his relationship with the Church. Galileo was the first of six (or seven, according to some) children born to Vincenzo Galilei, a musician, and Giulia degli Ammannati; his family belonged to the nobility although they weren't wealthy. At the University of Pisa, he studied and obtained a teaching position. He then joined the faculty of the University of Padua.

Galileo learned the physics of Aristotle, but also challenged that approach. Aristotelians believed that heavier objects fall at a more rapid rate than light objects. Galileo eventually disproved this idea and asserted that all objects, regardless of their density, fell at the same rate through a vacuum. In one of his famous experiments, Galileo rolled balls down a gently sloping inclined plane and then determined their positions after equal time intervals: these results provided the evidence and gave rise to the law I discuss below. He wrote about the findings on motion in his book *De Motu* ("On Motion").

Galileo was also intrigued by the back-and-forth motion of a suspended weight. His biographer, Vincenzo Viviani, stated that he began his study of pendulums after watching a suspended lamp swing back and forth in the cathedral of Pisa while he was a student—the coherent motion I spoke about before, but here for *one* object. Galileo's discovery was that the period of swing of a pendulum was independent of its amplitude, the arc of the swing. This discovery had important implications for the measurement of time intervals. He realized its significance for clocking and one of his friends, a physician in Venice, began using a pendulum, which he called a *pulsilogium*, to measure the pulse of his patients. However, the distinction for completing the first working pendulum clock fell to Christiaan Huygens, the Dutch astronomer who with the new clock was going after one of the greatest scientific problems of his time—Longitude.

There is one more contribution by Galileo that is relevant here—the telescope—and this was used in an analogy with the femtoscope by Professor Bengt Nordén when he introduced the 1999 Nobel Prize in Chemistry; the text, published in *Les Prix Nobel*, is in the Appendix. The telescope, which is an optical instrument that uses lenses to make distant objects appear nearer and larger, was one of the central instruments of what has come to be called the Scientific Revolution of the seventeenth century. It revealed hitherto unsuspected phenomena in the heavens and had a profound influence on the controversy regarding the then current belief in the centrality of Earth in the motion of the planets.

The telescope, therefore, helped shift authority in the observation of nature from human senses to instruments, and brought into view invisible, far-from-reach objects. The telescope was known before Galileo, as lenses were the products of craftsmen. But it was Galileo who made the instrument famous. Beginning in 1609, he turned his telescope toward the heavens and resolved mountain-type structures on the moon, resolved nebular patches into stars, and discovered four satellites of Jupiter. That an astronomical body could revolve about a planet other than Earth convinced him of the heliocentric theory of Copernicus, as opposed to the earlier geocentric theory. He outlined the discoveries in his *Sidereus Nuncius* ("Starry Messenger") in March of the following year.

Galileo made it possible to observe and study a whole new world, but ironically toward the end of his life he couldn't see the one around him. When Galileo lost his sight at the age of 70, he reflected on his life to a friend:

> Alas . . . your dear friend and servant Galileo has been for the last month hopelessly blind; so that this heaven, this earth, this universe, which I by marvelous discoveries and clear demonstrations had enlarged a hundred thousand times beyond the belief of the wise men of bygone ages, henceforward for me is shrunk into such small space as is filled by my own bodily sensations.

It is also ironic that the man who changed the way we think about motion and whose telescope changed the way we view the universe was pressured by the Inquisition to change his own way of thinking. The Inquisition of the Roman Catholic Church was charged with the eradication of heresies. A committee of consultants declared to the Inquisition that the Copernican proposition that the sun is the center of the universe was a heresy. With the printing in 1632 of Galileo's book, *Dialogue Concerning the Two Chief World Systems* (i.e., the Ptolemaic, Earth-centered, and the Copernican, sun-centered), Galileo had to face the Inquisition, and he was found guilty of heresy. He was confined to house arrest at his home near Florence until his death in 1642. In 1984 in a pronouncement by Pope John Paul II the Vatican finally exonerated Galileo.

The two prime issues in Galileo's work, observation and motion, are at the heart of our work, though they are not of heavenly bodies but of atoms and molecules. These two worlds of the very big and the very small obey different rules. The vocabulary is quite different: classical physics describes planets' motion, but quantum physics describes atoms; the time scale of a pendulum is seconds, the same scale as the heartbeat, while for molecules it is a million billion times shorter—the world of the sub-, sub-, . . . second. As discussed in the following chapter, planets and atoms have some similarity in their motions, even though the time scales are vastly different. But how can we reach time scales beyond the second, in the world of the sub-, sub-, . . . second?

Until 1800 the ability to record the subsecond timing of individual steps in any process was essentially limited to time scales amenable to direct sensory perception—for example, the eye's ability to see the movement of a clock or the ear's ability to recognize a tone. Anything more fleeting than the blink of an eye (~ 0.1 second) or the response of the ear (~ 0.1 millisecond) was simply beyond the realm of inquiry. In the nineteenth century, technology changed drastically, resolving time intervals into the subsecond domain. The famous stop-motion pictures by Eadweard Muybridge (1878) of a galloping horse, by Etienne-Jules Marey (1894) of a righting cat, and by Harold Edgerton (beginning in 1931) of a bullet passing through an apple and other objects are examples of these developments, with millisecond to microsecond time resolution, using snapshot photography, chronophotography and stroboscopy, respectively.

Only in the 1980s did the resolution reach the femtosecond scale, the scale of atoms and molecules in motion, and such achievement was made possible, in part, by advances in laser technology. The prelaser era was dominated by research on the millisecond to microsecond time scale, and for studies with this resolution in chemistry, the 1967 Nobel Prize was shared between Manfred Eigen in Germany and R.G.W. Norrish and George Porter in the United Kingdom.

The laser, an acronym for *l*ight *a*mplification by *s*timulated *e*mission of *r*adiation, was invented in 1960, following the seminal work by

Charles Townes in the United States and Nikolai Basov and Aleksander Prokhorov in the USSR in the development of the maser (microwave amplification by stimulated emission of radiation), which led to the development of the laser. For this work, Townes shared with Basov and Prokhorov the 1964 Nobel Prize in Physics. With lasers, it is possible to generate short pulses of light by methods known as Q-switching and mode-locking, and pulses as short as a few picoseconds in duration were part of research activities in many labs in the 1970s.

The invention of the dye laser, developed independently in Germany and the United States, broke the barrier to the subpicosecond pulse generation. With dye lasers, the first femtosecond pulses were generated by researchers at Bell Labs in the United States, creating excitement for their potential applications. A breakthrough took place in 1991 in Scotland where femtosecond pulses were generated using solid-state lasers, known as titanium-sapphire lasers, and these lasers have now replaced dye lasers because of the ease of their operation and versatility in specifications.

With the femtosecond time resolution that is appropriate for the invisible atoms, what new concepts and techniques were needed in order to catch them in the act? And why would we want to do so? When Muybridge demonstrated the movements of the horse in motion, he was studying the behavior of animals in motion. Such direct studies of motion could lead to confirmation of a proposed theory or give rise to new surprises. One such surprise in the nineteenth century resulted from striking observations made about the same time as Muybridge, not on horses but on cats in motion.

In France, Etienne-Jules Marey, a professor at the Collège de France, was working on a different solution to the problem of action photography: chronophotography, a reference to the regular timing of a sequence of images. In contrast to Muybridge's successive pictures at regular intervals with an array of cameras placed along a track, Marey's idea was to use a single camera and a rotating slotted-disk shutter, with exposures on a single film plate or strip that was similar to modern motion picture photography. Marey was interested in investigations of humans and animals in motion, including a subject that had puzzled people for many years, namely the righting of a cat as it falls so that it lands on its feet.

You can see this for yourself: it's amazing anatomy, but it's even more amazing physics that allows a cat to do this—in less than a single second! Cradle your cat with its four paws in the air or, alternatively, grasp the four paws and hold the cat upside-down about three or four feet from the floor—don't do this from high distances because you could annoy or injure the cat—and the important action takes place in the first hundredths of a second. Release your arms without pushing the cat in any direction, otherwise you will add what is called spin, potentially interfering with the elegant action you will see next. Actually, you probably won't be able to see the individual movements—you'll just see your cat, slightly miffed perhaps, land on all four paws as if nothing serious was amiss.

The average cat standing on all fours may be about a foot at the shoulders from the floor, and a fall of three or four feet is about three to four times its normal standing height. If you were to be dropped from a proportional height from an equivalent position (head first?), you would *not* be able to walk away. You would certainly be more than miffed. So the cat's anatomy is special; it has an extremely flexible spine, which enables it to twist its back about 180°. But in the macroscopic world in which people would drop cats from three- or four-foot heights, no person, animal, or thing can violate Newton's laws of motion, which specify that a body in static equilibrium and in the absence of an external force cannot rotate, no matter how miraculous and mysterious the action is. So how can the cat do it? Is it physiology or new physics or what?

First the cat rotates the front of its body clockwise and the rear part counterclockwise, a motion that conserves energy and maintains the lack of spin, in accordance with Newton's laws. It then pulls in its legs, reverses the twist, and with a little extension of the legs, it is prepared for final landing. The cat instinctively knows how to move, and high divers, dancers, and some other athletes learn how to move in the absence of torque (the pushing force that gives you momentum in one direction or another), but scientists needed photographic evidence of the individual stopped-action steps to understand the mystery. The answer to the puzzle was that the moving body was not rigid, and Newton's laws prevailed. Marey provided the results in a paper presented to the Paris Academy in 1894 and published in the journal *La Nature*. Two sequences of photographs each showed the cat righting itself during a fall. Marey's photographs were grainy and of rather poor quality by today's standards, but the motions he caught were clear, just as they were with Muybridge's horse photographs.

What determines the required time resolution? As a starting point, we may consider the historic experiments in stop-motion photography performed more than a hundred years ago by Muybridge. We can estimate the duration of the shutter opening, Δt, that Muybridge needed for his camera by considering the necessary spatial resolution and the speed (v) of the horse. For a clearly defined image of a horse's legs, a resolution (Δx) of 1 cm is reasonable; that is, 1 cm is small compared to the relevant dimensions of the problem, the dimensions of the leg and its displacement during the course of a stride. Taking v to be about 10 meters per second (m/s) for the speed of a horse (the legs will, in fact, at times be moving several times faster), and using the simple relation between distance and time, $\Delta x = v \, \Delta t$, we find that the 1 cm divided by 10 m/s gives Δt equals 10^{-3} s or 1 millisecond. Indeed, Muybridge was able to achieve this necessary resolution to capture an image of a trotting (and galloping) horse with all four feet in the air.

In these studies, Muybridge sought to provide not only the isolated images required to answer questions such as those that first attracted his interest, but also to document the entire sequence of an animal's leg motions during its stride. To establish the required absolute timing of the photographs, he had initially set up a row of equally spaced cameras along a track at the Palo Alto farm, as noted in the previous chapter. The shutter of each camera was activated by a trip-wire stretched across the track in front of the camera. Thus a horse running down the track at speed v recorded a series of photographs, and the point in time associated with the *i*th photo could be calculated as d_i/v, where d_i is the distance from the starting gate to the *i*th camera. The separation in time between frames, τ, equals $\Delta d/v$, where $\Delta d = d_{i+1} - d_i$, so the number of frames per second is $v/\Delta d$.

Although the absolute timing of the frames of the series was imperfect, tied as it was to the speed of the horse from camera to camera, the images nonetheless permitted detailed analysis of the motion. The imprecision of the chronology of images obtained in this manner was the subject of some criticism, and in his later studies, Muybridge used cameras with shutters triggered sequentially by a clockwork mechanism to obtain photographs regularly spaced in time. He also used a sequence of the snapshots to create the impression of a moving picture. In 1991 I gave the Faraday Public Discourse at the Royal Institution, which Muybridge gave a hundred years earlier, and I used his old demonstration to make a connection, from the horse to the atom!

In Marey's experiment with the cat, the timing was regular, so the snapshots are taken at equal time (t) intervals, but the distance (x) intervals traveled by the cat were not equal, due to acceleration. We can estimate the required resolution in the following simple way, but using some numbers. If the cat makes its total flight in say 0.5 second, then we may use ten frames to track the motion by "slicing time." To "freeze" the motion, to "see" the in-between, or "stop" time—all terms used in stop-motion photography—the shutter duration needs to be much shorter than $0.5/10 = 50$ ms, the time between frames; the number of frames is 10 in the flight time of 0.5 second, or 20 per second.

The required duration that the shutter must be open to freeze the motion in the trajectory of the cat fall can be calculated. First we need to know the travel distance under the influence of gravity, which can be determined according to Galileo's law[1]—the distance traveled by the cat

---

1   Galileo's law states that $x(t) = (g/2)t^2$, where g is the universal acceleration, which for bodies falling on earth equals ~9.8 meters per second square—g is the product of Newton's gravity constant G (6.67×10^{-11} Nm²/kg²), which has the same value for any two bodies in the universe, and the ratio of the mass of the Earth (6×10^{24} kg) and the square of earth's radius (6.4×10^6 m). The universal nature of these relations explains the motion of cats as well as planets, and the independence of $x(t)$ on the mass of the object indicates why bodies of different masses arrive at the Earth at the same time.

after 0.5 second is 1.225 meters, or four feet. The velocity is not constant—the average value during this time is 2.45 m/s and the terminal instantaneous velocity, which is the limiting value, is 4.9 m/s. For a distance resolution of $\Delta x = 0.5$ cm, the shutter duration becomes 0.5 cm divided by 4.9 m/s, which is near 1 ms, to provide sharp images of the cat in falling motion; if the righting motion is similar in speed then the shutter duration is the same.

An alternative approach to the study of rapid motions, which has also proved capable of reaching much shorter time scales than was possible with fast shutters, is the use of short light flashes, which make an object moving in the dark visible to a detector (observer's eye or photographic plate, for example) only during the light pulse. Thus the pulse duration, Δt, plays the same role as the opening of a camera shutter and could be thought of in just the same way. An instrument that provides a series of short light pulses is a stroboscope (*strobos* from the Greek word for "whirling" and *scope* from the Greek for "look at," show the original use of the apparatus in viewing rotating objects). Combining a camera with an open shutter with an appropriately chosen Δt for the light pulses, a stroboscope can produce a well-resolved image of an object as fast as a bullet. In the mid-nineteenth century, spark photography had been demonstrated to stop rapid motions. The development of stroboscopic photography in the mid-twentieth century was greatly advanced by Harold Edgerton, a professor at the Massachusetts Institute of Technology (MIT) and cofounder of EG&G electronics, through the development of electronic flash equipment capable of producing reliable, repetitive, and microsecond-short flashes of light.

An example of the use of a stroboscope is that of a precisely timed sequence of images of a falling apple, which has a historic linkage to the legendary picture of Newton under a tree—eureka, gravity! With the speed of the apple taken to be v = 5m/s and a value for $\Delta x = 1$ mm needed for a sharp image, the Δt of the flash must be 1 mm divided by 5 m/s, which equals 2×10^{-4} s (200 microseconds), well within the stroboscope's range. An absolute time axis can be established by electronic timing of the flashes.

Such a series of pictures shows the effect of gravity, which can be quantified by analyzing the successive positions in which the light illuminates the apple. According to the law of uniformly accelerated motion, which I just expressed, flashes equally spaced in time would record images of uniformly increasing separation; the slope of the plot of image separation versus time is equal to $g\tau$, where g is the acceleration of gravity (for Earth it is close to 9.8 m/s^2) and τ is the spacing of the flashes. For a known τ, the value of g can be determined.

For the world of molecules, if the above ideas of stop-motion photography can be carried over in a straightforward manner, then the requirements for a femtochemistry experiment can be identified. For a molecular structure in which atomic motions of a few angstroms (an angstrom, Å, is 10^{-8} cm) typically characterize chemical reactions, a detailed mapping of the reaction process will require a spatial resolution (Δx) of less than 1 Å (about 0.1 Å), more than nine orders of magnitude smaller than was needed for Muybridge's or Marey's stop-motion photography. Therefore, the Δt required to observe with high definition the molecular transformations in which atoms move at speeds of the order of one kilometer per second, 1000 m/s, is 0.1Å divided by 1000 m/s, which equals 10^{-14} s or 10 fs.

If this resolution can be reached and if the above classical Newtonian description is valid, this time scale will provide, for the first time, the necessary resolution to freeze motion and enable us to directly see the detailed steps in molecular transformations. However, such minute times and distances mean that molecular-scale phenomena should be governed by the principles, or language, of quantum mechanics, which are quite different from the familiar laws of Newton's mechanics that were used in the description of the motion of the horse and cat. This fundamental difference will be addressed in the next chapter, where we shall see that the atom on its femtosecond time scale becomes a classical particle, making the bridging of the quantum to the classical world a natural transition. For now we continue to discuss how we can we photograph atomic action.

The use of laser pulses to "stop the motion" of atoms and obtain instantaneous molecular structures may be called *femtoscopy*. This term and its sibling *femtoscope* are introduced in analogy with the telescope—in this case we "look at" (*skopeo* in Greek) the far-from-visible atomic world with femtosecond time resolution. The femtoscope is an apparatus made of a complex assembly of optical elements with the femtosecond laser as an essential ingredient. Professor Nordén presented the same analogy between the femtoscope and the telescope in the Nobel address (see Appendix), and his reference to "the fastest camera in the world" actually characterizes the femtoscope.

Flashing a molecule with a femtosecond laser pulse can be compared to the effect of a stroboscope flash or the opening of a camera shutter. Thus a pulse from a femtosecond laser, combined with an appropriate detector, can produce a well-resolved "image" of a molecule as it passes through a specific configuration in a process of nuclear rearrangement, as Muybridge caught the horse with all four feet in the air and Marey caught the cat righting itself. The detection step is based on spectroscopic or diffraction techniques, and the measured signal can be analyzed to give information about the positions of the molecule's atoms, as discussed below.

The pulse that produces such an image is called a *probe* pulse, as it is used to probe the molecule's structure just as a shutter opening and a stroboscopic flash probed the positions of the horse and cat. Molecular structures determined at different stages of a reaction process can be treated as the frames of a motion picture, allowing the motion of the atoms to be clearly visualized—the number of frames in a molecular movie could then be as high as 10^{14} per second.

Probing is not the whole story. For the entire course of any motion to be recorded, that motion must be initiated so that it takes place in the time span accessible to a sequence of probe snapshots. In photographing the horse and cat, the processes were initiated by opening a starting gate for the horse and by releasing the cat. The respective probing sequences were arranged to coincide closely in time to those actions. For femtochemistry, the analogous operation is realized by launching the molecule on its path using a femtosecond initiation, or pump, pulse passing through the sample. This establishes a temporal reference point (time zero of the clock) for the changes that occur in the molecular motion or reaction.

The timing relative to the probe pulses is accomplished by generating the pump and probe pulses from a common source and sending either the pump or probe along an adjustable optical path to the sample. The difference between pump and probe path lengths divided by the constant speed of light, 299,792 km/s, precisely fixes each probe image on the time axis established by the pump. This use of optical path differences to measure transient phenomena dates back at least to 1899, when H. Abraham and J. Lemoine reported their measurement in France of what was known as the Kerr response of carbon disulfide.

A fundamental difference in the analogy between femtoscopy of the atom and the millisecond photography of the horse or cat is the fact that in femtochemistry experiments one probes typically millions to billions of molecules for each initiation pulse and/or repeats the experiment many times to provide a signal strong enough for adequate analysis. A comparable situation would arise in stroboscopy of the apple if the capture of a distinct photographic image could be accomplished only by using many different apples and/or repeated exposures. It is clear that success in such a case would require precise synchronization of the strobe (probe) pulse sequence with the release of the apple to less than or about the same duration as the strobe pulse for optimum resolution, as well as a precisely defined launching configuration of each apple accurate to a fraction of an apple diameter.

By the same reasoning, in order to synchronize the motion of many independent *molecules* so that they have all reached a similar point in the course of their structural evolution when the probe pulse arrives to capture the desired impression, the relative timing of pump and probe pulses has to be of femtosecond precision, and the launch configuration has to be defined to subangstrom resolution. It is only by means of such synchronization that the signals from many molecules could be added together without hopelessly blurring the molecular structure derived from the measurement. The use of pulses generated by the same source and the optical path delay described above provides the required degree of timing precision; a typical optical path accuracy of 1 micrometer corresponds to absolute timing of the molecular snapshots of 3.3 fs, since the speed of light is very close to 300,000 km/s. Of equal importance is the required definition of the launch configuration. This definition is realized because the femtosecond pump pulse snaps all members of the molecular ensemble from their ground states, which have a single well-defined structure. Moreover, on the femtosecond time scale, moving atoms are coherent, particlelike in their trajectories, as shown later in the following chapter.

But in reality, how did we achieve such coherent localization of atoms in motion in an ensemble of millions to billions of molecules, and what were the needed new concepts? The experimental and theoretical foundations took many years to build, and we had to walk through many alleys and avenues for the efforts to culminate in exciting and rewarding discoveries. Following our work in the late 1970s on coherence phenomena and in the mid-1980s closing in to resolve reaction dynamics in real time, our thirst for better stroboscopic resolution was clear. We needed a whole new apparatus, a whole new "camera" with unprecedented time resolution. We needed to interface femtosecond lasers and molecular beam technology, which required not only a new initiative but also a quantum leap in funding, not just an incremental addition to what we had already acquired at Caltech.

A piece of good fortune came my way. Professor Shaul Mukamel invited me to a workshop in Rochester, New York, in October of 1985. The topic was intramolecular vibrational energy redistribution (IVR) and chemical reactivity, which was part of our research at the time. In the audience were two program directors from the U.S. Air Force Office of Scientific Research, who were intrigued by my presentation. They introduced themselves after my talk as Larry Davis and Larry Buggraf and suggested that I immediately send a preliminary proposal for my work. I sent a preliminary proposal outlining future directions of research, and followed it with a complete one in January of the next year.

We were approved for funding, and my laboratory components for the femtosecond laser were on order to build the new apparatus. One thing was still missing, however—a place to put the new equipment. My lab space at the time was already crowded with equipment and there was just no free space for the new apparatus, so Fred Anson, the division chairman at Caltech at the time, arranged for a new space for us by renovating an existing lab that housed the old x-ray machines of Linus Pauling. Murph Goldberger, then president of Caltech, provided the funds for the renovation without any delay. By Thanksgiving of 1986, we began setting up our apparatus, including the new laser, a Bell Labs designed colliding pulse mode-locked (CPM) ring dye laser. The system was in operation in time for our "femtosecond party" on December 11 of the same year.

Everything was now set up: we had the new light probe, we had the molecular beam, or reaction cells, and equipment for taking "snapshots" of the molecular changes. We just needed to get the "actors" in place. The "actors" in our little production, of course, were simple substances that would undergo a reaction to create a new substance. But our production wasn't going to be a two-act story with only a beginning and an end—we wanted to put on center stage what goes on *between* the beginning and the end. For molecules, that in-between action was on my mind, and I had already written about such a wish in the 1985 paper mentioned in the preceding chapter.

Our first successful experiment was on a molecule of three atoms, iodine, carbon, and nitrogen (ICN), the same molecule used in the 1985 experiment. We went back to the ICN dissociation reaction, snapping away at 10 fs intervals, which were fast enough to record enough frames of the I–C bond breaking, little by little, the first time such a thing had ever been witnessed in real time. Those were thrilling moments with my students and postdoctoral fellows, and I wasn't sleeping at night! Those slow-motion movies were composite pictures in more ways than one. We used the frequency of the light absorbed by atoms and molecules as the "fingerprints" of their change—the frequency absorbed by a free CN molecule is different from that of CN next to a foreign atom (the I atom). In other words, on the path to dissociation the music listened to, in our case the frequency of spectra, changed with time. This *tuning* was a new idea that worked so beautifully that I had a hard time believing it when the first results were successfully obtained.

Because the exact frequency that a molecule (or a bond) absorbs light depends on, among other things, the distance between the atoms, we set the probe laser to a frequency that corresponded to some arbitrary distance, and then marched through a complete set of, say, 150 delay times to see when that particular bond distance showed up. Then we reset the probe to a slightly different frequency and did it all again. Once we compiled the appearance and disappearance times for all the bond lengths into a single data set, we then saw the bond stretch till it snapped. And snap it did—ICN fell apart in a mere 200 femtoseconds. There was an additional check that confirmed our observations in the ICN experiment. When we tuned in on the free CN fragment, whose spectroscopy is well known, we observed the reaction in real time to its final destination. For this reaction we could record the time for the entire journey and its transition states when the CN was in close proximity to the I atom—frame by frame—just like the horse or the cat at the final stage of the motion and during their transient flights.

The reaction of ICN occurred on the so-called repulsive surface, that is, the I atom and CN diatomic molecule dislike each other from time zero, and by breaking the I–C bond they released their energy of frustration and ended up with a divorce. Such a change in the potential energy of atoms as bonds are broken and formed is called the energy landscape or the potential-energy surface. Some atoms like to attract each other and fall in deep love (a potential well); others repel each other and remain repulsive—attraction and repulsion as in human interactions. Many do both simultaneously when forming new bonds and breaking old ones, and in the process, the reactants climb up an energy mountain. As described by Doug Smith, a writer for *Engineering & Science* at Caltech, this reaction barrier is generally pictured as a mountain separating two valleys. In one valley, or state of minimum energy, lie the reactants; the products lie in the other. The reactants have to have enough energy to hike up the mountain before they can ski down the other side.

These are like landscapes, but unlike the latitude and longitude coordinates one uses to navigate cross-country, the axes of a potential-energy surface are the distances between the atoms involved in the reaction. When only two atoms are involved, the potential-energy surface becomes a curved line on a piece of paper: a two-dimensional plot of energy versus bond length. When one bond breaks and a different bond forms, the surface is three-dimensional, like a relief map, and as additional atoms get involved, the surface can occupy still more dimensions. And complex reactions may have several intermediate products in alpine valleys scattered through a canton's worth of peaks and passes. Each summit (in two dimensions) or saddleback (in three or more dimensions) in the potential-energy surface is what chemists call a transition state—that point when the molecule is in between, no longer a reactant and not yet a product, its bonds, like Richard III's physique, scarce half made up.

In this case, the transition state is a razorback ridge, not a broad plateau, and molecules don't dally there. But this definition is narrow—historically, it was important to invoke it in order to derive theoretical expressions for rates of reactions. More descriptive of the reactivity and the entire reaction journey is the whole family of transition states between reactants and products. These transition states were considered fleeting, and before our work, they had never been observed directly, even though they had been postulated to exist since the 1930s. As the first such observation, the ICN experiment demonstrated the ability to observe these ephemeral transition states—the heart of chemical reactivity—and opened the door for a myriad of new studies.

Next we tackled a molecule with a more complex landscape, sodium iodide, a molecule that I call the "drosophila" of our field, and it turned out to be a paradigm case for the field of femtochemistry. Sodium iodide, a sibling of the table salt sodium chloride, exists in its ionic form when left unexcited. When neutral sodium and iodine atoms approach one another to within 6.9 Å, the greedy iodine steals an electron from the sodium and becomes negatively charged, leaving the sodium ion with a positive charge. The two ions cling together electrostatically in a deep, steep (attractive) energy well at a bond length of 2.8 Å.

But it's also possible for the two atoms to share the electron in what chemists call a covalent bond, whose potential-energy surface lies at a higher elevation and has only one sidewall, like a ledge on the mountain's face. At distances of greater than 6.9 Å, the covalent potential-energy surface is actually lower in energy. In other words, the ionic and covalent potential-energy surfaces—parallel universes, if you will, that occupy the same space—intersect at that distance. And, as any viewer of any incarnation of *Star Trek* will tell you, where parallel universes cross, there's a portal from one to the other. In other words, the *real* potential-energy surface—the solid ground on which the system hikes—is ionic at short range and covalent farther out.

The pump laser punts the bond onto the unused, high-energy portions—covalent close up and ionic afar—that float above the low-energy landscape where the system normally lives. The laser also sets the atoms flying away from each other, and as they pass the magic 6.9 Å mark, the iodine snatches the electron, reverting to ionic form. Charges don't like to be separated and a femtoscale version of static cling starts pulling the atoms back inward. They woosh together again, and at 6.9 Å the iodine gives the electron back.

Experimentally we could see for the first time a chemical bond transforming in real time from covalent to ionic, covalent, ionic, covalent, ionic—in this case, by the way, they were in love for about nine or ten cycles before they divorced each other at the end. With each cycle came a chance that the outbound system would stay on the covalent potential-energy surface beyond the crossover point, in which case the two electrically neutral atoms would part company forever. The sodium-iodide marriage took about eight picoseconds to fall apart—a long-term commitment on the atomic scale, if not the human one!

With such striking observations of atoms moving in real time, and in concert among the billions of molecules studied, we had to ask questions regarding the concepts involved and formulate some theoretical framework for the physics behind the observations. In the process we learned a great deal about dynamics and we published papers on the classical picture of motion, the one used to describe the horse and cat in motion, and why such a picture emerges from the quantum one on the femtosecond time scale. There were some skeptics to the validity of this general picture, and they even questioned the general applicability of the approach to complex molecular systems. The belief is that quantum uncertainty, which is discussed in the following chapter, and quantum dephasing, which reflects the inability of molecules to stay coherent, will limit the value of femtochemistry. I was convinced of the opposite viewpoint, and we went on to do more studies of different systems—I had the feeling that the sky was the limit for the world of molecules and the femtoscope was ready for new discoveries in several of our laboratories at Caltech.

Across the hall, we were studying the happy marriage of two molecules. We were filming an even tougher assignment—determined to observe the simultaneous bond making and bond breaking in a chemical transformation, the so-called bimolecular (atom–molecule or any two-body) collision. One such transformation was a reaction essential in atmospheric chemistry and to the process of combustion: $H + CO_2 \rightarrow OH + CO$—an atom of hydrogen and a molecule of carbon dioxide changing to a hydroxyl radical and a carbon monoxide molecule. Dick Bernstein, who had become a familiar face at Caltech, had a special passion for bimolecular reactions, and almost every day we were together having intense discussions on their dynamics. How can we bang two molecules together so that they will react?

Most collisions are fruitless—the atoms or molecules just ricochet off each other. To react, they need to be in just the right orientation, and have to hit each other hard enough to stick. And how do you start the clock consistently with each fresh pair of molecules? Unlike Muybridge's camera, there are no trip wires for the inbound molecules to cross. However, if we shot a mixture of carbon dioxide and hydrogen iodide (HI) into the vacuum of the molecular beam chamber, when the two gases went supersonic and lost energy, some of the molecules would pair up into loosely bound complexes that put the atoms in the proper relative positions at a fixed separation, ready to be zapped with the pump laser. Now that one bond (in this case, the H–O) was forming while another

(C–O) was breaking, we got into questions of the sequence and timing. Did both happen at once? Were there intermediate products?

We discovered that once the H had collided with the O in hundreds of femtoseconds, leading to the H–O bond formation, the atoms clung together for a picosecond as they overcame the attraction energy and moved on the energy landscape. The intermediate HOCO, the presumed ephemeral collision complex, hung around, quivering like jello, for a picosecond or so as the excess collisional energy worked its way into the C–O bond in order to blow it apart. The exact timing was then compared to the detailed quantum-mechanical predictions numerous researchers were making from first principles—a rigorous test of the theory.

Hans Christian von Baeyer gave the following eloquent description of this study and the analogy with Marey's cat: For carbon dioxide to form hydroxide and deadly carbon monoxide, "how does it work? Does the carbon dioxide molecule shed an oxygen atom for the passing hydrogen atom to catch? That seems improbable, because if carbon dioxide spontaneously decayed into carbon monoxide, we would die of our own exhalations. If, on the other hand, hydrogen hits the carbon dioxide, the system becomes, at least temporarily, a congeries of four atoms—hydrogen, carbon, and the two oxygens. Then how do they reach their final outcome? In what manner do they twist and turn as they reassemble?"

Continuing with the questions, do they briefly form some new molecule hitherto unknown to chemists? If so, what is its shape? How long does it live? These questions were as urgent to modern chemists as the motion of a falling cat was to physicists during the Victorian age, as von Baeyer has commented. Described by the chemical formula HOCO, like all complex molecules that have just undergone a violent trauma—birth, in this case—it vibrates and rotates through space. The tumbling, shivering HOCO molecule is a quantum mechanical Cheshire cat, a short-lived enigma about which little was known.

Femtochemistry took off in the 1990s in many new directions. Our group moved to the next level of complexity—organic chemistry, the chemistry of carbon atoms and therefore of life. The group started with organic molecules of more than ten atoms and soon worked all the way up to DNA and proteins. And our lab continued its tradition of figuring out how to develop new instrumental methods, bringing in such techniques as mass spectrometry to femtochemistry. Organic molecules are complex enough that a reaction starting with a given molecule will often proceed along several routes at once, giving a family of similar-looking products that absorb and emit similar frequencies of light.

But mass spec, as it's called, separates molecular fragments by their mass-to-charge ratio (the m/e of J.J. Thomson), allowing us to discriminate between two variants that differ by as little as one hydrogen atom. An advanced version measures the arrival time, energy, and spatial orientation of each piece—vital clues for reconstructing the molecule's history and its femtoscape. Chemical theory comes in for its fair share of scrutiny as well, because femtochemists can make stringent tests of theoretical predictions by using one of those complex molecules that can follow many reaction paths, and comparing what actually happens to what the theory says should occur. Theory can also aid the experiments and we maintained the strong connection between theory and experiment.

One of the projects the Nobel committee mentioned in its citation had to do with stilbene, which has two benzene rings at opposite ends of a double bond. Double bonds don't spin freely, so the rings are locked into position—if you think of your shoulders as being the double bond and a tennis racquet in each hand as the benzene rings, you can hold both racquets up (what chemists call the *cis* configuration) or hold one up and one down (the *trans* configuration). However, zinging the right laser pulse at the bond unlocks it and flips the rings. This is Doug Smith's metaphor, which I like.

We were studying *cis*-stilbene in 1992, and found that not only did the shoulders move, but the wrists turned at the same time, and the entire process was coherently completed in 300 femtoseconds. Work at the University of California at Berkeley on biological molecules with a similar double-bonded structure showed that retinal, a light-sensitive pigment in the eye, undergoes a similar reaction with 70% efficiency in 200 femtoseconds as the first step in transforming a photon of light into a nerve impulse. The fact that the reaction happens so quickly and so efficiently (a vital attribute for good night vision!) indicates that the incoming light goes effectively to the double bond rather than being spread throughout the molecule—a theme that runs straight back to those early coherence experiments. It's identical in concept to sodium iodide. The twisting motion of the double bond is coherent between two configurations with coherence persisting for the high-efficiency process of vision—Alhazen would have been delighted to know about this microscopic picture! Other researchers tell the same story about photosynthesis, the process by which plants harvest energy from sunlight, and the phenomenon is now known to be common in other physical, chemical, and biological changes.

Currently, there are seven *femtolands*, as our laboratories are affectionately called. In our labs over the years, members of the group—graduate students, undergraduates, postdoctoral fellows, and visiting associates—have studied a variety of molecular reactions from different branches of chemistry and biology. The research groups of colleagues all over the world have also contributed significantly to studies of many other systems and in the different phases of matter. As the Nobel citation reads:

> Scientists the world over are studying processes with femtosecond spectroscopy in gases, in fluids and in solids, on surfaces and in polymers. Applications range from how catalysts function and how molecular electronic components must be designed, to the most delicate mechanisms in life processes and how the medicines of the future should be produced.

Following the announcement of the Nobel prize, the Philadelphia-based Institute for Scientific Information, which uses how often a researcher's papers are referred to in their peers' publications as an indicator of how influential the cited work is, announced that femtochemistry had been footnoted 50,000 times since its inception. Robert Paradowski, the noted biographer of Linus Pauling, among others, and a professor at the Rochester Institute of Technology, wrote about the contribution in a recent article from the following interesting perspective: "By inventing these methods Zewail was the Christopher Columbus of the femtoworld, becoming the first to witness chemical events that occurred in quadrillionths of a second." I take great pride that my entire professorial life has been spent at Caltech, and the development of the field of femtochemistry is truly part of Caltech's heritage. It all started here.

I take even greater pride in being at the same institution where Linus Pauling did his own Nobel prize–winning work on the nature of the chemical bond. (As the forces of history would have it, both of us were the same age, practically to the day, when we won the prize.) Pauling worked from crystallographic data, and his bonds were static, stable, and enduring. Now, forty-five years later, we have set those bonds in motion, making them as alive and dynamic as chemistry itself. I think this connection from the structure of the chemical bond to the dynamics of the chemical bond is a wonderful legacy for Caltech to give the world. In his article Paradowski gave a detailed analogy, part of which says: "Just as Pauling had used the techniques of X-ray crystallography and electron diffraction to figure out the structures of molecules, so Zewail used sophisticated laser techniques to describe how atoms move during the process when new molecules are created." It is at special institutions like Caltech that it is possible for us, with our students and associates, to provide such a legacy.

Being in the right place at the right time helped us achieve some of our initial goals and made us venture into new territories we hadn't planned originally. We didn't anticipate the huge activity in the field worldwide. And no one would have anticipated the widespread applications of femtosecond lasers, either in chemistry and biology or in other fields such as metrology, microelectronics, and medicine. In microelectronics, for example, the analogy with molecules is direct. Because of the ultrashort time duration of the pulses, energy can be deposited selectively and there is no spillover in micromachining on the nanometer scale of chips—clear patterns are obtained which are far superior to those obtained by nanosecond (or longer) lasers. The same principle applies to uses in dentistry, where tooth drilling is not accompanied by pain when energy has no time to reach the nerve with ultrafast femtosecond machining. In medicine there have been a number of applications now used in hospitals for the imaging of tumors and for the direct view of our cells and their changes with time.

There's no doubt that the unique features of these pulses—their duration, frequency range, and intensity—are bringing about new applications and opening new frontiers. One such frontier involves very intense pulses. The peak power density of a state-of-the-art femtosecond pulse is now in the range of 10^{21} watts per square centimeter (focused laser beam); unfocused power is about 10^{15} watts. The average electric power consumed per person in the United States is about 1 kilowatt, and thus for the entire population on planet Earth, the average power cannot exceed 10^{13} watts, only 1% of the laser power. The sun gives us on Earth 1.3 kilowatts per square meter, and for the entire state of Texas (678,000 square kilometers) the total solar power is the same as that of the femtosecond laser. Colleagues in the United States, Europe, and Japan are reporting on these and other exciting applications.

In retrospect, it's remarkable that the initial idea introducing the importance of coherence in the studies of molecular dynamics, which I outlined in the proposal to Caltech for my 1975 job search, remained vital to the development of the field. The last paragraph of the proposal is worth repeating here—it emphasized the importance of coherence for large molecules, beginning with studies of these molecules in solids:

> The coupling of the excited state levels to the radiation
> field whose frequency spectrum spans the transition
> width could result in the observation of quantum
> coherence effects. . . . In fact, one can measure the opti-
> cal transverse and longitudinal decay times by forming
> a superposition of states. Furthermore, quantum inter-
> ference effects will lead to the observation of the opti-
> cal 'rotating frame' phenomena. . . . These techniques

will open up a new field of 'beat spectroscopy' in solids with large molecules occupying their sites. . . . Ultimately this could shine some light on how the excited state is created.

Now that we can see the once invisible motions of atoms and now that the race against time is at its end for tracking coherent atomic motions in the femtouniverse of molecules, we must ask: What new concepts and principles can we offer to the sciences of time and matter?

Receiving the award from the king,
Stockholm, December 10, 1999

The banquet arrangement at the city hall
in Stockholm, December 10, 1999

The Nobel awards ceremony of 1999; I am in the front row, third from the left

Dema and I meet
King Gustav
and Queen Silvia
of Sweden

Giving the Nobel banquet address, December 10, 1999

My family, dressed for
the evening's big event

The Nobel medal

The design by artist Nils
G. Stenqvist on the inside
of the Nobel diploma

The Grand Collar of the Nile

At the presidential palace

With President Mubarak on the occasion of the receipt
of the Grand Collar of the Nile, December 16, 1999

Postage stamps
issued on the
occasion of the
Franklin prize
in 1998, and the
Nobel prize
in 1999

With President Clinton,
January, 2000.

With Pope John Paul II,
November, 2000

With the laser setup
in the laboratory

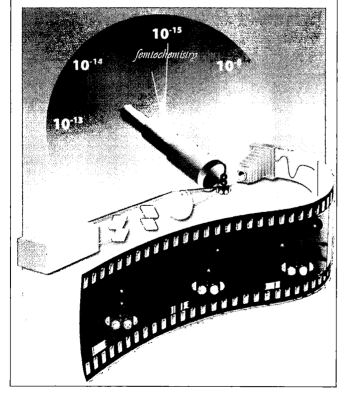

An artist's rendering
of the femtoscope
capturing atoms in
motion

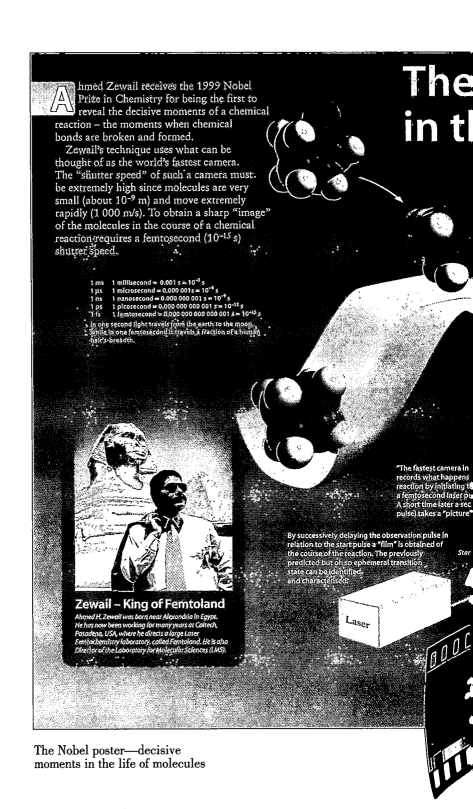

The Nobel poster—decisive
moments in the life of molecules

ecisive moments
life of molecules

A chemical reaction – up hill and down dale

Like everything in nature, molecules strive to reach the lowest possible energy state. This makes it practical to describe reactions using energy surfaces. A molecule on an energy surface tries, like a child in a water-slide, to reach the lowest point. You need enough speed (high energy) to get up over the crests.

The picture to the left shows the ring opening of a cyclobutane molecule to form two ethylene molecules. Zewail studied this reaction by exciting cyclopentanone molecules with a femtosecond pulse. He could show that this reaction occurs via a transition state living a few hundred femtoseconds. This experiment settled an old argument over whether the reaction takes place in one step with simultaneous breaking of both bonds or in two steps, one bond breaking before the other.

We need to know the properties of the transition state if we are to understand, predict and perhaps modify the course of a reaction. For almost a hundred years the transition state remained a hypothetical species that few chemists believed could ever be observed. But this is precisely what Zewail has succeeded in doing.

The experiment gives no direct image of the molecules. Instead, the reacting molecules are observed by measuring certain characteristic properties, e.g. an optical property (a spectrum is obtained) or by recording the molecular masses (mass spectrometry).

Molecular beam

rvation molecules.

Spectrum

Observation pulse

The picture shows part of Zewail's "camera". It is a complex array of lasers, mirrors, lenses, prisms, molecular beams, detection equipment and more.

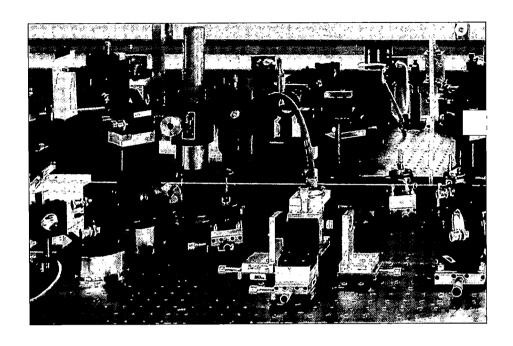

Two views of the femtoscope
apparatus, taken in the first
femtosecond laboratory at
Caltech—Femtoland I

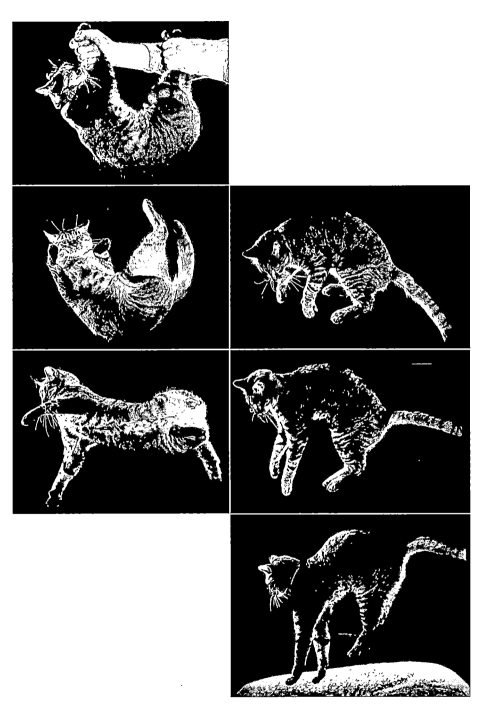

Stop-motion photographs of a falling cat
(©Stephen Dalton/NHPA/Photo Researchers Inc.)

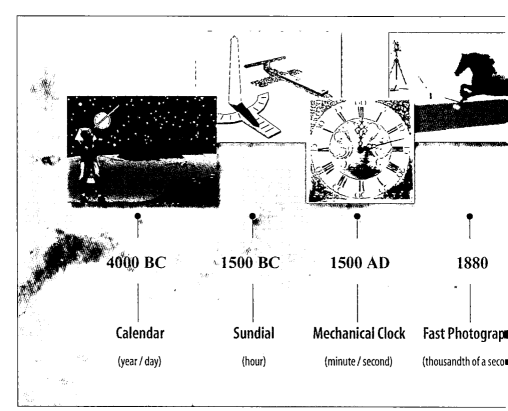

4000 BC	1500 BC	1500 AD	1880
Calendar	Sundial	Mechanical Clock	Fast Photograph
(year / day)	(hour)	(minute / second)	(thousandth of a seco

A boll of
Egyptian cotton

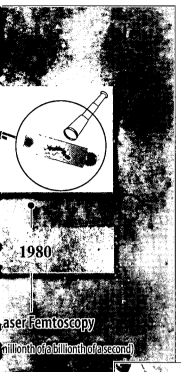

1980

Laser Femtoscopy
(millionth of a billionth of a second)

A modern Greek
ten-drachma
coin showing
Democritus (top)
and the atom
(bottom)

Freezing time:
six millennia
of history to the
femtosecond

Galileo Galilei
(courtesy of
Galleria degli
Uffizi,
Florence, Italy)

A quiet moment with my family in Pasadena

7

Time and Matter

The Femtouniverse in Perspective

reeman Dyson, a well-known physicist and science writer, quoted one of his mathematics teachers at Cambridge, Professor Godfrey Hardy, as saying: "A mathematician, like a painter or a poet, is a maker of patterns. If his patterns are more permanent than theirs, it is because they are made with ideas." I think the same description applies to scientists in general, but what is meant by ideas—*new* ideas? Some scientific revolutions arise from the invention of new tools or techniques for observing nature; others arise from the discovery of new concepts for understanding nature. Historians seek to explore in depth the process of scientific discovery and to define what constitutes new ideas.

Thomas Kuhn, in his influential book, *The Structure of Scientific Revolutions*, suggests that the process of scientific discovery is driven by new concepts, new paradigms. On the other hand, Peter Galison in his book *Image and Logic* takes a different view—the process is driven by new tools. Dyson is more on the side of Galison than Kuhn—he rejects the idea that scientific revolutions are primarily concept-driven, but rather that new tools are more often the sparks that ignite scientific discovery.

I believe that the fusion of the two—the development of new tools or techniques and new thinking about new concepts—is what creates harmony in observing and understanding nature. Some are gifted in developing tools for observing and they need the help of those interested in developing new concepts, or vice versa, and some have the ability to do both. At the end, the creation of a beautiful pattern results when the communication between the two becomes clear and even critical. The first thing that a good scientist does when confronted with an important discovery is to try to prove it wrong, either in the process of observation or in concept.

In our work, we have experienced this fusion between observations and concepts, and it was important to our understanding of the marriage between time and matter or, more accurately, of the behavior of matter—the transformation from one form to another—at the limit of time. The Nobel citation (given in the Appendix of this book) is more specific, as it is written for the scientific community, but it conveys this point about the fusion of observations and concepts. The academy went on to detail the historical progression of events in an extended version of the write-up, and the following words describe the intermingling of techniques and concepts in the development of the field and its applications:

> He had realized in the 1970s that molecules could be brought to vibrate in pace. Coherent preparation of a sample system is thus a key point in all his experiments. At the end of the 1980s, [he] performed a series of experiments that were to lead to the birth of a new research field called femtochemistry. . . . Studies according to Zewail's concept are being intensely pursued the world over. . . . Femtochemistry has fundamentally changed our view of chemical reactions.

Instruments can be invented and even be widely available, but until their use is directed to address significant conceptual questions, major breakthroughs are unlikely to be made—of course, serendipity may be part of the practice, but as Louis Pasteur said, "Chance favors a prepared mind." As I mentioned in the preceding chapter, Galileo didn't invent the telescope, but rather developed it for the purpose of looking at the heavens and directed it the right way! Concepts relating to the dynamics of motion were surely part of Galileo's thinking. Whether we look at the heavens (telescope) or molecules (femtoscope), the newly observed phenomena give rise to new knowledge that helps us conceptually understand nature—we then look farther. Another example comes from the work of one of the greatest twentieth-century scientists. Linus Pauling didn't discover x-rays or quantum mechanics, but his success in elucidating the nature of the chemical bond was the result of using these tools and applying and developing new concepts.

In our work, the excitement initially stemmed from the ability to observe, for the first time, atoms in motion and to bring to view the transformation of molecules from one structure to another, and from one substance to another—a fundamental property of matter. Clearly, the role of new tools and instrumentation was critical. The integration of newly developed picosecond and femtosecond lasers to the molecular beam was an essential advance for us to be able to make such observations. But what lie hidden are the concepts behind the design of new experiments and the developed concepts that are formulated from the new observations. The fusion of observations with concepts is what led to the establishment of the new field and to the real change in the way we think of the dynamics of matter in real time.

In my mind, there are four significant elements that are the basis for this change in the way we think and answer the question, why is observing in real time important? They are: the new world of knowledge, the new field, the new concepts, and the new prospects. First, *the new world of knowledge.* Science, which has its roots in the Latin word *scientia,* meaning "knowledge," is the systematized study of phenomena that are concerned with the material and functions of the physical universe. As students of science we begin research to acquire new knowledge, and in the process we may make new discoveries and we may find applications for our society. To know something useful about the unknown or to uncover its secrets is a gratifying feeling for a scientist.

For me, the new knowledge about atoms in motion is a big thrill.

Since their birth as a concept nearly 2,500 years ago, Democritus' atoms had not been observed, and femtochemistry made it possible to observe and study these once hypothetical atoms. The physicist Hans Christian von Baeyer describes the significance in his book *Taming the Atom:* "Femtochemistry represents the latest link in the reductionist program begun by Leucippus and Democritus . . . of describing nature in terms of the motion of its irreducible constituents."

Motion is fundamental, as all molecular transformations and properties are governed by the forces between atoms, the forces of hate and love between them. Isaac Newton, in the preface to the first edition of his *Principia Mathematica*, described his perspective on the subject:

> I wish we could derive the rest of the phenomena of Nature by the same kind of reasoning from mechanical principles, for I am induced by many reasons to suspect that they may all depend upon certain forces by which the particles of bodies, by some causes hitherto unknown, are either mutually impelled toward one another, and cohere in regular figures, or are repelled and recede from one another.

Motion and its forces are what dynamics is all about, and many fields of science are defined with dynamics and mechanics in their titles: thermodynamics, statistical mechanics, electrodynamics, classical mechanics, quantum mechanics, and molecular dynamics. Motion is at the root of many phenomena, and femtochemistry provides a magnifying glass for the study of the dynamics of invisible phenomena in the microuniverse of molecules.

Second, the *new field*. In all of chemistry's rich history of over two millennia, the actual atomic motions involved in chemical reactions had never been observed in real time. Thus, the transition states between initial reactants and final products were not amenable to direct observation. This "black box" was represented by an arrow with a question mark on it, since these transition states were considered elusive and ephemeral.

Understanding the dynamics of transition states is understanding the heart of chemistry—understanding how atoms are involved in the elementary processes of bond breaking and bond making, understanding matter and its reactions. This is the concern of the field of femtochemistry. To appreciate the significance of the development we should look at the history of chemistry, which goes back to the place where I received my university education.

As a term defining a field, "chemistry" has its roots in Alexandria, when it was called *chemia*, a word apparently derived from a much earlier pharaonic word, *kmt*, meaning the "black land" of Egypt; Egypt took this name for its dark, fertile soil and for the changes in the topsoil that accompanied the annual flooding of the Nile. Chemistry was thus the art of change, the Egyptian art. (Historians make the point that it wasn't meant as the "black art" of magicians.)

In fact, the Stockholm Chemical Papyrus, written about AD 300 in Greek, records a recipe for making a new substance (which turned out to be for coloring stones) that derives from the much older pharaonic period and is indicative of the long roots of interest in chemical change. Research advances of *chemia* in Alexandria were the result of an amalgamated effort between the Egyptians, who were consumed by the practical transmutation of metals and workings of glasses and substances ("technology driven"), and the Greeks who were occupied with the philosophical definition of what the meaning of an element was ("concept driven").

The era of *chemia*, which lasted until into the Roman period in Egypt, had its roots in the rich period of about 3500 BC during the ancient cultures of Egypt and Mesopotamia. Metals, glasses, and dyes were extracted, worked, and improved. The Egyptians extracted gold, perhaps the first metal found, from areas in the vicinity of the Nile Valley; obtained copper from the malachite (carbonate) of Sinai by reducing it in charcoal fires (around 3500 BC); and made bronze alloys of copper and tin (around 3000 BC), and later discovered iron and its workings. Similarly, they made advances in the working of pottery and glasses: melting natron, the sodium carbonate found near Alexandria, and quartz to make glass; heating silica with malachite and lime to make "Egyptian blue"; and extracting indigo dye from plants. We might call this ancient "divine art" the "art of applied chemistry."

These advances, reached during the era of *chemia*, defined an interest in achieving control over the transmutation of metals and in the observation (and trial) of many chemical changes. As a result, new types of chemical apparatus were designed for distillation, filtration, heating, and crystallization. When the Arabs came to Egypt in AD 639 they studied *chemia* adopting and Arabizing the word as *al-kimia'*, which in turn was brought into English and other Western languages as *alchemy*. The Arabs contributed significantly to the field and the works of Jabir ibn Hayyan, al-Razi, and Ibn Sina became known during the period 700–1100.

In about 1100, throughout Spain, the works of Arabs and translations of earlier works from Alexandria and Greece were transferred to Europe, forming the basis for what we now know as chemistry. The work on gases, combustion, and other phenomena by Robert Boyle (1627–91), Joseph Priestley (1733–1804), and Antoine Lavoisier (1743–94), among others, started modern chemistry and its modern techniques. Alchemy, which was also known in China, India, and other cultures, had an impact on Europe's medicine, metallurgy, and other fields, but perhaps most importantly, it triggered the studies of chemistry as an *exact* science.

The research of John Dalton (1766–1844), Amadeo Avogadro (1776–1856), Dmitry Mendeleyev (1834–1907), and many other notable scientists has reduced the understanding of chemistry to its atomic and molecular descriptions. I would like to define four key concepts that define many modern fields of study over the past three hundred years. These are: composition (atomic, molecular weight, synthesis, etc.); energetics (thermodynamics, heat, entropy, etc.); structure (stereochemistry, chirality, etc.); and dynamics (rates, transition states, etc.). At the heart of these concepts were the questions: What are molecules? How are atoms glued together to form molecules? And how does molecular behavior determine reactivity? The discovery of the electron by J.J. Thomson in 1897 was of paramount importance in answering some of these questions.

Structure and dynamics have benefited greatly from the natural evolution of the scientific progress in: 1) the development of new techniques and observations; 2) theoretical understanding; and 3) generalizations to explain and exploit the phenomena (sometimes points 1 and 2 are interchanged). Two years before the discovery of the electron, in 1895, Röntgen discovered x-rays. (Remarkably, about the same time, three other important discoveries were made: radioactivity in 1896, quantum theory in 1900, and special relativity in 1905.) The Braggs' (father and son) work in the 1910s established x-ray crystallography as a new experimental technique for studying the structure of molecules, as noted before.

The road to the dynamics of the chemical bond started before the discovery of the electron with the question: How do reactions proceed and what are their rates? In Sweden, Svante Arrhenius gave the description of the change in rates of chemical reactions with temperature and formulated in 1889 the familiar mathematical expression describing this change. Arrhenius introduced the concept of a hypothetical body, now known as the activated complex or transition state. In the 1930s, the atomic description of this picture was provided by Henry Eyring and Michael Polanyi, then in Berlin. In the 1930s, no one could have dreamed of observing the transient molecular structures of a chemical reaction, since the time scale for those far-from-equilibrium activated complexes in the transition state were estimated to be less than a picosecond. Only in the late twentieth century could we observe and study transition states.

The third of the four elements that illustrate the impact femtochemistry has made is the *new concepts*. Observations made on the femtosecond time scale have resulted in the crystallization of new concepts regarding the *femtoscape* of molecules and the dynamics of chemical and biological change. Some of these concepts are fundamental to the behavior of matter on this time scale, and have, during the infancy of the field, raised several questions in the minds of skeptics. These concepts relate to the duality and uncertainty of matter at this time scale and the brevity of the phenomena observed.

Generally speaking, one would like to know the answer to the following questions, which we raised in the preceding two chapters: Given that atoms and molecules follow the language of quantum mechanics (their position in space is probabilistic, not deterministic), how is it possible that we can speak of their motion as classical particles? What about the uncertainty principle paradox? (Because of the brevity of time, we lose knowledge of where the atoms are going. This uncertainty was thought to be a real obstacle for the usefulness of this time scale). Finally, why do all molecules behave in the same way during the time of observation?

Knowledge in our universe is not always certain. In everyday life we are familiar with classical mechanics and its description of macroscopic systems—the motion of objects with a precise knowledge of where the object is (position, x) and where it's going (momentum, p, or speed, v), as noted before. In contrast, within the microscopic world, governed by the laws of quantum mechanics, we cannot predict the position and momentum with the same precision simultaneously; such quantum effects also have a signature in phenomena of the very big—cosmology. Mechanicians of both worlds, classical and quantum, accommodate the difference by recognizing two of the most powerful and not easily digested concepts: the uncertainty principle and the particle–wave duality of matter. Particles, even molecules, can behave as waves. The same duality holds for light—waves can behave as particles.

In 1864, James Clerk Maxwell showed the nature of light to be that of an electromagnetic wave made of electric- and magnetic-field disturbances. Then in 1905, Albert Einstein described light as particlelike with a quantum of energy, later dubbed a photon by G.N. Lewis. This idea of quanta has its roots in the earlier 1900 work of Max Planck—it relates the energy (E) to the frequency (v) of radiation by $E = hv$, where h is Planck's constant. For matter, the analog of light's duality—matter's duality—was introduced by Louis de Broglie in a brilliant contribution. In 1924, he described the wavelike character of a particle (with a wavelength now known after him, $\lambda_{de\ Broglie}$) and related it to the momentum of the particle (p), simply through the relationship $\lambda_{de\ Broglie} = h/p$. The complementary nature of the two descriptions, waves and particles, becomes clearer when the concept of coherence is introduced.

Coherence in light has been known for the two hundred years since the 1801 experiments by English physician, natural philosopher, and linguist, Thomas Young. (Incidentally, Young also studied hieroglyphs and was the most serious rival to Jean-François Champollion in deciphering the ancient Egyptian writing system.) In a simple way, Young demonstrated what unique properties light has. When he poked a couple of pinpoint holes in a window shade, light fell on the opposite wall in a curious pattern, instead of as a pair of spots. What Young saw was an oval patch of equally spaced light and dark vertical areas. When he covered one of the holes, the interference pattern disappeared—there was just one light spot on the wall, as you might expect. Young concluded that light behaved like a wave, that light waves entered each of the slits, met and interfered—in other words, the light beams were alternately in phase and out of phase with each other.

This principle works for all types of waves—light waves, sound waves, and radio waves—and even electrons, which behave as waves; all demonstrate their "waviness" through adaptations of Young's experiment. Matter can show its waviness when interacting with x-rays or electrons. When x-rays interact with a crystal, they get diffracted producing an interference pattern, through which the molecular structure can be obtained. Electrons can do the same and produce diffraction patterns. These interferences of waves are the result of adding the amplitudes, *not* intensities, of their field, and this adding is called superposition.[2]

For matter, superpositions analogous to those of light waves can be

---

2   This superposition results in a group of waves localized in space (Δx). For all waves, the group generally obeys $\Delta x \, \Delta k \sim 1$, where Δk is the resultant wave number, and k is given by the inverse of the wavelength. Invoking the duality expression makes $\Delta x \, \Delta p$ equal to $h/2\pi$, or $\hbar$. For light waves, this behavior, which has also been observed for electrons, embodies many abstract concepts from the microscopic world such as the superposition of waves, particle and/or wave behavior, quantum measurements, quantum electrodynamics and the uncertainty principle, and the connection to macroscopic systems as in a thought experiment that is called "Schrödinger's cat."

formed from the so-called wave functions. These wave functions are the solution to the famous quantum-mechanical Schrödinger equation. They and their probability distributions are diffuse over position (x) space of the nuclei. But if these waves are added up coherently with well-defined phases, something remarkable emerges—the probability distribution becomes localized in space, as Schrödinger showed in 1926 using the quantum states of a harmonic oscillator, such as a vibrating spring. The resultant wave packet, with its associated de Broglie wavelength, has the essential character of a classical particle: a trajectory in space and time with a well-defined (group) velocity and position; just like a moving marble but at atomic resolution.[3] (For a free particle $E = p^2/2m$, it's evident that the group velocity of the packet, that is, the derivative of energy with respect to momentum, dE/dp, is simply the classical speed v.)

If the concepts are clear, what created the perception that quantum uncertainty would limit the importance of femtosecond resolution? Two lines of argument dominated the thinking. The first was the use of the uncertainty relationship between time and energy, $\Delta t\, \Delta E \geq /2$. On the femtosecond time scale, the energy uncertainty is relatively huge and considered poor by the standards of high-resolution spectroscopy in the energy domain. For instance, a 50 fs pulse has an energy width ΔE of about 300 cm^{-1}, which is larger than the spacing between the vibrational-

---

3   The association of a wave character to a particle motion through de Broglie's relationship, which leads to $\Delta p = \hbar \Delta k$ (as discussed above), is entirely consistent with Heisenberg's mechanics (1925) in which the uncertainty in measurement is defined for all quantum systems—an imprecision in position, with a standard deviation ($\sigma_x \equiv \Delta x$), and in momentum, with a standard deviation ($\sigma_p \equiv \Delta p$); both are related by $\Delta x\, \Delta p \geq \hbar/2$. When the equality holds, the packet is termed uncertainty- or transform-limited. Similarly, there is the analogous uncertainty for energy measured over a finite period of time, $\Delta t\, \Delta E \geq \hbar/2$. This is the crux of the whole matter. With femtosecond resolution, it is possible to make $(\Delta x/x) < 1$ and $(\Delta p/p) < 1$ and the key concept is the coherent superposition and coherent state (wave packet) probing, in accord with these joint uncertainties.

rotational energy states of the molecule—it seems as though we would be "ruining" the quantized vibrational-rotational states by using femtosecond excitation or probes! The second issue is that of the spreading of localized wave groups, or packets, in microscopic systems, which was thought to be wide enough, due to interactions within and between molecules, to prevent localization.

With these two issues in mind, there were predictions made in the literature that femtosecond resolution for studies in chemistry and biology would be of limited utility. Had the energy states been pumped by the laser incoherently, this would have been true, but obviously it is not. In the energy range of the packet, the dispersion in time scales gives a dephasing, or spreading time,[4] that is long when compared with that of the nuclear motion—once again the uncertainty is in our favor!

The very small size of Planck's constant $\hbar$, 1.05457 x 10^{-27} erg sec, means that the fuzziness required by the uncertainty principle is imperceptible on the normal scales of size and momentum, but becomes important at the atomic scale. For example, if the position (x) of a stationary 200-g apple is initially determined to within a small fraction of a wavelength of light, say 10 nm, the apple's position uncertainty (Δx) will spread by ~ 40% only after 4 x 10^{17} s, or 12 billion years—the age of the universe! On the other hand, an electron with a mass twenty-nine orders of magnitude smaller would spread by 40% from an initial 1 Å localization after only 0.2 fs. The much greater masses of atomic nuclei com-

---

4   For a Gaussian (free particle) wave packet having the minimum value of the uncertainty product, $\Delta x\,\Delta p = \hbar/2$, the momentum distribution is also Gaussian, and the contribution of the momentum uncertainty to the widening of the packet as it moves is easy to express. We can calculate the time needed for an appreciable spreading (by $\sqrt{2}$ or ~40%) to take place and express this time as: $t_s = \Delta x(0)/\Delta v = 2m\Delta x^2(0)/\hbar$, where t=0 is the time of minimum uncertainty, m the mass, and $\Delta v = \Delta p/m$. When a free particle wave packet is initiated by an ultrashort light pulse so that it has the minimum value of the $\Delta x\,\Delta p$ uncertainty product, one can calculate the relationship between the pulse duration and the wave packet spatial width. It turns out to be quite simple: $\Delta x = \langle v \rangle \Delta t$.

pared to the electron make their wave packets spread at a rate that is orders of magnitude slower than 0.2 fs, and in fact this spreading is relatively minor on the femtosecond time scale.

We are now in a position to see the consequence of the joint uncertainty relations between time (Δt) and energy (ΔE) and between distance (Δx) and momentum (Δp). Since momentum and energy are related, then time and distance can be related—small Δt is the way to obtain small Δx and hence *localization*! To study classical-like motion in quantum systems, we need to shorten time, but maintain coherence. What is useful to keep in mind is the relationship of energy uncertainty (ΔE) to the binding energies of atoms—for a 50 fs pulse, ΔE is a relatively small fraction of a typical binding energy, and that is important.

Femtochemistry makes this transition from quantum to classical mechanics a clear one, because of the following point. According to the correspondence principle for the two worlds, as Planck's constant goes to zero, i.e., as the states of the system become infinitely close in energy (the continuum limit), then quantum mechanics reaches the classical limit. On the femtosecond time scale, the energy uncertainty, ΔE, makes the states of the system, even with finite energy spacings, reach the classical limit, provided ΔE is larger than the energy spacings of states and that coherence among states is introduced—contrary to a simple view that the ΔE uncertainty would be an obstacle. This is a key to the understanding of atomic-scale dynamics, which, as discussed in the preceding chapter, have been observed and studied in all phases of matter and spanning phenomena from the simple to the very complex, from gas phase to condensed media and from diatomic to protein molecules.

The paradigm case of sodium iodide elucidated many of the concepts involved. The wave packet was observed to oscillate periodically (resonance motion), exhibiting a particlelike behavior during the entire course of the reaction. The packet was found to be very robust, with relatively minor spreading (dephasing), and the ensemble of molecules behaved in harmony and exhibited "single molecule" motion. Theoretically, by constructing the superposition of wave functions with their appropriate phases, we reproduced the experimental observations that showed that the initial packet is indeed highly localized on the subangstrom scale and remains intact for many periods of its motion. The de Broglie wavelength is also consistent with subangstrom localization. Observations made in the condensed phase and in biological systems can be described similarly. We could then address the nature of chemical and biological forces of the dynamics and provide new concepts for the behavior of atoms in complex systems.

Why is coherence robust in molecular systems? The observation of motion in real systems requires not only the formation of localized wave packets in each and every molecule, but also a small spread in position among wave packets formed in the typically millions to billions of molecules on which the measurement is performed. The key to achieving this condition is generally provided by the well-defined initial equilibrium configuration of the molecules before excitation and by the "instantaneous" femtosecond launching of the packet. The spatial confinement (typically ~ 0.05 Å) of the initial ground state of the system ensures that all molecules, each with its own coherence, begin their motion in a bond-distance range much smaller than that executed by the actual motion (typically 5–10 Å). The femtosecond launching ensures that this narrow range of bond distance is maintained during the entire process of pumping. Unless molecular and ensemble coherences are destroyed by molecular perturbations, the motion of the ensemble is that of a single-molecule trajectory.

At the 1972 Welch Conference, in a lively exchange between Eugene Wigner and Edward Teller, the uncertainty paradox for picosecond time resolution was debated. But, as has been seen, the uncertainty paradox is not a paradox even for the shorter time scale of femtoscience and certainly not for the dynamics of physical, chemical, and biological changes. Coherence in the femtosecond time regime—the vibrational time scale of a bond—is essential to the formation of localized, nonequilibrium molecular structures, which then evolve with time and in complete harmony with the uncertainty principle.

Historically, coherence was also not appreciated in the realization of the maser. Charles Townes encountered objections because of concern about the uncertainty principle—the claim was that molecules spend about one ten-thousandth of a second in the cavity of a maser and that it was therefore impossible for the frequency of the radiation to be narrowly confined. When recognized, coherence of photons in the stimulated emission-feedback process removed this concern.

The last of the four elements regarding the impact of femtochemistry is the *new prospects for the field.* Predicting the future is not wise, as many new discoveries will be made without linear extrapolation from work already done. I am reminded of predictions made by some famous people that turned out to be far off the mark. In around 1885, the distinguished Lord Kelvin said, "Radio has no future; x-rays are a hoax." Another distinguished scientist, Lord Rayleigh, said in 1889, "I have not the smallest molecule of faith in aerial navigation other than ballooning." Finally, in the United States, Thomas J. Watson, founder of IBM, said in 1943, "I think there is a world market for about five computers."

Nevertheless, I will still make some predictions. I see three areas of research where the field of femtochemistry is already providing us with new prospects. One such area is the control of reactions. In a paper published in 1980, I suggested a new concept for controlling chemistry with lasers, namely, through the use of ultrashort pulses—to localize the energy in certain chemical bonds and to fulfill chemists' dreams of doing "surgery" in a localized part of the molecule—laser-selective chemistry. Due to the efforts of many colleagues, the field has become active in many labs, and I expect to see further substantial progress in the coming decades. This control of reactions is intellectually exciting, both theoretically and experimentally, and some successes have already been made. On the horizon are numerous extensions, although control hasn't yet reached the desired industrial applications. One important question to ask is: Can we *force* molecules to yield new products, not the ones dictated by the given energy landscape?

An exciting frontier is in biology, which is the second area of research that holds great prospects. Caltech, being small by choice and interdisciplinary by inclination, is a good place for collaborations. Since 1996, I have been the director of the National Science Foundation's Laboratory for Molecular Sciences (LMS) at Caltech. There are eight faculty members involved. Together, we are doing truly exciting interdisciplinary work on very complex systems, from electrocatalysis to DNA, from photoelectron spectroscopy to protein structure and dynamics. Among the recent new studies published are those concerned with the conduction of electrons in the genetic material, the binding of oxygen to models of hemoglobin, molecular recognition of protein by drugs, and the molecular basis for clinical studies of the cytotoxicity of anticancer drugs. In the future, new extensions are anticipated. The nature and control of enzymatic reactions, the catalytic function of the transition state, and the design of artificial biological functions seem to be areas of great promise for dynamical studies.

In the third area of research, I have my eye on the Next Big Thing: using ultrafast electron diffraction can we actually take a direct image of a molecule as it undergoes structural transitions? Once we break a bond here or a bond there, how does the architecture of the whole molecule change with time? This is a dream I have shared with some members of my group since 1991, and it has become a major effort lately. Recently we showed, for the first time, that we can actually see *images* of the chemical structure of the molecule changing with time, and we are currently developing a new apparatus and the methodology to tackle the most complex of all molecules, the biological. Spectroscopic techniques focus on one bond at a time and even the most patient grad student would balk at the prospect of looking at every blessed bond among the several thousand atoms of an average small protein. But a diffraction pattern, in principle, gives the three-dimensional location of all the atoms in the molecule, even when they are complex and large in size, and it gives them all at once—a true 3-D snapshot!

Our setup uses the usual femtosecond pump laser to start the clock. However, the probe, after going down its variable-length path, is focused on a photocathode, which emits electrons when hit by light. This adds an electron beam to the intersection of the pump beam and the molecular beam or the molecule in a condensed medium. It is just like a chest x-ray—when we look at a molecule's diffraction pattern we can "see" the structure. Our ultimate goal is to see how the atoms move as they perform a biological function. You can imagine watching a protein, for example, moving around as it catalyzes a reaction, or as it recognizes and binds to an antibody. With diffraction you see the entire ensemble at once, in real time. Indeed, an exciting prospect, especially when we cover all relevant time scales.

As the ability to explore shorter and shorter time scales has progressed from the millisecond to the present stage of widely exploited femtosecond capabilities, each step along the way has provided surprising discoveries, new understanding, and new mysteries. Developments will continue to emerge and new directions of research will be pursued. Surely, studies of transition states and their structures in chemistry and biology will remain active areas of exploration into new directions, from simple systems to complex enzymes and proteins, and from the probing to the controlling of matter.

Since the current femtosecond lasers now provide the limit of time resolution for phenomena involving nuclear motion, one might ask: is the race against time at its end? Subfemtosecond or attosecond (10^{-18} s) resolution may one day allow for the direct observation of the electron's motion. I made this point in a 1991 article and, since then, some progress in the generation of subfemtosecond pulses has been made with a focus on applications in physics and technology. In the coming decades, this may change and we may view electron rearrangement, say, in the benzene molecule, in real time, bringing Kekulé's serpent to life!

Additionally, there will be studies involving the combination of the three scales: time, length, and number. We should see extensions to studies of the femtosecond dynamics of single molecules and of molecules on surfaces (for example, using STM). Combined time and length resolutions will provide unique opportunities for making the important transition from molecular structures to dynamics, to functions. We may also see that all of femtochemistry can be done at micro-to-nano-Kelvin temperatures, utilizing lasers and other cooling techniques.

It seems that on the femtosecond to attosecond time scale, we are reaching the inverse of Big Bang time (12–15 billion years), with the human heartbeat situated in the middle as the geometric average of the two limits. The language of molecular dynamics is even similar to that of cosmic dynamics. Cosmologists speak of energy landscapes and transition states for the Big Bang and for the inflation of the universe. Perhaps we are approaching a universal limit of time!

Originally, I did not expect the rich blossoming of the field in all directions. What is clear to me is that my group and I have enjoyed the odyssey of discovery, seeing what was not previously possible, acquiring new knowledge, and developing new concepts. Perhaps the best words to describe this feeling are those of the English archaeologist Howard Carter on November 25, 1922, when he got his first glimpse of the priceless contents of Tutankhamun's tomb: "At first, I could see nothing . . . then shapes gradually began to emerge." Lord Carnarvon, who was financing the excavation and stood just a few feet behind Carter, anxiously asked, "Can you see anything?" And Carter replied, "Yes. Wonderful things!" This is the thrill of discovery in science, too. It seeks to unveil the hidden simplicity and beauty of nature's truth. On a visit with my wife to the Los Angeles County Museum of Art, I stood in front of Van Gogh's masterpiece "Almond Blossom" wondering about the beauty of the big picture and the unpredictability of its details. That, also, is in the nature of scientific discovery.

The future of femtoscience will surely witness many imaginative and unpredictable contributions. I hope that I will be able to enjoy the future as much as I have the past. Benjamin Franklin once wrote:

> The progress of human knowledge will be rapid and dis-
> coveries made of which we at present have no concep-
> tion. I begin to be almost sorry I was born so soon since
> I cannot have the happiness of knowing what will be
> known in years hence.

Scientists have a feeling when they make a significant contribution. This feeling is usually strengthened when recognition is received from

On the Road to Stockholm
Festivities and Fairy Tales

H ow did you win a Nobel prize? This is one of the common questions I am asked in many places, including Stockholm, the
mother city of the award. The process of scientific recognition
and the culture of prizes and awards in the sciences may not be familiar
to many, especially in the developing world. After all, it was not familiar to me until I became part of the academic community in the United
States. So in this chapter I want to go into some detail that may not be
of interest to those familiar with this culture, although some may find
enlightening the appreciation for scientific achievement in the developing world. Some of the experiences shared here include the most joyful
moments for my family and for my research group.

In our science endeavor, the thrill of discovery is the real fuel for taking off but the flight becomes satisfactory and enjoyable when recognition of the contribution by peers, perhaps the most significant reward,
becomes evident. The process begins with publication of scientific work
in peer reviewed journals. In my case, the observation of femtosecond-
scale molecular phenomena generated excitement not only in scientific
journals, but also in the general press. Although we had submitted our

papers in the early part of 1987, Caltech didn't announce the break-through discovery until November 30 of that year—the scientific papers had to be accepted first for publication and had to pass the scrutiny of the review process.

The *Los Angeles Times* broke the story to the general public on the front page of its December 3 edition, with an article by Thomas H. Maugh II, headlined "Unprecedented Step: Scientists Able to See 'Birth' of New Molecules." In his report, Maugh highlighted how we were able to see chemical reactions while they were happening, an unprecedented achievement that had "opened up a new branch of chemistry." A day later, *The New York Times* covered the story with an article by Malcolm W. Browne entitled "Snapshots Taken as Chemicals Bond." Numerous other newspapers and magazines followed suit. I was particularly pleased to see that distinguished expert colleagues like Dick Bernstein, Ken Eisenthal, Jim Kinsey, John Thomas, and others were publicly endorsing the significance of the development, and with enthusiasm.

Within a year, professional journals began to feature the topic of femtochemistry even on their covers, as seen in *Chemical & Engineering News* in 1988 and *Mosaic*, a publication of the National Science Foundation, in 1989. The prestigious US journal *Science*, which publishes in all areas of the sciences, featured femtochemistry on the cover in 1994, and by that time it was evident that a new field had in fact emerged; we had published a review article entitled "Laser Femtochemistry" in *Science* in 1988, but it didn't make the cover. In the equally prestigious *Nature* of London, several commentaries were written, and we also published some of our early work there. The *Journal of Physical Chemistry*, which had published our original report of 1985, had illustrations of femtochemistry work on its cover several times. The topic received in-depth treatment more than once in a number of articles and in special issues of the journal, including the one that celebrated "Ten Years of Femtochemistry," edited by Will Castleman and Villy Sundström, which provided a historic overview. In this same issue, Craig Martens first wrote the now oft-quoted statement: "All chemistry is femtochemistry."

This issue was published in June 1998, one year before the Nobel prize. Many books were also published during this period, and in the years that were to follow.

The field began its international broadening with the inauguration of a series of conferences dedicated to femtochemistry. The first one was held in Berlin on March 1–4, 1993, with about two hundred attendees, and the series continues to this day, held every other year, with the most recent one in Toledo (Spain). These international exchanges culminated in the Solvay Conference of 1995 in Belgium and in the Nobel Foundation Symposium on Femtochemistry and Femtobiology, held in September of 1996, almost three years before the prize was awarded. The well-known Solvay series has been in existence since the beginning of the century—it was the 1911 Solvay Conference that brought together Einstein, Rutherford, Planck, de Broglie, the Curies, and other giants to discuss the birth of the new field, quantum mechanics.

The subject of a Nobel conference is decided by members of the Swedish Academy of Sciences and the Nobel Foundation to examine topics that are "hot" and perhaps worthy of a prize. I vividly recall the dynamics at this Nobel conference for femtochemistry and femtobiology. The atmosphere was very tense, especially since all the scientists who could be candidates for the prize were invited to speak and several members of the Nobel Committee were present! We stayed in the home (and laboratory) of Alfred Nobel in Björkborn, Sweden. I gave the opening lecture, in which I overviewed the progress in the field.

My work wasn't yet known in Egypt. In December of 1988, I was invited to be a Distinguished Visiting Professor (DVP) at the American University in Cairo (AUC) to give a series of public lectures on the campus in downtown Cairo on Tahrir Square. I stayed in one of the AUC apartments in Garden City and the school generously provided a cook and a driver as well. During the time I was at AUC I attended a New Year's Eve party in the Fayoum at a hotel that had a number of distinguished guests. One of them was Mme. Amal Fahmy, who is well known for her Friday afternoon radio broadcasts, *'Ala al-Nasia* ("On the Corner"), which have been popular since I was a boy. I had met Mme.

Fahmy earlier in March of 1988 in Los Angeles, and she recorded a broadcast with me about our scientific work at Caltech, and we became better acquainted. The first report on our work to the Egyptian people, however, was made in 1987 when the *al-Ahram* correspondent in Los Angeles, Mme. Thuria Abu Sa'ud, wrote a full-page article after she read the report in the *Los Angeles Times*. I first spoke to the public about femtoscience, among other things, during my visit to AUC in 1988 and the lectures were well received.

Those events took place at an exciting and busy time for me. I received many invitations to speak to scientists, students, and public audiences and to receive honors from scientific societies and universities. From 1987 on, I made trips all over the world: to Japan and Europe, across Africa and the Middle East, and other places. My lectures were devoted mostly to the new science of laser femtochemistry and I was pleased that our contribution was appreciated. I hoped to inspire the young people to consider careers in science and the public to understand the science of time and matter.

On one trip to Saudi Arabia, the honor I received was doubly pleasing for its international scientific recognition and for creating new family ties—it was a fairy tale that began on the day I was scheduled to leave Cairo: after ending my DVP stint at AUC, *al-Ahram* announced on the front page that I had been awarded the King Faisal International Prize in Science, although I had not yet been officially contacted. Hours later the president of Caltech, Thomas Everhart, called at my residence to congratulate me, but still I hadn't heard from Saudi Arabia. He said, "They're expecting you in Saudi Arabia soon, and the faculty will have a celebration for you at Caltech when you return to Pasadena, before you receive the prize." The prize ceremony was scheduled for March of 1989. I decided to delay my return flight to absorb the good news and also to celebrate for a few days in Egypt.

The King Faisal Prize is a major award; it's an international prize and is given not just to people from the Middle East. Arabs and Muslims had often received it in literature and in Islamic studies, but in science and medicine it was usually awarded to Americans, Europeans,

Japanese, Australians, . . . in short, to scientists outside the Arab world. I was the first Arab to receive the prize for work in the sciences or medicine. The hosts in Saudi Arabia were proud and they received me with a warm welcome. Following its inception in 1977, the King Faisal International Prize has quickly established itself as one of the world's most prestigious awards. This reputation couldn't have been accomplished without, first, strict adherence to nomination and selection procedures that ensure that winners are selected on the basis of merit, and second, the continuous support of academic institutions both nationally and internationally.

The winners are usually announced in January, but receive their awards two months later at a special ceremony held in Riyadh in the presence of the king of Saudi Arabia. This ceremony is one of the most important annual events organized by the foundation. The prizes are given in the following five categories: service to Islam, Islamic studies, Arabic literature, medicine, and science. Many who have received the prize in medicine or science have gone on to receive the Nobel prize, including Gerd Binnig of Germany; Heinrich Rohrer of Switzerland; myself of the United States and Egypt; and Steven Chu and Günter Blobel of the United States. In 2001 four others joined this list: Carl Wieman, Eric Cornell, Ryoji Noyori, and Barry Sharpless; I am sure there will be more in the future.

Caltech put on a sumptuous party in honor of the occasion at the Athenaeum. Speeches in a personal tribute were made by Francis Clauser, Dick Bernstein, and Rudy Marcus. Dick and his wife, Norma, were so happy with the news that they put on a party at their house. Dick expected that I would begin to receive more international awards for my scientific work, and he said so in his speech at the Athenaeum:

> This is a very significant award which anyone would be
> very proud to receive. Nevertheless, it is only the first in
> a series of important awards which you will surely be
> getting over the next years in recognition of your inno-
> vative forefront research achievements.

In mid-March, I arrived in Saudi Arabia for a week of festivities that culminated in the laureates' meeting on March 17 in Riyadh and the awards ceremony two days later. At the ceremony I received the golden medal and the diploma. The citation, in English, from the book of laureates reads:

> Professor Ahmed Zewail is the pioneer of ultrafast laser chemistry with femtosecond resolution. Thanks to his brilliant and landmark works, chemists worldwide are now able to explore real-time dynamics of bond-forming and bond-breaking in the transition state. . . . His work holds the prospect of a new type of applied chemistry in which the course of a chemical reaction can be controlled to create hitherto unimagined useful materials for the benefit of humankind. Zewail has opened the eyes of the world to a truly fundamental and profoundly fascinating aspect of nature at the atomic level.

Prior to this time I was not planning to get married. I had been single for nearly ten years. I was traveling around the world and working late hours, and in a sense, science became my wife. But every now and then Stephan Isied, a friend from the Berkeley years, and I would get together in my condominium and we would discuss the marriage situation; after all, we were both entering our forties. Yehia El Sanadydi, another friend who lived in Santa Monica, was in a similar situation and we too used to discuss the issues while hiking in the mountains. In Egypt, I was introduced to several women and their families, but nothing materialized, and although I contemplated the idea of engagement to a lady from the Middle East, I wasn't really ready.

My professional life was rich and kept me busy, and I also wanted peace in my children's lives. I saw my daughters on weekends, and we did different things together. I worried that a new marriage would affect their well-being and my devotion to science. This situation changed when I met, upon arrival in Riyadh, a young lady by the name of Dema

Faham. Like me, Dema had gone to Saudi Arabia without any intention of getting married. And like me, she had been married, but for a very short time, in her case only for a few months. Shortly thereafter, she had come to Riyadh because her father, Dr. Chaker Faham, had won the King Faisal Prize in Literature.

Dr. Faham had been the Syrian Minister of Education, the Minister of Higher Education, and president of the University of Damascus. He held other important posts, such as that of ambassador to Algeria. Today Dr. Faham is the president of the Arabic Language Academy in Syria. Besides these administrative posts he is a scholar in his own right. During the period of Taha Hussein and other great Arab literati, he wrote his doctoral thesis on an Arab poet, al-Farazduq, at Cairo University, where he did both his undergraduate and graduate work. In all, he lived in Egypt for ten years, loving the country like his home.

Destiny was in the making. Dema and her parents had just returned to Syria from Cairo and, like her father, she loved Egypt too. Now when she thinks I'm not spoiling her enough, she jokes, "I thought *all* the Egyptians were like the ones I met in Cairo." Ironically, she wasn't originally going to go to Saudi Arabia, because her older brother, Bashar, a physician in the United States, was planning to accompany their parents. He couldn't make it at the last minute, so they asked Dema. In Riyadh, all the laureates and their families stayed at the same hotel, al-Khuzama, which is named for a flower; the hotel complex is owned by the King Faisal Foundation. It was during this week of festivities at al-Khuzama that Dema and I got to know each other. The foundation had organized a full program, including a trip to the desert where there was a big tent with many tasty Arabic delicacies, such as roast lamb, and we all had a great time.

Dema's mother, Mediha Anbari, is equally impressive. She is university educated and a worldly person. I saw the caring and love between her and her husband. We have a saying in Egypt, *Iqlib al-qidra 'ala fummaha, titla' al-bint ummaha*, literally, if you turn the pot of *ful* (Egyptian beans) upside down, the daughter is like the mother, meaning whatever the mother is like, the girl will be similar. Dema, who is very intelligent, in many ways reflects her parents' intellect and their strong, loving relationship—this is good and bad, good for the wonderful traits and bad because her standards are very high with little tolerance for error! She is a deep person, solid about her roots, and a cosmopolitan and worldly woman. She speaks Arabic and English, knows French and Spanish, and is at home wherever she goes.

I called her frequently when I returned to Pasadena and after doing this for a while, with the telephone bills beyond our budgets, I made a trip to Syria in May of 1989 ostensibly to visit my friend Dr. Chaker Faham in his capacity as a fellow laureate. I also visited the rest of the family—Dema has three brothers and a sister all in the United States, but her family in Damascus is big. There, we recited the *fatiha*, the opening chapter of the Quran, which signaled our commitment to each other. We had the engagement party in July of the same year at her sister's home in Port Huron, Michigan, and we married on September 17 of the same year, also in Port Huron.

Our wedding party was held on September 30 at the Athenaeum in Pasadena, with about 120 family and friends in attendance, especially those from Caltech and the Los Angeles area. It was the first time the president of Caltech and many of my good friends were able to witness a real Middle Eastern wedding, and they found it interesting. The vice-president of the institute, David Morrisroe, commented that for all those years at Caltech he had never attended as exciting a wedding as this one—I think the belly dancer did it! It was the entertainment and the wedding itself that made the event truly Egyptian, since the food and the cake were Western. We had an Egyptian band for the *zaffa*, the bridal procession— we came down the stairs of the Athenaeum accompanied by music, which was played on the drums. Members of my research group were present and they displayed on a screen words like "Thank you, King Faisal," "Dema, welcome to Pasadena," "Ahmed, we love you," all projected by a laser. At this party both Maha and Amani were beaming, and I was particularly touched by the thoughtful words Maha asked to say publicly.

We took up residence at our new home at 566 Winston Avenue in San Marino, where I had moved from the condominium earlier in the summer, and began the transition from single to married life. Friends and neighbors welcomed us, and so did members of the Caltech community; Roxanna Anson, the wife of the division chair, Fred, arranged a special welcome party for Dema. After the wedding festivities, life returned to normal and to science. Not much later, in October, I arranged for two first-class tickets to Cairo for a honeymoon trip. When I think back on that trip, I must have been difficult. First we had to make a stop in Rochester, New York, where I was to receive the Harrison-Howe Award. So here was the bride sitting in on my lecture for one hour, and she didn't understand anything of what I was saying! From there we went on to Jordan for a five-day conference with scientists.

Finally we went to Cairo so she could meet my mother and some other members of my family. But I guess I was still a little distracted. Dema reminds me of an incident that she never forgets. One night we were sitting on the balcony of a suite in the Semiramis Hotel, overlooking the Nile, which provided a romantic ambiance. She saw that I was preoccupied, and she was probably pleased to see me in a romantic mood, so she asked, "What are you thinking about?" "Do you want the truth?" "Yes." "My group at Caltech," I replied. It was a terrible thing to say. So now she tells me that I'm brutally honest, a polite way of expressing her dissatisfaction.

Dema had received her M.D. from Damascus University before we met, and when she came to the United States she thought of continuing as a physician at first. She realized, however, that she really didn't care much for medicine, and with my busy schedule it would be very hard to work as an M.D. She decided to go to UCLA for a master's degree in public health, which took a few years of study and going every day from San Marino to UCLA for classes. We also traveled quite a bit together. Dema became pregnant before she was able to take a job in the field of public health, and the two boys were born one year apart.

Our first son, Nabeel, was born on April 29, 1993, at the Huntington Hospital in Pasadena, and I must say it was a different feeling with this child, because in the two previous deliveries of Maha and Amani, both born in the United States, I didn't get to be at my wife's side as they were born. It's the same in Egypt—a new father doesn't get to see his babies for the first time until the delivery is completed. Hospital staff come out and congratulate you by saying you have a girl or a boy. With the birth of the two girls in the United States, the situation was somewhat better; there was a window for the expectant fathers to look through. But with Nabeel, it was the first time for me to be in the same room with my wife as she was giving birth. I don't actually know how I handled it, because I'm not good at these things usually, but Nabeel came while I was there, and I was the first one to hold him after the doctor.

The same thing happened with Hani, our second son, born on July 29, 1994. I can't exaggerate the powerful feelings I had with this new experience, seeing the births of Nabeel and Hani. Nabeel weighed nine pounds and ten ounces and he made us wait for about twenty-four hours before he finally appeared! Today I joke with him, telling him that he had a big head. Hani's delivery was shorter and he was smaller, eight pounds and six ounces. The boys came at a time that was quite different from when the girls came. I was now a chair professor, and even though I'm busier than I used to be, I'm more in control and can make time to enjoy them more.

In fact, I changed my working habits; for example, I don't work on Sundays, unless it's really critical, so I can be with them. I see them in the evening and we do many things together, including traveling around the world, and I particularly like swimming with them. Dema is a devoted mother. All her time is given to them, taking them to different places, even if they start whining and don't want to do anything. Dema wants to keep both cultures alive in the boys, so they have had to speak Arabic, in the Syrian dialect, which is different from the Egyptian! They have no choice; almost every summer they take lessons in Arabic. Besides learning languages they take violin, art, and soccer classes. The two are close friends despite their different personalities. Nabeel is a deep thinker and has an inquisitive mind. He reads voraciously and likes to play electronic games. Hani is a very bright and charming boy and is full of energy—he too likes to read and play. They bring a real joy to our lives. On several occasions, traveling with all four children has made those trips special; the children enjoy being pampered at ceremonies for awards and prizes. I too enjoy the special treatment, but most special is the appreciation for my group's scientific contributions honored by the awards.

In our world of science, recognition comes in different forms. I had the opportunity to meet kings and queens, heads of states and first ladies, princes and princesses, and popes, and such meetings are memorable experiences. Big celebrations are a real treat for me and my family. For one thing we all have to buy new clothes, especially the ladies. Before the Nobel feast, four prizes were in this special category: the King Faisal, the Wolf, the Welch, and the Benjamin Franklin prizes.

The Wolf Prize, which I received in early 1993, is considered a major scientific award, and like most major awards, is a step on the ladder to the Nobel. The Wolf Foundation, established by the late Dr. Ricardo Wolf, inventor, diplomat, and philanthropist, seeks to "promote science and art for the benefit of mankind." Born in Germany in 1887, Dr. Wolf immigrated to Cuba before World War I, and served Cuba as one of its ambassadors until his death at the age of 93. The Wolf Foundation began awarding its prizes in 1978; since that time Caltech faculty have won five of these prizes. Of the 140 Wolf Prize recipients, thirteen of the winners in physics, chemistry, and medicine have gone on to become Nobel laureates. Nominations are made by the scientific community, and self-nominations aren't credible. The selection is made by an international committee whose names are not publicly disclosed. I received the news while I was at a conference in Cairo, and the official citation stated that the award was

> for pioneering the development of laser femtochemistry.
> Using lasers and molecular beams, femtochemistry has
> made it now possible to probe the evolution of chemical
> reactions as they actually happen in real time.

Once again the Caltech president telephoned me. Caltech had a grand party, but this time it was at the Ritz Carlton in Pasadena. All Wolf prizes are awarded, according to the bylaws in the Knesset, and I delivered my speech on May 16, addressing the scientific and the humanistic dimension of the recognition. Egypt's ambassador accompanied me, and held a reception at his residence. Four years later, I received another major award from the United States.

Because of my relatively young age I wasn't expecting the honor of the Welch Prize, which I received in 1997—it recognizes "lifetime achievements." But I was pleasantly surprised to hear that the prize committee, composed mostly of Nobel prize winners (Glenn Seaborg, E. J. Corey, Joseph Goldstein, Yuan T. Lee, William Lipscomb; the other members—Peter Dervan, W. O. Baker, and Norman Hackerman—are all distinguished and prominent scientists), had decided to select me for the Robert A. Welch Award in Chemistry, given for "outstanding contributions in chemistry for the betterment of humankind." I was pleased with this recognition of our work and the committee's detailed write-up announced by the foundation, whose chairman, Richard Johnson, wrote:

> Dr. Zewail has given birth to a new era in chemistry. . . .
> This is an enormous accomplishment with wide-ranging
> implications for expanding chemical knowledge.

Norman Hackerman, chairman of the Scientific Advisory Board, added:

> The fundamental nature of his work can be seen in biol-
> ogists' and physicists' adaption of femtochemistry tech-
> niques. This ability to actually observe material
> rearrangement has already stimulated important new
> theories and understanding by scientists in many fields.

My family was given a great party in Houston and another one at Caltech.

In spite of glowing words of praise, I had a funny, humbling experience on my way to receive this award. The party was in Houston, and a huge limousine came to the hotel to pick up my family and me and take us to a meeting with the board for dinner. On the way, I noticed a lot of people were waving to us as the limo wound its way through the streets. Well, my heart was warmed to see so many people in Houston impressed with my scientific achievement, but I found it a little hard to believe. The truth was that people thought our limo was carrying movie stars to the opening of the city's Planet Hollywood café, located close to where our meeting was being held. Even more embarrassing, Maha and Amani, who were with us and very well dressed, said they would rather go to the Planet Hollywood café than attend my award ceremony. I hope they were joking!

The year before I received the Nobel prize, I was awarded a prize that was also very special in scientific terms, revolutionary in the response in Egypt, and disappointing in a human dimension. The Benjamin Franklin Medal in Chemistry brought me back to the City of Brotherly Love, in April of 1998, and it was particularly special to me because of my personal admiration for Benjamin Franklin, the inventor, scientist, educator, and statesman. The institute founded in 1824 in his name initiated an awards program the following year that continues to this day. Among recipients of the Franklin Medal are Marie Curie, the Wright brothers, and Albert Einstein.

In that same year, also in Philadelphia, I was elected to the American Philosophical Society, America's first learned society, which has played an important role in American cultural and intellectual life for 250 years. It too is connected to Benjamin Franklin's legacy. In 1743, in establishing the society and contextualizing the role of knowledge in the new nation, Franklin wrote:

> The first drudgery of settling new colonies is now pretty well over, and there are many in every province in circumstances that set them at ease, and afford leisure to cultivate the finer arts, and improve the common stock of knowledge.

The scholarly society he advocated became a reality that year. By 1769 international acclaim for its accomplishments assured its permanence.

He was a true visionary—something I deeply revere in individuals—and he had the spirit of science in his soul.

The Franklin prize committee was composed of some forty members from different disciplines, as awards are given in several categories. Because of the history and distinction of the award, the committee feels that it should be only Nobel-level people who receive the Benjamin Franklin Medal. The ceremony took place at the Franklin Institute and it was done with class. More than a thousand people attended, and among the list of patrons were former US presidents and distinguished leaders in the arts, sciences, and business. I received a beautiful gold medallion that depicts the Benjamin Franklin National Memorial located in the Franklin Institute of Science Museum in Philadelphia; the year 1824 is engraved on it. The press release emphasized that close to one hundred recipients over the prize's history had gone on to receive the Nobel prize, and provided the citation for our work, which read: "Professor Zewail's ingenious methodology has made it possible to probe directly, in real time, the dynamics of chemical bond changes with atomic-scale time resolution."

With the medal, I was given a report on how the decision was made. I was surprised by this, but apparently that is the tradition. The report was detailed and thorough in assessing the contribution. It also contained a surprise. I had been considered in previous years and they had contacted scientists to evaluate the contribution. All but one were positive, and strangely, this person, whose name was given in the report, had been writing to me for years about the—in his words—"breakthrough contribution" we had made. This revelation was disappointing, but it was clear from the report that he had an alternative motive—he was recommending one of his own former students for the prize. Ironically, when the committee contacted the student, who is now a distinguished scientist, he was very positive about our contributions. In the year I received the prize, the committee was unanimous in awarding it to me, unshared.

The Benjamin Franklin prize caused an earthquake in Egypt. My first official recognition from my mother country had been from AUC in 1988, when I was invited to be a distinguished visiting professor; in

1993, the school also awarded me my first honorary degree from Egypt. I received the medal and shield of honor of Cairo University in 1992 and a similar honor from Ain Shams University in 1997. In 1995, H.E. President Mohammed Hosni Mubarak bestowed on me the Order of Merit, First Class, in Sciences and Art, an honor that was indeed special and the first from the government.

At the time of the announcement of the Franklin prize, Egyptian newspapers were full of reports on Egypt's winning of the African Soccer Cup. President Mubarak received the victorious team at the airport. *Al-Ahram* newspaper, in its March 2, 1998, issue, published a small box on the front page announcing my selection as a recipient of the Benjamin Franklin Prize; Mr. Atef al-Khamry, who was in Washington, D.C., had written the piece, following the announcement in February. In editorial after editorial and in most of the newspapers, this subject was covered using my case to emphasize the lack of appreciation for achievements in science. Headlines such as "Egypt only knows how to celebrate soccer and arts, not science" appeared everywhere. Another was "Zewail should shave his hair to look like Hosam Hassan [a famous soccer player] to get the same recognition."

I visited Egypt in June of 1998 and found an incredible and heartwarming reception from the people, the governor of Behira (to which Damanhur belongs), the governor of Kafr al-Sheikh (where Desuq is located), and from the prime minister. I believe that the prime minister was doing his duty, but the emotion I saw in the people on the street was beyond my expectations. There were thousands of people on the streets in Damanhur and Desuq, and everywhere I went people welcomed me. One touching experience was in the area of al-Hussein mosque in Cairo. When a handicapped man in a wheelchair, who was selling gardenia necklaces to make money to live, caught sight of me, he wept and gave me all the gardenia necklaces he had. I tried hard to give him money for them, but he wouldn't accept it. At the end we compromised—he didn't take money and I took only one necklace. It was from the heart.

On this same trip, it was announced that a pair of postage stamps would be issued in my honor for the scientific contributions and for the awarding of the Benjamin Franklin Medal. These stamps, which show my portrait, were made in ten-piaster and one-pound denominations and their official date of issue was June 14, 1998. This was indeed an honor of historical magnitude, especially since stamps in many countries, including the United States, are issued posthumously. The chairman of our division at Caltech (and my friend), Peter Dervan, commented in Caltech's press release that my contributions to molecular science, "like the pyramids, will be long lasting."

The stamps, however, were only a part of this tribute; they also renamed a major street in Damanhur after me. In Desuq, the high school I attended was renamed after me, as was a street; this road runs from Desuq to Fuwwa in the north, near Rosetta. At the rededication in Desuq, we visited Sidi Ibrahim's mosque and the police lost control as the people tried to reach me with a hero's welcome. Never before had I seen anything like this. Some reporters called this unusual celebration *Farah Zewail* or *Mulid Zewail*—the "Feast of Zewail."

It was as if the Egyptian people were anticipating the Nobel prize, the crown jewel for a scientist. Since 1987, colleagues had been telling me that the work was deserving of the Nobel prize. But of course, no one knows what the Swedes will do and this is part of the prize's mystique and cachet. The nominations, which are sent every year to nearly four thousand scientists around the world, are based on individual solicitation and there is an agreement of secrecy—the deliberations do not become available to historians until fifty years after the awarding of the prize. In recent times, the committee has received up to four hundred nominations. A nomination by a scientist is supposed to be top secret. However, people do whisper in your ears and send you a copy of their nomination—they do so because they are convinced (or wish) that you will be awarded the prize.

The official announcement that I had won the Nobel Prize in Chemistry in 1999 came on October 12 at 5:30 in the morning, California time. The news was chilling and in a way unbelievable—at least for a while. The secretary-general of the academy, Dr. Erling Norrby, said: "Is this Dr. Zewail?" I said yes. He said, "Sorry we have to disturb you this early but I have some interesting news. I am the secre-tary-general . . . " He didn't have to complete the sentence—by his title I knew they were calling about the Nobel prize. He told me that I was receiving the prize unshared and read the citation. Twenty minutes to six o'clock—he said the famous words that I repeated at the press confer-ence: "These are the last twenty minutes of peace in your life."

After we called members of our families in the twenty-minute inter-val, our phones and faxes were all jammed and my e-mail accounts were crammed with congratulatory messages. Reporters, scientists, and friends from around the globe were trying to reach us. The Caltech pres-ident, David Baltimore, was near the Los Angeles airport on his way to Washington, D.C. A Caltech public relations officer called him and he returned to Pasadena, and tried to call me but without success. He then decided to come to our house directly, knocking on the door, but we did-n't open it: I thought it was one of the many reporters at our door and I was simply overwhelmed with all the telephone calls coming in. Moreover, I was still in my pajamas and unshaved—David had to go to his office to wait for me. Dema, who hadn't slept well that night, woke Nabeel and Hani, and we contacted Maha and Amani—we were all very excited to say the least. I must confess, I told Dema that I had to see the academy's write-up at exactly 6:00 A.M. on the Internet, when it was first posted—I wanted to see what would go down in history and whether the word *femtochemistry* would become part of the scientific lexicon. The write-up was superb and femtochemistry was there!

In the company of my wife, I went to the press conference at the Athenaeum organized by our very able public relations office, headed by Bob O'Rourke. The room was packed. I had had a cold over the weekend, but by the time I went to the press conference at 10 A.M., I was no longer feeling its effect. The president, the provost Steve Koonin, and the chairs of chemistry and physics, David Tirrell and Tom Tombrello, respectively, were with me on the stage and we had an exhilarating conference. At the press conference, one reporter asked me if I lived a normal life. I said I did. I went with my family to do this and that, we ate Chinese food, we went to the theater. . . . In Japan, this reply was published, but the Chinese food was replaced by Greek! The news traveled so fast it seemed to me from the succession of calls I received that the story was spreading in femtoseconds. The flurry of calls continued endlessly, and I received nearly five thousand messages by snail and electronic mail—Caltech's server was jammed. Indeed life changed!

The Nobel prize is now one hundred years old, with the first prizes awarded in 1901. The Nobel Foundation administers the prizes in accord with the will of Alfred Nobel, the inventor of dynamite, who had amassed a fortune during his life, in part from the inventions he had patented. Alfred Nobel died on December 10, 1896, and this is the reason the awards ceremony takes place annually on that date. His last will and testament, which took five years to execute after the removal of some obstacles, was remarkable in many ways. Friends and relatives received a good share of his fortune, but the larger portion went toward the prizes. The part of Nobel's will that dealt with the prizes and with those who should award them was indeed visionary:

> The whole of my remaining realizable estate shall be dealt with in the following way: The capital, invested in safe securities by my executors, shall constitute a fund, the interest on which shall be annually distributed in the form of prizes to those who, during the preceding year, shall have conferred the greatest benefit on mankind. The said interest shall be divided into five equal parts, which shall be apportioned as follows: one part to the person who shall have made the most important discovery or invention within the field of physics; one part to the person who shall have made the most important chemical discovery or improvement; one part to the person who shall have made the most important discovery within the domain of physiology or medicine; one part to the person who shall have produced in the field of literature the most outstanding work of an idealistic ten-

dency; and one part to the person who shall have done the most or the best work for fraternity between nations, for the abolition or reduction of standing armies and for the holding and promotion of peace congresses.

The prizes for physics and chemistry shall be awarded by the Swedish Academy of Sciences; that for the physiological or medical works by the Karolinska Institute in Stockholm; that for literature by the Academy in Stockholm, and that for champions of peace by a committee of five persons to be elected by the Norwegian Storting. It is my express wish that in awarding the prizes no consideration whatever shall be given to the nationality of the candidates, but that the most worthy shall receive the prize, whether he be a Scandinavian or not.

The money that is awarded comes from a stock portfolio and from real estate holdings maintained by the foundation, and in recent years, award payments have become the highest in the world for such prizes. In addition to the accolades and the tremendous honor of the award, the cash award of almost one million dollars is to be divided *at most* among three winners—this is the maximum number of persons who can share the prize in physics, chemistry, physiology or medicine, and in literature; the peace prize can sometimes be awarded to an organization. The foundation spends almost one million dollars on each prize for all the activities and selection expenses, making the real cost to the foundation around two million dollars for each prize every year. In the United States, the prize is considered taxable Federal and state income, making its net worth about half the total amount. In my case, some of the prize money has gone to the establishment of merit prizes for the best students graduating from the American University in Cairo and to a prize honoring the best student graduating from my high school, which is now named after me; a portion of the endowed fund is to help the school with equipment and infrastructure.

The ceremony itself is an experience of a lifetime. It is part of a week of celebrations—the Nobel week. From the moment they welcome the laureate and his or her family at the airport to the departure from Sweden, one has the feeling that it is a fairy tale. As I said in my speech, I know of no other country that celebrates intellectual achievement with such style and class. Laureates of the prizes of physics, chemistry, physiology or medicine, literature, and economics and their families stay at the fabulous Grand Hotel in Stockholm—the peace prize is awarded in Oslo—and are escorted by a limousine, one for each laureate. In my case we had twelve members in my family and, because the ladies had to be in long gowns and the men in white ties, we must have had fifteen suitcases that felt like fifty—most of the men rented their tuxedos, but the ladies, of course, did not rent their gowns. Throughout the week, we had an attaché from the Swedish Foreign Ministry, Ann Måwe, with us and she did a fine job, taking care of every move, including the escort of the children to the banquet. Ann, who is Swedish born, spoke Arabic, and this choice by the Swedish Foreign Ministry is symbolic of the meticulous way in which everything was arranged. Members of the Nobel Foundation were gracious and exceptional in their welcome and we have become members of the family.

The laureate gives a Nobel lecture to present the work for which the prize was awarded, some days before the Nobel ceremony—I gave mine on December 8. This was an exciting lecture to give as hundreds of people attended to learn of the significance of the work and, of course, the whole event was upbeat; I asked the youngest, Hani, if he understood the lecture. "Yes," he said, "you spoke about the horse," in reference to my mention of Muybridge. We participated in a variety of other functions, such as press conferences, TV interviews (including a live program, "Nobel Minds" for BBC World), lunches, dinners, and visits by the family to Stockholm and its surroundings. There were also other special events: the dinner and lunch given by the ambassadors of Egypt and the United States, the party arranged for by the Student Union of Stockholm University, and the Sankta Lucia—queen of light—day of festivities on December 13, which included a 6:00 A.M. breakfast in bed, when we were serenaded by lovely girls and boys who brought us goodies, and a dinner at the university, where laureates are knighted by the honor of the Green Frog! But of course, everybody was waiting for the event on December 10, the day of the awards ceremony at Concert Hall and the banquet at City Hall.

At the prize ceremony, members of the academy and the selection committees and the laureates sat on the stage in Stockholm's Concert Hall and behind and above them was the orchestra. Laureate family members and invitees sat in the hall, which was elegantly arranged with flowers everywhere and music in the background. Everyone was again in formal attire and the gala sparkled with the delighted eyes of family members, colleagues, fellow scholars, ambassadors, government officials, and other dignitaries.

His Majesty King Carl XVI Gustaf, Her Majesty Queen Silvia, and Her Royal Highness Princess Lilian, Duchess of Halland, entered the hall at 4:30 P.M., after which the royal anthem was played. The laureates proceeded onto the stage after everybody had taken their place; Professor Nordén accompanied me. Only on this occasion do the king and queen stand up to receive the laureates; normally the people stand up for their royal majesties whenever they enter or are standing. The ceremony proceeded according to a detailed program that included musical interludes. Speeches were given by the chairman of the board of the Nobel Foundation and then by members of the academy who introduced the laureates.

In my case, Professor Bengt Nordén outlined the reasons for the academy's selection of me as the 1999 laureate in chemistry. As he walked to the podium, my mind wandered back to my youth—the boy from Egypt was about to receive the highest science prize in the world and our work would be recognized by this highest honor. I was also eager to hear the content of the speeches at this historic moment. It was *exhilarating* to hear my work compared to the father of modern science—Galileo. This analogy makes any scientist pleased: very few people can name the heads of state during Galileo's lifetime, but most people have heard of Galileo.

Professor Nordén then said: "May I convey to you my warmest congratulations on behalf of the Royal Swedish Academy of Sciences and ask you to come forward to receive the Nobel Prize in Chemistry for 1999 from the hands of His Majesty the King." These were moments that seemed almost unreal, but then they became real. With the applause in the background and my blood pressure shooting way up, I went to the king to receive the prize—the medal and the diploma, which on one side has a brief citation and on the other an original piece of art, in my case a painting, designed by the artist Nils G. Stenqvist, of pyramids and molecules streaked by the light of a pair of laser beams. I returned to my seat walking backward facing the king, a protocol we were told about in the rehearsal. The "Egyptian March," Op. 335 by Johann Strauss Jr., was playing in the background and I was overwhelmed by my emotions, but calm.

The medal, designed by Erik Lindberg in 1902, is a work of art. It's a big gold coin, almost two inches in diameter, with a portrait of Alfred Nobel on the face and on the reverse two concepts depicted as ancient goddesses stand in clouds: Nature, shown as Isis with an austere face, holds a cornucopia, and a veil that covered her face and body is lifted by the second goddess, the Genius (or Spirit) of Scientia—Science—who holds a scroll in her right hand and wears a laurel wreath on her head. The meaning is clear: Science uncovers the beauty and bounty of Nature. She writes down her findings for others (hence the scroll) and she is rewarded with a crown of laurel, representing the Nobel achievement of the winner, who is called *laureate*—one crowned with laurel.

In ancient Roman times, only individuals who had achieved a great triumph were technically permitted to wear a crown of laurel leaves, so there is a sense of *triumph* in Science's laurels. But laurel was also associated with the Greek god of wisdom and truth, Apollo, and some of that sense is also present in the meaning of the medal. Around the edge of the medal is a Latin phrase taken from Virgil's *Aeneid*, "Inventas vitam iuvat excoluisse per artes," which means "And they who bettered life on earth by new-found mastery" (also translated as "Inventions enhance life that is beautified through art"). Then at the bottom is a nameplate, where I found my name, "Ahmed H. Zewail," in raised relief, along with the date in Roman numerals, MCMIC.

At the end of the ceremony, Nabeel and Hani were brought to the stage by Ingmar Grente, a member of the Nobel Committee, and he sat them on the chairs of the king and the queen—Nabeel and Hani's photo on the chairs was a front page story in many newspapers the next morning. I thought that with the power of the Nobel prize I had impressed them and their sisters—this wasn't the case. At first, Hani, who looked handsome in his tuxedo, followed the ceremony. But then he fell asleep—and stayed asleep right through the time when I was receiving the prize from the king. Maha and Amani, dressed like princesses for the week's festivities, were everywhere, excited to have their pictures taken with my fellow Nobel laureates, but not with their own father. Nabeel, who had behaved like a gentleman during the whole week, hadn't done so after the announcement of the prize in October. Before going to Stockholm, we were invited to Palm Springs to meet with the Caltech Board of Trustees at their annual meeting. Nabeel, who was just six years old, was in a bad mood one evening and this mood escalated when Harold Brown, former Caltech president and US Secretary of Defense, noticed it, commenting, "Ahmed, you're just a dad to him, not a Nobel laureate." Nabeel's mood kept getting worse, to the point that we called him *ghazala* ("little wild deer"), and culminating with him telling me "you're a dumb chicken." To Nabeel, at the age of six, it meant that I wasn't paying attention to him; to me it meant that he put me in my place! He's now embarrassed when I remind him about this episode, especially when I promise him that this story will be told to his children!

After the award ceremony at the Concert Hall, we went by limousine to the City Hall for an amazing feast—the Nobel banquet. In the company of the king and queen we entered the hall, masterfully decorated with elegant china with polished silverware and crystal glasses, colorful flowers, plates of inviting food, perfectly attended to in every detail. I accompanied Princess Lilian, a very lively person, in the procession line. The seating was in accordance to a protocol for the different prizes and there were about 1,500 people in the hall. I sat next to Princess Lilian and across from the queen; when we visited the palace the next day for a royal dinner, Dema sat next to the king and I was next to Princess

ever, Egypt and the Arab world, which gave to science
Ibn Sina (Avicenna), Ibn Rushd (Averroës), Jabir ibn
Hayyan (Geber), Ibn al-Haytham (Alhazen), and others,
have had no prizes in science or medicine. I sincerely
hope that this first one will inspire the young generations
of developing countries with the knowledge that it is possible to contribute to world science and technology.

This speech and the entire award ceremony were broadcast live on
Egyptian television and radio and was watched, I am told, by millions all
over the world. People said that in Cairo there weren't many people on
the streets. It was as if there was an important soccer game between Ahly
and Zamalek, the two leading soccer teams in the country. To many, this
was a triumph for science and for the country. To me the highest praise
was when I felt that I could contribute to the well-being of the nation and
thus give hope for the future. People made the analogy between the
Nobel broadcast evening and a concert evening by Umm Kulthum, and
this too was high praise.

Egypt celebrated in a big way and so did Caltech. Every home in
Egypt shared in the celebration and the national feeling was clearly evident in the generosity of President Mohammed Hosni Mubarak and in
the people of the country. The day after the announcement of the Nobel
Prize in October, President Mubarak telephoned me at home in
Pasadena, congratulating me on the award and inviting us to Egypt for,
as he said, a big celebration. On December 11, the day after the awarding of the prize, it was announced that President Mubarak, by a decree
of the republic, had decided to award me the Order of the Grand Collar
of the Nile, the highest state honor.

We left Sweden on December 15, after I gave lectures at Lund and
Göteborg/Chalmers universities, and arrived in Cairo, by way of
London, on EgyptAir. This was an important choice since the airline had
lost a plane in a tragic crash over New York in October. Our arrival at
Cairo airport was much like that of a soccer team returning home victo-
rious. My children, all of them American born, were in awe of the huge

reception, which at times became unmanageable. The Minister of Higher Education and Scientific Research, Professor Mufid Shehab, tried to organize the "media frenzy," but the vast crowd of reporters were so enthusiastic that they were oblivious to the chaos surrounding us. After a press conference, we went to the Semiramis hotel, and we had another two weeks of celebrations—Egyptian ones.

In Egypt, I was awarded keys, shields, and medals from many organizations and cities, including the House of Representatives, the Shura Council (similar to the US Senate), the Arab League, the Opera House, and the City of Alexandria. I was also awarded an Honorary Degree from the Arab Academy for Science and Technology and from Alexandria University. A third stamp was issued with my portrait next to the pyramids to commemorate the occasion. I made many public appearances and gave addresses at such places as AUC, Alexandria University, Cairo University, the Opera House, *al-Ahram*, and *al-Akhbar*. Dr. Shehab was a gracious host and accompanied me on many of these invitations.

On December 16, my wife and I were invited to the Presidential Palace where the president and Mrs. Suzanne Mubarak were to receive us first in private and then in the company of Egypt's distinguished scholars, scientists, journalists and artists, and, of course, members of the cabinet, which included the prime minister and the ministers of state. The religious leaders of the Islamic and Coptic faiths were also present. The ceremony was broadcast nationally, and began with a speech by Dr. Shehab. Then came the announcement of the decree of the republic to grant the Order of the Grand Collar of the Nile, and I was asked to come on stage so the president could bestow the honor and place the beautifully decorated (and substantial) collar around my neck to the applause of the dignitaries present and, I am sure, that of the country. The declaration by President Mubarak read: "For the high esteem and great respect we hold for you and in recognition of your outstanding services to the nation and to science." This elegant ceremony took place after *iftar* during the month of Ramadan and there was something special about the serenity of the event during the peaceful month of remembrance for the best in human behavior and enlightenment.

The Grand Collar of the Nile (Qiladat al-Nil al-'Uzma) is unique in the history of the country. It can be traced back thousands of years to when it was bestowed on pharaohs and other honored persons. The modern version was created by law in 1953, and it was amended by another law in 1972. It's presented by the president and conferred on heads of states—it's the highest Egyptian decoration. On the death of the holder, he is accorded a funeral with military honors; holders who are living rank after the president, former living presidents, and vice-presidents. Indeed, it is a grand honor, which touched me deeply.

The collar is a necklace of gold, in which three square golden units follow each other alternatively, each one bearing a pharaonic symbol: *ankh, wadja,* and *seneb* (life, prosperity, and health; I learned this from my friend, Francis Clauser). The first unit symbolizes saving the country from evil; the second symbolizes the prosperity and happiness brought about by the Nile; and the third symbolizes welfare and continuity. The connecting link between these units takes the form of a circular golden flower, decorated with turquoise and rubies. The collar has a golden ornament connected to the chain by a clasp, and ornamented by pharaonic flowers as well as by turquoise and rubies. In the center is a relief design symbolizing the Nile as it unifies the north, represented by the papyrus, and the south, represented by the lotus.

With the collar around my neck, I gave my acceptance speech, and thanked the president and the nation, but I also had a message—Egypt should be directing its attention to the development of a science and technology base. President Mubarak gave the final words of the ceremony in a moving speech. He commented on the importance of my winning the Nobel Prize in Chemistry, a first in the sciences or physiology or medicine for Egypt and the Arab world. Among President Mubarak's thoughtful remarks were the following statements:

> I would like to start on a personal note, and on behalf of
> the great people of Egypt, by expressing our sincere
> congratulations to the devoted son of the land of Egypt,
> Dr. Ahmed Zewail, on the occasion of his receipt of the

Nobel Prize in Chemistry for 1999. . . . The Egyptians
and Arabs were most deeply thrilled by the great event
because they instantly realized its significance—namely, we are capable with the help of God of contributing
to the accelerating scientific revolution and its marvelous achievements.

President Mubarak characterized my work as a "gift to the world,"
and me as a "son of this ancient Egyptian civilization, which continues
to produce achievements that even until today strike the world with awe"
—the full text is given in the Appendix. He commented on the meaning
of the award, my educational background in Egypt, and the power of
Egyptian intellectuals in world scholarship, and he listed a number of
great Arab and Islamic thinkers who were our predecessors. He also
referred to my 1995 receipt of the Egyptian Order of Merit. He then mentioned his commitment to developing science and technology in Egypt in
an organized way, and ended his speech by saying:

I reiterate my congratulations to the devoted son of
Egypt and its distinguished scientist, Dr. Ahmed Zewail,
for his winning this distinguished prize. I am confident
in the ability of our people and our nation to attain the
progress we deserve. I am sure that there will be gatherings like this in the future to celebrate further achievements of the loyal children of Egypt for the sake of their
homeland and future of their descendants. By so doing,
they are fulfilling lofty human principles laid down by
their ancestors at the dawn of human civilization.

President Mubarak's speech stirred the crowd with enthusiasm and all
burst into applause when he concluded. The ceremony was followed by
a reception.

During the reception I asked for a special meeting with the president
to discuss future plans for science and technology in Egypt. I met the

president a few days later and at this meeting I outlined the need for a new center of excellence for science and technology, with a specific suggestion—the inauguration of a new university and technology park. On December 31, 1999, at a special event celebrating the new millennium at the Giza pyramids, the president was so enthusiastic about the project that in the private company of the prime minister and myself he mentioned that this project was important and should be realized promptly. On January 1, 2000, we had a groundbreaking ceremony for the new University of Science and Technology (UST) on the outskirts of Cairo in October 6 City, on a parcel of 300 acres, a subject to which I shall return in the last chapter. The festivities of the Nobel prize in Stockholm and of the Grand Collar of the Nile in Cairo ended when we returned to Los Angeles on January 8, 2000, the day of 'Eid al-Fitr, which marks the end of fasting during the month of Ramadan.

In the United States, the highlights of celebrations, before and after our trip to Stockholm, were at the White House and at Caltech. We had an invitation from the White House to visit with President William Jefferson Clinton. On our way to Stockholm we had stopped in Washington, D.C., for the White House reception as well as a black-tie dinner hosted by the Swedish ambassador to the United States at his residence. The visit to the White House was quite an experience, for both the protocol and the politics. The party was attended by many members of the cabinet, senators, science leaders, such as the directors of the National Science Foundation and the National Institutes of Health (NIH), and other dignitaries. The president had to leave at the last minute before the reception for a campaign speech! But the real "treat" actually occurred before the event, when the Nobel guests—Günter Blobel and his wife Laura, my wife Dema and I, together with the Swedish ambassador and his wife—tried to get through White House security checkpoints on the way to our own party. It took some time to get in. We were freezing in Washington's winter air, especially the ladies in their fancy gowns.

I met President Clinton at Caltech on January 21, 2000, when he gave a brilliant speech announcing his national policy on science and technology. I mentioned to the president our experience with security. He laughed, and in a shrewd move avoided the issue by suggesting that we should have a photograph taken together. I met the president again on March 27, 2000, at the White House for close to two hours, in connection with discussions on the Middle East.

At Caltech, a week after we returned from the Stockholm trip, we had a welcome-home party—the faculty dinner at the Athenaeum—where about five hundred attended. Colorful flower arrangements perfumed the sparkling dinner setting at the Athenaeum that night and the convivial atmosphere was charged with spirited congratulatory remarks. Speeches were given by the president, the provost, several faculty members, and friends. Vince McKoy gave a thoughtful speech about the scientific journey and contribution, and several friends were beaming when they expressed their happiness for the recognition. I was particularly pleased with the presence of current and former "AZ Group" members—students, postdoctoral fellows, associates, and staff. Former group members came back to join in the celebration and we reminisced about the old days; we ended the evening with a souvenir group photograph.

That evening in my speech, I spoke about Caltech's uniqueness and about the future. I mentioned three phrases that characterize the forces that made it possible for our Nobel prize work to be accomplished only ten years after my being hired as an assistant professor: "The sky's the limit," an expression that summarizes the attitude of Caltech and its administration; "The selection of my own research direction," a tradition at Caltech that allows for total freedom with no pressure to chase funding sources or the latest fads of research; and "The support by students, staff, and scholarship," a defining character in the make-up of the institute. It is my hope that these unique Caltech features remain the same in the future and that we do not follow the prevailing fads. After this party we had another one that was elegantly organized by the Associates of Caltech, held at the Ritz Carlton in Pasadena; my friend Jack Roberts gave the after-dinner speech. Festivities continued with parties at our home for members of my research group and for family and friends.

One of the most satisfying aspects of these festivities was sharing these special moments with my family, with my wife, with Maha and Amani, and with Nabeel and Hani. I only wish that my father had been alive and that my mother had been able to attend these celebrations with us. While the celebrations were focused on me, they presented an opportunity to reflect with my wife on the good fortune of having such a wonderful family in good health, and with children who are high achievers themselves. Maha, now a happy mother, is a Ph.D. graduate from the University of Texas at Austin, with a B.S. degree from Caltech, and Amani is currently a graduate student at UCLA, with a B.S. degree from the University of California at Berkeley. Nabeel and Hani are happy and have all the signs of equal promise. In the walks of life, the happiness and success of one's family members are among the most valuable treasures.

Moving beyond the festivities, I now face new challenges and responsibilities. I still have my passion for starting new areas of research at Caltech and exciting young students and the public about science. I must now think about how Egypt can build its science and technology base. But the following question is on my mind now as it has been for many years: How can we help the have-nots?

9

A Personal Vision

The World of the Have-Nots

With the laurel of the Nobel, I was bombarded with requests for advice on almost everything—from infertility and birth control to the hole in the ozone layer and to life on Mars. Through e-mails and the Internet, I received questions about life, money, and health—as if I had become Superman with a solution for everything. I even received personal requests, such as one man's e-mail proposal of marriage to one of my daughters, Amani—his curriculum vitae looked good to me, but this approach wasn't pleasing to Amani! There were also requests for my signature on the petitions of numerous organizations and for my autograph by thousands of individuals.

In addition to the pleasure of being a scientist, there are duties that I recognize and intend to carry out with vigor and diligence. The Nobel honor comes with important responsibilities and opportunities for aiding progress in the world. It is not the end of the road for achievement. I was surprised by the comments of many to relax, meaning that nothing is higher than the honor of the Nobel. While this is true from a profession-al perspective, there are the intrinsic rewards that result from a true pas-sion about one's work, family, and humanity in general. For those who seek to acquire new knowledge, this passion is a continual process. One of Egypt's greatest scholars, Dr. Taha Hussein, admonished people who rested on their laurels with the following words: *Wailu li-talib al- 'ilmi al-radi 'an nafsihi*, which means "Woe to the satisfied scholar!" And he's right—we have to continue to seek and we have to take the responsibility to help other seekers of knowledge.

I have, however, made a decision not to be involved in everything, but to limit myself to three areas that I feel would benefit from my efforts and would keep me content with my life in its voyage through time. These are, as it were, three angles that define the triangle of a vision. The first of these is to keep our research effort buoyant. Indeed we have done so. My group at Caltech is larger than ever and we have developed a new area of research, ultrafast electron diffraction, which allows us to record images of molecular structures transforming in time with unprecedented time and space resolution. We also have a strong initiative in the biological and medical sciences and in the area of organic materials. In these research directions we are exploring new frontiers and we expect an exciting time ahead. It is hoped we'll have some breakthroughs.

The second angle of this triangle is the popularization of science. I've been involved in many public lectures, TV interviews, and meetings with youth, and these events are exciting as I can see the thrill on the faces of young people, just as I had been thrilled when I was their age. The hope is to inspire not only the young people but also the public about the beauty of science and of new knowledge.

The responses so far have been gratifying. On several occasions in the United States and in Europe, a student has come up to me and said, "I was planning to go to medical (or law) school, but I have decided to become a scientist," and I even received gifts from people who attended my lectures in Chicago, Basel, Stockholm, and other places. In Crete, the theater was crammed with a public clamoring for news of the latest scientific research. In Egypt, thousands of students are eager to hear about science, and my lectures there have drawn huge gatherings of the public at the American University in Cairo, at the annual Egyptian National Book Fair, and at universities nationwide. Last year I spoke at the Opera

House about the mapping of the human genome, and it too was packed—the Opera House is nominally for musical and art events and I was pleased to see that science can generate equal enthusiasm.

Perhaps the one part of this triangle that consumes the lion's share of my time, and that isn't as straightforward as the other two, is my involvement in what I call science for the have-nots. With my experience in two cultures I feel that I may be able to make a contribution in the developing world in fostering science and in the developed world in creating a serious partnership with the developing world. This involvement is particularly relevant to Egypt and to peace and prosperity in the Middle East, along with the development of the Arab and Muslim world. In my speech at the celebration of the Collar of the Nile, I stressed the importance of education and a science-based society using the following words—this part of the speech is translated from Arabic:

> The world today stands on two primary supports that are the foundation for power, influence, and progress. These two supports are advanced scientific knowledge and the productivity of the people in line with this knowledge base. The developed world of today relies on science and productivity to change the standard of living and to be positioned as a world force on this planet.
>
> For developing states to attain a similar level of progress and development requires the building of a science base and a scientific culture. With these keys, it is possible to escape the 'import mentality,' the trap of relying on importing goods only for consumption, and it is possible to join in technological competition with the outside world in the new system of globalization. Such a powerful scientific base needs true and unified participation—the Egyptian people need to believe in the role of science in creating a new and advanced position for the country.
>
> Egypt now has the ability to take that great scientific

and technological leap forward that will boost it into the twenty-first century, because of the success of your wise leadership, Mr. President, in courageously embarking on the difficult task of building the infrastructure and strengthening Egypt's political position in the world.

My perspective on these issues was recently summarized in a commentary published in *Nature*. A more detailed version was presented at the Pontifical Academy of Sciences at the Vatican on the occasion of its jubilee celebration, which happened to coincide with my induction into the academy; the article was published in the special proceedings, *Science and the Future of Mankind*. These papers were published weeks before the tragic attacks on the World Trade Center in New York City and on the Pentagon in Washington, D.C., on September 11, 2001, which were followed by a new type of attack, a biological one involving the anthrax bacterium.

I don't agree with the view that the current state of the world is primarily due to a "clash of civilizations" or a "conflict of religions," as many authors and commentators have recently claimed. Instead, I believe that economic and political forces are playing a fundamental role behind world instabilities. Poverty, illiteracy, and the huge injustice of the division of the world into haves and have-nots, into powerful and powerless—these are the real causes that threaten our peaceful coexistence. I will attempt to address these issues, with a focus on what I term a *proposal for partnership*. It is not my intention to project knowledge of the absolute solution. These thoughts are given from a personal perspective based on my experiences in both worlds.

On our planet, every human being carries the same genetic material and the same four-letter genetic alphabet. Accordingly, there's no basic genetic superiority that is defined by race, ethnicity, or religion. We don't expect, based on genetics, a person of American or French origin to be superior to a person from Africa or Latin America. Moreover, it has been proven repeatedly that men and women from the so-called developing or underdeveloped countries can achieve at the highest level, usually when they are in developed countries with the appropriate atmosphere conducive to such achievements. Naturally, for any given population, there exists a distribution of abilities, capabilities, and creativity.

In our world, the distribution of wealth is skewed, creating classes among populations and regions. Only 20% of the world's population enjoy the benefit of life in the developed world, and the gap between the haves and have-nots continues to increase, threatening a stable and peaceful coexistence. According to the World Bank, out of the 6 billion people on Earth, 4.8 billion live in developing countries; 3 billion live on less than $2 a day and 1.2 billion live on less than $1 a day, which defines the absolute poverty standard. About 1.5 billion people have no access to clean water, with health consequences like waterborne disease—and about 2 billion people are still waiting to benefit from the power of the industrial revolution.

The per capita gross domestic product (GDP) in some developed Western countries is $35,000, compared with about $1,000 in many developing countries and significantly less in underdeveloped countries. The GDP in US dollars is the total unduplicated output of economic goods and services produced within a country as measured in monetary terms. Taking the GDPs of a sampling of countries, from data compiled by the UN Statistics Division, we can see that this standard measure of a country's development varies considerably across nations: Yemen (354), North Korea (430), Angola (528), China (777), Egypt (1,211), South Korea (6,956), Israel (17,041), Canada (19,439), Hong Kong (24,581), United States (31,059), and Switzerland (35,910). This difference in living standards by a factor of up to 100 between the haves and have-nots ultimately creates dissatisfaction, violence, and racial and ethnic conflict. Evidence of such dissatisfaction already exists and we have only to look at the borders of developed with developing or underdeveloped countries, for example, between the United States and Mexico and between Eastern and Western Europe, or between the rich and the poor within a nation.

Overpopulation of the world and its anticipated disasters represent a major problem because of limited resources and increased conflicts on the globe, but the problem is not new. This has been a concern for millennia, from the time of the ancient Egyptians and Babylonians to this day. In his book *How Many People Can the Earth Support?* Joel Cohen provides a scholarly overview of the global population problem.

Some believe that the new world order and globalization are the solution to problems such as the population explosion, the economic gap, and social disorder. The standard conclusion regarding world order and globalization is questionable. Despite the hoped-for new world order between superpowers, the globe still experiences notable examples of conflict, violence, and violation of human rights. The world order is strongly linked to political interest and national self-interest, and in the process many developing countries continue to suffer and their development is threatened. Globalization, in principle, is a hopeful ideal that aspires to help nations prosper and advance through participation in the world market. In practice, however, globalization is better tailored to the prospects of the able and the strong, and, although of value to human competition and progress, it serves only that fraction of the world's population who are able to exploit the market and the available resources.

Moreover, nations have to be ready to enter through this gate of globalization and such entry has its requirements. Among these requirements are the following: computer and Internet literacy; a minimal level of bureaucracy; the accessibility of sources of knowledge and information; the entrepreneurial spirit; efficiency in management; and the clear and just application of the law. The picture one should have in mind is that a country is like a global company, with the aim of becoming prosperous in a timely manner. Accordingly, organization, management, and technical know-how are essential for a country to prosper; location, history, natural resources, or even military might are no longer the only deciding factors!

Before attempting to address solutions, it's important to examine the origin of the problem by looking at the anatomy of the gap. In my view, there are four main forces that contribute to the barriers to achieving developed-world status:

Illiteracy: In many countries, especially those in the ⁃Southern

Hemisphere, illiteracy reaches 40–50% in the general population. Even worse, in some countries, illiteracy among women is above 70%. These rates reflect the failure of educational systems, and are linked to an alarming increase in unemployment. One cannot expect to seriously participate in the world community with this state of unpreparedness. In the West, illiteracy on this scale has been essentially eliminated, and today the term often means a lack of expertise with computers, not the inability to read and write! Of course, some developed countries of today had high illiteracy rates when they began their development, but we must remember that a significant portion of the population possessed some basic level of technical know-how.

Incoherent Policy for Science and Technology: The lack of a solid science and technology base in the world of have-nots is not always due to poor capital or human resources. Instead, in many cases, it's due to a lack of appreciation for the critical role of science and technology, an incoherent methodology for establishing a science and technology base, and an absence of a coherent policy addressing national needs and human and capital resources (even in some developed countries, we have witnessed the consequences of the latter). Some countries believe that science and technology are only for rich nations. Others consider scientific progress a luxury, not a basic need, that should be pursued only after the country has solved other demanding problems. Some rich, but developing, countries believe that a base for science and technology can be built through the purchase of technology from developed countries. These beliefs translate into poor or, at most, modest advances and in almost all cases the success is based on individuals, not institutional teamwork. Such complex problems are made worse by the fact that there are many slogans, reports, and showcase efforts that fail to address the real issues and are intended for local consumption alone.

Restrictions on Human Thought: Real progress requires the participation of knowledgeable people working together to address key problems and possible solutions. In the West, this participation involves senior and junior people and their different areas of expertise in the exchange of human thought and knowledge. The result is a planned recommendation, designed to help different sectors of society. In many developing countries, although this practice is true on paper, in reality it's usually not followed. There are many reasons, including hierarchical dominance and strong seniority systems, which limit people's ability to speak freely. Although Western democracies aren't the only successful models for government, a lack of democratic participation suppresses collective human thought and limits the due process of the law, which unfairly stifles human potential.

Constitutional Law and Fanaticism: Confusion and chaos result from the misuse of the fundamental message of religion, namely the ethical, moral, and humanistic ingredients in the life of a significant portion of the world population. For example, in Islam the message is clear: it's fully expressed in the Holy Quran to Muslims, who number close to one billion people in the world. The Quran makes fundamental statements about human existence and integrity, on everything from birth and death to science and knowledge. "Read!" is the first word in the first verse of the direct revelation to the Prophet (Quran, 96:1), and there are numerous verses regarding the importance of knowledge, science, and learning. There is also a *hadith*, or saying of the Prophet, that runs: "God makes a path to Paradise easy for anyone who journeys in search of knowledge." Seeking knowledge is only a first step. The Quran also emphasizes the critical role that humans must play in the struggle to achieve and develop: "Truly, God will not improve the conditions of any people until they improve them themselves." (Quran, 13:11).

All societies and religions experience some degree of fanaticism, but when such a phenomenon exploits constitutional laws and threatens national security, it ultimately leads to a crippling of the society. Exacerbating the situation is the dominance of the West with its inconsistent politics, jumbled together with invasive modern media and the current disparity in the world economy. With all of this in the background, there is a real fear of the erosion of religious and cultural values. This situation, coupled with increased unemployment, results in a rigid attitude toward progress and forces the release of frustration in less than productive ways.

What is needed to solve these multidimensional problems? The answer to this question is not trivial because of the many cultural and political considerations that frame the total picture. Nevertheless, I believe that the four issues mentioned above point to the essentials for progress, which are summarized in the following goals: 1) *building the human resources*, taking into account the necessary elimination of illiteracy, the active participation of women in society, and the need for a reformation of education; 2) *rethinking the national constitution*, which must allow for freedom of thought, minimization of bureaucracy, development of a merit system, and a credible (enforceable) legal code; and 3) *building the science base*. This last essential of progress is critical to development and to globalization and it is important to examine this point further.

In order to thrive, a healthy scientific structure must rely on the interconnectivity of its fundamental components—the science base, technology, and society. First, *the science base*. The backbone of the science base is an investment in specialized education for the gifted, the existence of centers of excellence for young scientists to blossom, and the opportunity to use knowledge to impact the industrial and economic markets of the country (and, it is hoped, the world). In order to maximize the impact, this plan must go hand-in-hand with that of general education at state schools and universities. The science base must exist, even at a modest level, to insure a proper and ethical way of conducting research in the culture of science, which demands cooperation and a team effort in search of the truth. The acquisition of confidence and pride in intellectual successes will lead to a more enlightened society.

Second, *the development of technology*. The science base forms a foundation for the development of technologies on both the national and the international level. Using a scientific approach, a country will be able to address its needs and channel its resources into successful technologies that are important, for example, to food production, health, management, information, and, hopefully, participation in the world market.

Third, *the society*—its science culture. Developing countries possess rich cultures of their own in literature, entertainment, sports, and history.

But, many have no or little science culture. The science culture enhances a country's ability to identify and address complex problems rationally, based on facts, while involving many voices in an organized, collective manner—scientific thinking becomes essential to the fabric of society. Because science isn't as visible or as easy to digest as entertainment, the knowledge of what is new, from modern developments in nutrition and genetics to emerging high-tech possibilities in the world market, becomes marginalized. With a stronger scientific base, it's possible to enhance the science culture, foster a rational approach, and educate the public about potential developments and benefits. The youth, the future of the nation, are the real beneficiaries of such a culture.

The mindset that such a structure is only for those countries that are already developed is a major obstacle for the have-not countries. Moreover, some even believe in a conspiracy theory that the developed world will not help developing countries and that they try to control the flow of knowledge. The former is a version of the chicken and the egg paradox because developed countries were once developing countries before they achieved their current status. Recent success in the world market in developing countries such as China and India is the product of their developed educational systems and technological skills in certain sectors—India is fast becoming one of the world leaders in software technology, and products "Made in China" are now all over the globe.

As for the conspiracy theory, I personally don't give significant weight to it, preferring to believe that nations "interact" to the best of their mutual interests. If the gap is too large, the interest, mutual or perhaps more on the side of the advanced countries, diminishes. If the gap narrows, the flow of information (including science and technology) becomes easier, even if the two nations involved don't really have an affinity to each other. Internalizing and living by a conspiracy theory does not lead to progress.

What is needed is acceptance of responsibility in a collaboration between developing and developed countries. In my proposal for partnership, I see two sets of responsibilities, which I summarize in the following outline.

Proposal for Partnership

Responsibilities of Developing Countries

1. *Restructuring education and science.* The force of expatriates in developed countries should be organized and used for assistance. Expatriates can help the exchange between developed and developing cultures and assist in bringing modern methods of education and research. This will be unsuccessful without the genuine participation of local experts.

2. *Creation of centers of excellence.* These centers should be limited to a few areas in order to build confidence and achieve recognition and shouldn't just be exercises in public relations. They are important not only for research and development but also in preparing a new population of experts in advanced technologies. This would also help reduce the brain drain that many developing countries are currently experiencing.

3. *Commitment of national resources.* These resources are needed to support research and development in a selective way, following well-established criteria that are based on merit and distinction. To guide national policy, government at the highest level should create an overseeing "Board for Science and Technology," composed of national and international experts. Without serious commitment to such an effort, progress will remain limited.

Some developing countries have made admirable progress in these areas, and the results from India, South Korea, and Taiwan, for example, reflect healthy educational reforms and excellence in some science and technology sectors. In Egypt, the University of Science and Technology (UST) was proposed as an experiment, with the hope that it will become a center of excellence that will satisfy the criteria of the above trilogy: nurturing the science base, developing technologies important to the region and the world, and fostering the science culture. This could be a unique experiment in which both developing and developed countries will be able to participate, helping a region rich in human capital and potential but in great need of peace and prosperity. By the time UST reaches its final stage, it should have satellites that will benefit other countries in the Middle East region. I shall revisit the UST project in the next chapter.

Responsibilities of Developed Countries

1. *Focusing of aid programs.* Usually, an aid package from developed to developing countries is distributed to many projects. Although some of these projects are badly needed, the number of projects involved and the lack of serious follow-up, not to mention the presence of corruption, means that the aid doesn't result in big successes. More direct involvement and focus are needed, especially to help centers of excellence achieve their missions, according to criteria already operational in developed countries.

2. *Minimization of politics in aid.* The use of an aid program to help specific regimes or groups in the developing world is a big mistake, and as history has shown it is in the best interests of the developed world to help the *people* of developing countries. Accordingly, an aid program should be visionary in addressing real problems and should provide for long-term investment in the development program.

3. *Partnerships in success.* There are two ways to aid developing countries. Developed nations can either give money intended simply to sustain economic and political stability or they can become a partner and provide expertise and a follow-up plan. This serious involvement would be of great help in achieving success in many different sectors. I believe that real success *can* be achieved provided a sincere desire exists with a serious commitment to a partnership that would be in the best interests of both parties.

What do rich countries get in return for helping poor countries? At the level of a human individual, there are religious and philosophical reasons that make the rich give to the poor—morality and self-protection motivate us to help humankind. For countries, mutual aid provides, besides the issue of morality, insurance for a peaceful coexistence and cooperation for preservation of the globe. If we believe that the world is becoming a village, especially in the age of information technology, then we must provide social security for the unprivileged in that village. Otherwise we may trigger a revolution—if the population is not in harmony, grievances will be felt throughout the village and in many different ways.

Furthermore, healthy and sustainable human life requires the participation of all members of the globe. Ozone depletion, for example, is a problem that the developed world cannot handle alone—it is not only the haves who use propellants with chlorofluorocarbons (CFCs). Transmission of diseases and the greenhouse effect are likewise global issues and both the haves and have-nots must address solutions and consequences.

Finally, there is the growing world economy. The markets and resources of developing countries are a source of wealth to developed countries and it is wise to cultivate a harmonious relationship for mutual aid and mutual economic growth. I recently heard the phrase "Give us the technology and we will give you the market!" used to describe the US–China relationship.

The Marshall Plan, named for George C. Marshall, US Secretary of State from 1947 to 1949, was a powerful example of visionary aid given by the United States to Europe after World War II. Recognizing the mistake made in Europe after World War I, in 1947 the United States decided to help rebuild the damaged infrastructure and to become a partner in Europe's economic (and political) developments. Western Europe is stable today and continues to prosper—as does its major trading partner, the United States. The United States spent close to 2% of its GNP on the Marshall Plan for the years 1948–51. As Joel Cohen pointed out, a similar percentage of the $6.6 trillion of the 1994 US GNP would amount to $130 billion, almost ten times the $15 billion a year currently spent for all non-military foreign aid and more than 280 times the $352 million the United States gave for all overseas programs in 1991. The commitment and generosity of the Marshall Plan resulted in a spectacular success story. The world needs a rational commitment to effective aid programs and to aid partnerships.

It is in the best interests of the developed world to help developing countries become strong and part of the new world order and market. Some developed countries are recognizing the importance of partnership, especially with neighbors, and attempts are being made to create new ways to support and exchange the know-how. Examples include the

United States with Mexico and Western with Eastern Europe. The rise of Spain's economic status is due in part to the partnership within Western Europe.

In the next twenty-five years, it is anticipated that 2 billion human beings will be added to the planet, with 97% of those 2 billion people living in the developing world. This uneven population explosion, with its impact on world resources, the deterioration of the environment, and regional conflicts, threatens our peaceful coexistence and calls for serious and active involvement. The consequence when developing countries acquire an underdeveloped status is ugly, not only because of the human costs and suffering, but also because of its negative impact on the world as a whole, including an increase in violence and terrorism. By the same token, it's in the best interests of developing countries to seriously address the issues of education, human resources, and the science and technology base, not through slogans, but with a commitment of both will and resources in order to achieve real progress and to take a place on the map of the developed world.

We may picture the current situation of the new world "dis-order" by likening it to a ship in a flood, keeping in mind that this analogy is not meant to quantify the problem. Underdeveloped countries are close to sinking under the deluge; developing countries are trying to make it onto the ship; and developed countries are sailing, *but* in a flood of the underprivileged. The choices are clear: the ship must seriously attempt to help those who are trying to get on board. Those trying to get on board shouldn't regard the ship without a willingness to put forth their own efforts, and shouldn't waste their energy on conspiracy theories—getting on the ship is more important! Meanwhile, all must attempt to rescue those at the bottom. To be part of a civilized planet, every human should matter. The notion of "us" and "them" is not visionary and we should speak of global problems and global solutions. At the heart are poverty, illiteracy, and the repression of liberty.

Maha's graduation
from Caltech, 1994

Amani's graduation from San Marino
High School in 1997

Halloween trick or treating with my sons; I am
wearing one of the honorary degree robes

Dema Faham on the occasion of the awarding of
the King Faisal International Prize in March of 1989

Wedding photo of Dema and me, with family,
at Caltech's Athenaeum in September, 1989

Professor Bengt Nordén introducing
me at the Nobel awards ceremony

My family and friends at a
reception in Stockholm, prior
to the awards ceremony

With Naguib Mahfouz
in Cairo, 2000

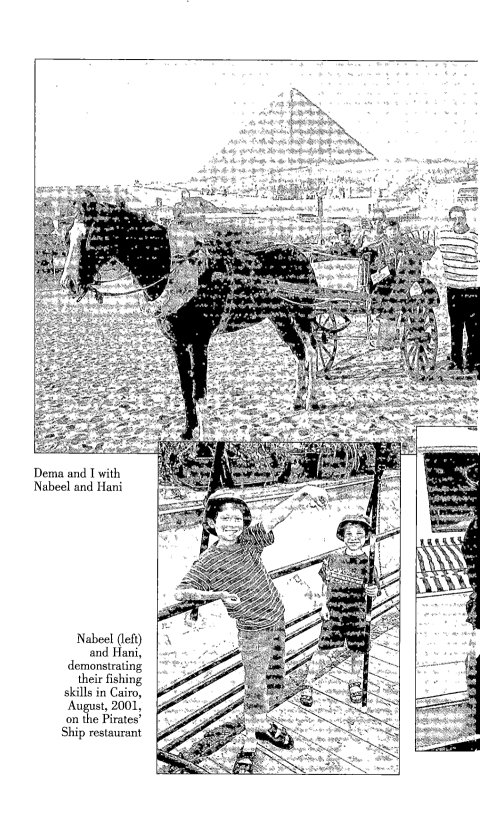

Dema and I with
Nabeel and Hani

Nabeel (left)
and Hani,
demonstrating
their fishing
skills in Cairo,
August, 2001,
on the Pirates'
Ship restaurant

Omar Batisha and I at al-Fishawi cafe in Cairo in 1997

My family on board a yacht on the Nile with Hesham, in December, 1999

In the Tea Garden of the Semiramis

With Mme. Amal Fahmy
in West Lost Angeles,
March 5, 1988, for the
recording of *'Ala al-Nasia*

Walking with Linus
Pauling on the
Caltech campus on
the occasion of
receiving the Pauling
chair, July 17, 1990

Dick Bernstein
and I sharing coffee
and points of view
in 1987, under the
portrait of Tutankh-
amun in my office

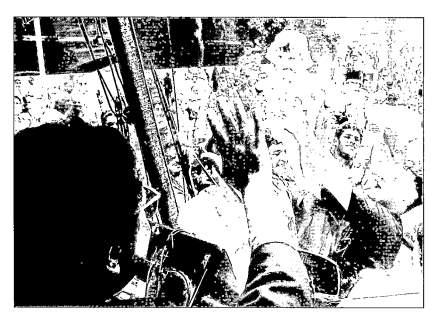

Street scene in Desuq at the dedication of a street in my name, inaugurated by Governor M. Abou Leil Rashed, in 1998

At the head of the street
named for me in Damanhur,
inaugurated by Governor
F. El-Tellawy, in 1998

Dr. Ahmed Zewail Square in Alexandria,
inaugurated by Governor M. A. Mahgoub, in 2000

My wife and I, with Nabeel and Hani, in front of the femtoscope and a pyramid
depicted on the Zewail Square open museum wall in Alexandria

The souvenir photograph taken at the Athenaeum on the occasion
of the Nobel prize celebration, January, 2000

Groundbreaking ceremony for the University
of Science and Technology on January 1, 2000

10

Walks to the Future
My Hope for Egypt and America

he arrow of time is well defined in its direction, and life is a transition state that is ephemeral on the time scale of the universe. This
seems to be a universal constant: the universe has been expanding
over its age of 12–15 billion years; stars age, and even our sun was born
4.6 billion years ago, and in 10 billion years it will shrink and become
white hot, a white dwarf, and eventually a dark dwarf—the life and death
of stars. The cause of the directionality of time is not obvious. In fact, for
some phenomena in the world of the very small, time reversal is allowed.
Scientists rationalize the irreversible behavior in our world by invoking
concepts that describe systems at equilibrium. One such concept, called
entropy, is the tendency of systems to become disordered, to increase in
randomness, as time goes on.

Not everything relating to time can be rationalized in a conceptual
manner, but one thing is certain—our feelings and perspectives change
with time. As youngsters we might not appreciate parents and teachers or
even our countries, but as adults we begin to appreciate them and to feel
the need for a stronger bond with our roots. In youth we think we are
immortal, but as we age we think seriously of mortality. A happy and ful-

filling life makes such a change with time easier to accept and to focus our perspective on what can be done to help others fulfill their lives. For me, time is of the essence—in science and in life. In science I focus on the shortest duration of time and ask questions like what would I see if I could travel on a femtosecond laser at the speed of light? Meanwhile, in life, I ask: how can I prolong a positive impact on the well-being of others, especially the have-nots? I have attempted in the preceding chapter to provide a personal vision of this mission.

Here, I concern myself with the two cultures I have shared in my voyage through time so far—Egypt and the United States. By my fiftieth birthday, I had spent almost equal amounts of time in these two countries, in the culture of the East and the culture of the West. I am a citizen of Egypt and a citizen of the United States, naturalized on March 5, 1982. Growing up in Egypt, the mother country that shaped my early life, gave me pride in the incredible achievements of my ancestors. The land of my birth was one of the first places in history that hosted human civilization, and that civilization has passed down through the generations its spirit of achievement and learning. Moving to America, the country that gave me opportunity, enriched my life with another culture; it is home to pragmatic innovation and a can-do Edisonian attitude that propels science and technology forward with vast leaps and a characteristic confidence. Although the history of the United States is much shorter than Egypt's, America's achievements are also of historic magnitude.

When I left Egypt at the age of twenty-three, I was fully aware of its impact on me in education and family values. But I was not fully aware of Egypt's contributions to world civilization, in almost every corner of knowledge. In the West, children are taught of Egypt's ancient civilization, illustrated by the best in architecture, namely the Great Pyramids and the Pharos lighthouse—two of the Seven Wonders of the ancient world. Through its written history of more than six thousand years, Egypt has enjoyed the continuity of a path full of different cultures and religions—the pharaonic dynasties, the era of the Ptolemies, the Roman and Christian eras, and today's Arab Muslim and Coptic cultures, not to mention the cultures experienced through colonization and invasions by outside powers.

Recently, I was reading a series of *Eyewitness Science* books with my children and discovered that in every topic we covered—light, time, matter, chemistry, paper, language, arts, and religion—Egypt was mentioned as the first or among the first to make a contribution to the world's knowledge of the subject. The situation is now different. Egypt's population is near 70 million and resources are limited. By world standards, Egypt is now considered a developing country and some call it a third-world country, a term that I do not find appropriate. So I ask myself: What happened to the Egyptians? Why can't Egypt be a developed country? Given that nations go up and down in their status, can Egypt recover its glory days? What is the future of Egypt?

I ask similar questions about the American culture for different reasons. Being in the United States for more than thirty years, I fully appreciate America's strength—the youthful character of the nation, the openness, and the democratic institutions that ensure the freedom and respect of the American people. I also appreciate America's achievements in science and technology and in creating new opportunities for the young—indeed, America is the country of opportunity.

America will be remembered for creating the atomic age, the space age (after the launch of the Soviet-manned satellite *Sputnik* in 1958), the electronic age, the information age, and now the age of the genome. But I ask myself: Can America maintain its leadership in a complex, interactive world? Can America maintain a balanced social structure but continue to establish "elite" institutions? Can the country continue to excel with its present educational system? And why is there violence in America and hatred from outside America?

For both cultures, these are complex and difficult questions, and I think I am in a position to reflect on them, at least from the perspective of a person who has hopes for both cultures. My experiences in both cultures are important to a dissection of the problems. I have been part of the educational system in America. I have taught undergraduate students and have had more than 150 graduate students and research associates in my research group—many are now working as professors and in leading industrial positions in the United States and throughout the world. I have also given more than five hundred scientific and public lectures in the United States and abroad and interacted with institutions of learning in many developed and developing countries. I have been an active member of various committees that direct the future of science at Caltech and in the United States and other countries.

I have also chaired or served on national committees affiliated with major science organizations in the United States, such as the National Science Foundation and the National Academy of Sciences, and helped to position Caltech in terms of the new changes and challenges that are taking place in science nationally and internationally. By being an active member of several boards of advisors and trustees, including the Max Planck Institute in Germany, the American University in Cairo, and others, I participate in a vision for improving education, research, and society. All of these experiences have given me the opportunity to see issues important to the development of institutions and nations and the problems that face science and education programs.

In Egypt, I have organized international conferences, beginning with the first one on photochemistry and photobiology, in Alexandria in 1983. I was involved with establishing the National Institute for Laser-Enhanced Sciences, which I named, with the acronym of NILES. Professor Lotfia El-Nadi, the first director of this Cairo University–based institute, made a major contribution to NILES. I interacted extensively with her to get this project finalized, and together we cochaired the international conference on lasers and their applications, in Cairo in 1994. I have given science lectures at NILES as well as at the American University in Cairo, and numerous public lectures; this broad outreach effort sparked excitement in Egypt about science and I used the opportunity to inspire and interact with young people.

I have visited essentially all the major research institutions in the country and feel comfortable in assessing the strengths and weaknesses of Egypt's science base. Knowing the true state of research and development in Egypt, I proposed an initiative for establishing an institution of higher learning in Egypt that should serve as a true center of excellence; this is the University of Science and Technology (UST), which I referred to earlier. UST is designed to bring about a strong research and development base that is capable of participation at the level of the advanced world, and to help Egypt be an active part of globalization through the development of critical technologies. By so doing, Egypt will also be able to retain some of the best university graduates in the country. UST is critical for the development of Egypt and below I shall return to the subject.

Egypt's barriers to developed-world status are in part historic. The modern history of Egypt began with the Arab conquest in AD 639. Egypt began its state system in 1805 at the end of the Ottoman period. During the reign of Mohammed 'Ali (1805–48), a man who landed in Egypt with the Albanian contingent of the Ottoman army, Egypt was propelled into a new age. Egypt modernized its army and changed the education system, and the country pushed forward the frontiers of modernization and industrialization. It is remarkable that 'Ali, who was illiterate until the age of forty-seven, believed in a strong education system that was interactive and open to the world. Mohammed 'Ali died in 1849 and unfortunately his successors had neither his energy nor his vision.

A succession of rulers was to culminate in King Farouk's ascent to the throne in 1937. During this time, the country witnessed turmoil and attempted revolutions. The British occupation had made Egyptians thirsty for a ruler of their own, and until 1952 the situation in the country was unsatisfactory—an unjust class system, the alienation of Egyptians from their rulers, and the deteriorating economic state of the country were forces pushing for change. The Nasser years from 1952 to 1970 gave people a sincere hope for such change. Unfortunately, the Free Officers movement headed by President Nasser, who was a "real" Egyptian, did not satisfy these dreams. Many good things came out of the 1952 revolution—these include the dream of Arab unity, made possible by Nasser's beliefs and charisma, the building of the Aswan High Dam that was crucial to Egypt's future, the nationalization of the Suez Canal, and the initial reforms in the educational and social policies. But there were mistakes committed, most importantly the absence of new democratic institutions and freedom of speech.

This era in the history of Egypt resulted in major changes among the Egyptians and in their society. Egypt had to deal with population explosion, with illiteracy, with education of a huge number of students (with no paid tuition), and with subsidies on most basic goods. Besides all of these problems, the remaining effects of colonization, the friction within the new socialist system, and the conflict with Israel over Palestine were draining the country in terms of its natural as well as its intellectual resources. A variety of ideologies and classes of ideologues emerged and the country was in a bind economically.

Something had to be done, and this is what President Sadat (1970–81) attempted to do by adopting the open door policy so that the country would become fertile soil for foreign investment. He also believed that achieving peace with Israel was important for progress, both national and international. In retrospect, his launching of the 1973 war was a historic move that allowed him to regain Egyptian land and secure a peace treaty. But because the country did not form a solid foundation for a governing system to deal with the new policies, corruption increased and the gap between the rich and the poor widened. Moreover, the infrastructure of the country reached a serious level of deterioration and was not attractive to foreign investment. President Mubarak, who took office in 1981, made the building of the infrastructure of the country one of his top priorities, and indeed Egypt's infrastructure has undergone a revolutionary change.

Egypt is still being drained because of the conflict in the Middle East and because of the social and economic problems facing the country, but I believe that these problems are not impossible to solve. Egypt has the human resources, the history, the respect of the world, and, I believe, the necessary financial strength. But there is one more factor, namely the Egyptian's love for Egypt, which makes my belief in Egypt's potential strong. Egyptians argue and joke about their country and its leaders, but they are sensitive, and even emotional, when it comes to attacking "Misr," which is the Arabic word for Egypt (and also for Cairo).

Egyptians are friendly and happy people by nature and they can tolerate hardship. They have faith. The Nile must have given people a sense of eternity, and as the notable Gamal Hamdan said, it is the "genius of the place." Egyptians possess another type of genius, good and bad, which in Egypt is called *fahlawa*, with the approximate meaning of "understanding things in a moment of flight." This is good because they are perceptive enough that it's not so easy to fool them, but is also bad because they might think that they understand things without knowing the facts, even if the flight time is femtoseconds!

Egyptians value education and intellectual achievements. I experienced this first hand when I saw the entire country celebrate on the occasion of the awarding the Nobel prize and the Grand Collar of the Nile. Even before those celebrations, they took note of some of the scientific discoveries that my group and I had made. Thus the appreciation for advancements in education and in science and technology are part of the Egyptian fabric. When I was a student, most of my fellow *mu'id*s were from the Egyptian villages—parents worked very hard as illiterate farmers to give their children the best education possible. The word *doctor* meant a lot in Egypt and, as I mentioned earlier, in those days if you had a postgraduate degree, you could marry into a financially well-off family.

With these traits and talents, one expects no intrinsic barriers to progress, and historically Egyptians were indeed able to cross barriers and achieve at the highest level. Even in modern times, once Egyptians believe in a cause and in their leadership they form a united force. Two experiences come to my mind. The first was the 1973 war. Egypt, after the 1967 war with Israel, was devastated in its military forces, economic status, and more importantly, its morale. Under President Sadat, the country was able to regain its strength. Despite the lack of modern equipment and the limited resources available, the leadership of the country, in a brilliant move, managed to mobilize the people and achieved a miracle, the crossing of the Suez Canal, which ultimately led to the peace treaty with Israel, backed fully by the United States. The people believed in this cause and despite the everyday hardships they stood up to the challenge. President Sadat must be given credit for his leadership role and President Nasser for his preparation efforts.

The second experience is my own. When I called for the establishment of a nonprofit science institution, UST, Egyptians in the thousands expressed their enthusiastic support for the idea and were willing to make donations. Ironically, some of the very rich were less willing to make significant contributions until they had weighed their personal benefits. The public sector was pushing me to begin a national donation campaign believing that every Egyptian should participate in this national cause. But of course, I could not do so without a new law that guarantees that UST will be able to function freely.

So if all these traits, talents, and resources are present in Egypt, what is missing? Other countries, such as India, South Korea, and China, have shown great progress in some sectors—why not Egypt? Egypt and Japan both began their modern renaissance around 1879, and Japan is now a part of the developed world—why not Egypt? Clearly there is no genetic reason that prevents Egypt from achieving this status. But there is one word that may say it all—the *system*. East Germans have the same genetic and cultural makeup as West Germans, but the former did not expand as far into the world market as the latter because of the system guiding people's lives and work. The same is true for the two Koreas.

Egypt is in a unique position to go forward, and it *can* go forward. Egypt is a leader in the Islamic world; it is the home, for example, of al-Azhar University, the distinguished institution of learning for Islamic studies. Egypt is also proud of its rich Christian heritage; today the Coptic Church is an integral part of Egyptian culture. Egypt is the most populous Arab country and its strength goes beyond its population—all Arabic-speaking nations consider Egypt to be central to Arab culture, arts, theater, and the very popular TV programs and films. Geographically, Egypt is at the crossroads of three continents, Africa, Europe, and Asia. This unique geographical position, together with the country's openness to the world, its appreciation of other religions, cultures, and civilizations, and the attraction of other civilizations to one of the first civilized cultures on Earth, make Egypt special indeed. On the occasion of the awarding of the 1978 Nobel Peace Prize in Oslo, the chairman of the Committee, Aase Lionaes, gave a thoughtful historical perspective of the region:

> It was in this part of the world that the cradle of our civilisation was to be found, more than 6,000 years ago. Here, communities with a high standard of culture, which were to exercise a profound influence on the development of human society in other parts of the world, grew up and flourished. Today, every single schoolchild knows from his or her history books that it was here that our written history first began; and adherents of three historically related religions—Islam, Judaism, and Christianity—have turned their gaze with unflagging devotion to that part of the world from which their religion sprang.

Egypt, in recent times, has relied on income from tourism, Suez Canal tariffs, oil-export revenues, as well as income from Egyptian expatriates working abroad, especially in the Arab world. But with its enormous potential, Egypt must go beyond these natural resources into the new world of science and technology and recover some of its past glory.

I see the following prescription as a way out of the present situation to a new future. I offer this "wish list" not as a criticism, but as a desire for my mother country to regain its rightful position among the nations of the developed world. I hope that instead of taking a defensive attitude toward these ideas we will all scientifically study their usefulness or inapplicability. But whatever we do—a change is needed. President Mubarak has done his best to build Egypt's infrastructure and the time is ripe to make the transition to developed world status. I am an optimist by nature and I believe it *can* be done!

For Egypt, I see three corners that form a triangle for change—*education*, *bureaucracy*, and the *law*. If this triangle is defined clearly, the people will fully support the building of a new and prosperous future.

Leadership must come by way of example, and I am confident that Egyptians would like to see their country led by exemplary authorities. I have met with President Mubarak several times and found him to be a sincere and devoted leader. But many authoritative bodies below the president have bureaucratic routines, which limit the speed of progress.

Egyptian priorities should be clear. First, *investment in the future* must focus on the creation of a functional and world-class educational system, the care for national treasures (such as the historic monuments), and the care for the environment and global climate change. Second, *a strong economy and GDP* are possible only if major changes are introduced, as discussed below. Third, *national security*, like the defense of the nation, must include two equally important objectives: the national unity of Muslims and Copts and the security of the Nile and associated water resources. These priorities cannot be seen by a few only, but must be shared by the population at large.

Everyone I meet in Egypt speaks of the need for a new educational system, but the picture is fuzzy—why and how? The "why" is perhaps more clear than the "how." Obviously, in order to create a world-class system, one needs to study the current system in detail. But I see that a change is needed when I look at the level of the university graduates and the work skills and ethics of students. Imparting concepts such as teamwork, reliability (and absence of *fahlawa*), and the ethics of work requires a new way of teaching and a new curriculum aimed at genuine synthesis of these values. These values and attitudes are needed in order to compete on the level of the developed world, but this goal cannot be achieved with illiteracy still close to 50% among the population.

I believe that Egypt must eliminate illiteracy and its roots in a determined national campaign—and in a very short time. I know that many efforts have been put into this problem, but it should be dealt with as an "enemy attacking the nation" and there's no other solution but immediate action. Another problem of similar magnitude is population growth. With these critical issues under control (or on the way to control), Egypt should change the educational system to a merit-oriented one. At the university level, the new system should have machinery in place to identify the very best students and to allocate this education to those who deserve to be there. Tuition should be charged to families who are able to pay and waived for financially strapped students who earn high grades. Technical schools should grow in number and in prestige in order to build a technical base in all sectors of the country.

On the graduate level, I see no way out but to create some centers of excellence. This is not a luxury. It is a necessity in order for Egypt to participate on the world level and to enhance national pride, as Germany does with its Max Planck Institutes, France with its Collège de France, the United States with Caltech and the Massachusetts Institute of Technology (MIT), Israel with its Weizmann Institute and the Technion, and India with its Indian Institutes of Technology (IITs) and the Indian Institute of Science (IISc). I was and am still ready to help in this endeavor. The description for UST (see the Appendix) gives some of my thoughts and efforts, but time is of the essence—bureaucracy has a reputation for erecting barriers so high that useful progress comes to a halt.

Bureaucracy is the second corner of the triangle. Some bureaucracy is probably needed in every system, but when it introduces a strict routine management of affairs and inhibits independence in thinking, then it impedes the implementation of visionary, progressive ideas. As I stated earlier, Western democracy is not the only way of governing, but it is clear to me that utilization of human resources in a collective teamwork effort requires a democratization process that is fundamentally antibureaucratic. I believe that the minimization of bureaucracy is crucial for any major economic and intellectual progress.

I have had first-hand experience with UST and other projects in Egypt and have seen how bureaucracy and the "power of the chair," or more accurately the power of position, can impede real progress. President Mubarak has enthusiastically endorsed the idea of UST because he sees that Egypt will not be able to be a partner in globalization unless its science and technology are on a par with the rest of the world. That means that young scientists should find active, productive research and development work in Egypt—they shouldn't have to leave Egypt to dream big and to engage in frontier science and technological advancements.

Although clear orders regarding UST have been issued, the slow implementation of the plan is enough to subdue the enthusiasm of any serious person with obligations and exacting demands on his time. We broke ground on January 1, 2000, in October 6 City, on the outskirts of Cairo, for a campus of some 300 acres. So far, I have completed the academic and administrative structures, as briefly outlined in the Appendix. I strongly believe that in order for UST to succeed, it needs to be a non-profit nongovernmental organization (NGO)—and it should have its own bylaws, with the books open to scrutiny, of course. UST should have an endowment and a board of trustees composed of outstanding individuals, from Egypt and around the world. But a fundraising campaign for such an endowment cannot begin without the operational support in place and the law enacted in a timely manner—time has no sympathy for bureaucracy. UST also has in its charter a plan for an adjoining technology park, which will aid the country in the advanced technologies proposed and trigger new high-tech industries.

The final corner of the triangle is the rigor in the constitutional system—the law. Egypt has a strong judicial system and the laws are written clearly. The problem, however, is in the implementation of these laws—from traffic violations to corruption involving billions of dollars, there seem to be cases in which individuals get around the law. This is serious, not only for its impact on the local population but also for the attraction of foreign investors. Egypt needs to revisit the legal system and make implementation of the law apply to *every* citizen—no *wasta* ("influence") and no *baksheesh* (forced tipping).

Problems of the sort I outlined above are not unique to Egypt and they are present in the Arab world at large, and in some developed countries. Even in the wealthy Arab oil-possessing states, the *system* needs change—money alone cannot build a developed nation. Although progress has been achieved in these rich countries, none has attained developed-world status. Moreover, among nations of the Arab world, there are no real strong economic ties, compared to, say, the European countries, and unless this unity is achieved in a common-market format, I do not see a collective impact of Arab resources on world markets. There is some unity in cultural exchanges and in entertainment, but it is essential to strengthen the economic and scientific investment among the Arab countries, in part through the Arab League.

America faces problems of another type, and new challenges. The questions are different and I have alluded to some in this chapter. I offer some reflections on these issues, again in the hope of a better future. America has democracy and despite all the faults in the system, it works for the Americans and the American culture. The clear separation between the state and the church and between the executive (President), legislative (Congress), and the judicial (Supreme Court) branches has given the American people a system of government that has the capability to force a standing president (as it did with Nixon) out of office.

America applies the law uniformly, from traffic violations to the levy of taxes—everyone is equal before the law. However, in many countries I have visited it is said of the United States that "if you have the money you can buy the law." Many cite the case of O.J. Simpson, a former football star, as an example. In that famous case, Simpson, who many believe murdered his ex-wife, hired a team of high-powered lawyers who successfully convinced the jury of his innocence. Of course, imbedded in the capitalist system is the important role of wealth—you can hire better lawyers and you can "buy" comfort in the society. But I think this is true everywhere and it would be naïve to think that democracy is the equal of an absolute and ideal system. Winston Churchill said: "Democracy is the worst form of Government except all the others that have been tried from time to time."

America also has educational institutions that are magnets to many in the world. Although the average American might not be educated about the world, the elite institutions and the broad-based school system form a society able to progress and to have one of the highest GDPs in the world today. America has a system with minimal bureaucracy and believes in the integrity of people, unless otherwise proven. I'm not saying that everything in America is perfect, but one should be cautious about generalizations without knowing America's foundation.

With all of the above, why then do I worry about the future of America? Three problems are now on my mind—education and research, violence, and a limited worldview. First, education and research. In the United States one can find the best education possible, but it's not available to the majority of citizens. Moreover, the country is slackening in its efforts to make science a part of everyone's education, rich or poor. The United States now scores seventeenth in global secondary school mathematics tests. To some degree the low score can be dismissed by noting that many countries submit the scores of the elite only, but nonetheless, I would expect the United States to score higher.

One aspect of the problem has to do with the educational system. Private schools serve a privileged class where young people learn the important skills to survive and excel in the modern technological world. They don't just have computers—they use them as an aid in critical thinking, in exploring the world, and in discovering new things for themselves and with the aid of trained professional teachers. These students, naturally, do well, and most of them become prepared for college and advanced careers. Meanwhile, in some districts, the public schools may lack resources and high-quality teachers. Many problems at these schools result in graduates unable to cope with societal advances and some even resent society in a violent way. This disparity in one of the richest countries in the world must be addressed, since the future demands that the majority of citizens perform productively within a competitive world.

Another aspect has to do specifically with science education. I am amazed by the paucity of coverage of science by the media, given the monumental achievements made by American science. I am also amazed by the lack of understanding of the purpose of science. I am amazed because I expect more from America, but I am also appreciative of how, in general, Americans educate themselves about the role of science in everyday life, particularly when it comes to medicine and defense, and when they observe achievements of major impact such as exploration in outer space. Some Americans are skeptical of science and its benefits to humankind, and I can see some points in their arguments, but there are always two faces to advanced technologies, the good and the bad.

Manipulation of nuclear energy gave us the bomb, but also power plants for modern life. The laser is used as a guide in weapons, but also as a tool in eye surgery. Even a kitchen knife that helps us with food preparation can be harmful. In all of this, we should not forget the profound importance of new knowledge that allows us to understand ourselves, what goes on around us, and the universe we are part of. Societies with scientific education can decide between the two faces of technologies and make the best out of them with the goal of achieving a better life for humanity. Undoubtedly some mistakes may be made in the process, but on the whole, progress is inevitable.

There is also the concern about dogmatism, which is a phenomenon not exclusive to the United States. Science and religion are not in conflict, provided dogmatic thinking on either side does not dominate. I don't see why parents object to their children being taught about evolution. The conflict started in 1925 when a biology teacher in Tennessee named John Scopes decided to teach Darwin's theory to his students, in defiance of an anti-evolution law; he was found guilty in a famous trial that pitted two of the most eloquent speakers of the day, Clarence Darrow and William Jennings Bryan, against each other. In a more recent case, the Kansas state legislature banned the teaching of evolution, and the effect has been profound. People must be permitted to believe what they want from a religious perspective, since the US constitution recognizes the separation of church and state, but teachers must also teach science according to the best scientific wisdom of the day. That means teaching evolution without shame or excessive concessions.

Finally, the support for scientific research. It is not at the level expected from a superpower, and this is of concern. When I came to the United States, support for science was at its acme, because the leadership in the country believed in its importance and power. Accordingly, graduate schools were attracting the best American students and the best from abroad. I now see problems with the new trends in funding research, with its emphasis on immediate pay-offs and so-called relevance to new applications. These constraints are not consistent with proven experience in making new discoveries, and the examples are numerous: the laser, the transistor, and the computer.

The second problem that I hope that America can tackle promptly is also related to education—violence. Danger in the schools and on the streets is becoming an American phenomenon and this worries my family and millions of others. Some people say it's the freedom of speech, but when I go north to Canada, where there are similar guarantees on speech and similar democratic institutions, I just don't feel the same level of violence. We live in one of the best areas of cosmopolitan Los Angeles, yet I would be scared to walk around at night. This is unfortunate and should not be the case in a country so rich in resources and natural beauty. I believe there must be a solution to this problem.

Some think that the origin of violence lies with the heterogeneity of the American society and/or the resentment of the rich by the poor. While these factors can cause some dissatisfaction, I do not see them as the only reasons, especially as the majority of the society belongs to the middle class. In Canada, many European cities, and in Australia there exists some heterogeneity in population, and in Cairo the poor are aware of the obvious gap between themselves and the rich—yet in these places I walk without the fear of violence. I think that the issues of social disorder, gun control, and punishment to suit the crime should be revisited in the US law. I understand that these are complex issues and that they touch the American soul and capitalistic ideals, but we live in a new world that requires new perspectives and new ways of dealing with such phenomena. This is an issue that a visionary leader must address for the sake of the future of the United States.

The third issue on my mind is the United States' limited worldview, which gives the appearance of governmental shallowness and arrogance in global affairs. As of the writing of this book, we see domestic and international terrorism scarring the landscape of America. The strongest country on Earth must play a fundamental leadership role in combating terrorism together with the international community. Equally important is the leadership role in working for human rights, and in reducing the gap between rich and poor, between haves and have-nots. The United States has a responsibility to lead the globe to become a united world, to get people all over the world to think of ourselves as humans. I am reminded of the American image in the 1960s of a man going to the moon for the sake of humanity. As Neil Armstrong said in his first words on the moon: "One small step for a man, one giant leap for mankind." The Marshall Plan and the Peace Corps are two other examples of visionary initiatives that are representative of that American image.

True, the United States cannot possibly solve every problem in the world, but being the most powerful nation, it should stand tall as a leader and be a role model for others. America cannot afford to alienate people around the world, but rather must apply the same standards of fairness at home and abroad—supporting corrupt regimes and following double standards in foreign policy are not in America's interests in the long run. The United States is in a position to revisit its foreign policy now and a visionary approach is badly needed. I do hope that such a vision will not be dismissed by shallow and simplistic arguments such as "The world hates us because of our wealth and democracy" or "We cannot solve every problem in the world." On the contrary, people around the globe look up to America and many people wish to have an American system of freedom. And America can be a real partner in helping solve many problems around the world.

A new vision will not come by building a missile shield. It will not come with isolationist policies. In this world, we need to build bridges between humans, between cultures, and between nations, to make people really feel that we are living on one globe with common objectives—even if we disagree on some issues. The key is not to ignore the have-nots, not to ignore the frustrated part of the world. Poverty and hopelessness are sources for terrorism and disruption of world order.

With American prosperity, I can see that the United States should invest in new plans to help the *people* in Africa, Latin America, and other needy parts of the world live in dignity. I would rather see America concentrate on such issues than on selling arms in the billions to countries that do not need to make such purchases. In the big picture, we should not divide the world into "us" and "them" and must not allow for the creation of barriers through slogans such as the "clash of civilizations" or the "conflict of religions" —we need dialog, not conflict or clashes!

I am an example of what can be done by bridging cultures and I am not alone. One of the smallest and most effective investments the United States has probably ever made is in giving scholarships to foreign students: if they stay in the United States, they are of significant benefit through their technological expertise and the enrichment they provide to the ethnic mix of the country, and if they go back to their homelands they are the best ambassadors abroad. They bring part of the US culture with them to their native countries. In fact, there are many people in leadership positions throughout the world who obtained their educations in the United States. Some turn against the system, but the majority of them cherish and value the US culture and system. These people help to bridge the gap between the cultures, and they take back a piece of their sponsoring institution and sponsoring nation with them.

I have seen this influence of cultural bonding all over the world, but a recent simple incident makes the point for even a local cultural experience. I was touring the Nobel Museum in Stockholm after its inauguration in the spring of 2001 to see the new exhibition on some thirty Nobel laureates, including one on our work. The Swedish director of the museum, Svante Lindqvist, who was a visiting scholar in the History of Science and Technology Office in 1986 at the University of California at Berkeley, mentioned to me that there was an exact replica of the museum that will be traveling to a number of cities around the world, with at least two stops in the United States. Out of curiosity, I asked him which two. "New York and San Francisco." "New York I can understand, but why not Los Angeles, especially since Caltech is there?" He continued with a smile, "My loyalty is to Berkeley." I think this type of bonding can be broad in its mission, making the world a better place. The international collegiality of science, with all its professional competition, is a powerful example of such a bonding of cultures and nations. Another investment that can pay back with high dividends is partnership programs, which I outlined in the preceding chapter.

These are some of my hopes for the future of the two nations that have played an important role in my life. These same hopes for living peacefully and in dignity in our world are indeed common to all cultures. The world is now more dependent on all of its parts than ever before in the history of humanity. Both the Egyptian and the American cultures have tasted the fruits of great achievements in their histories—I hope that the harvest of the new century and the new millennium will be bountiful for both of them, bringing about a renaissance to Egypt and a new perspective to American leadership, and for all of humanity. As I've said several times, I am an optimist!

Epilogue

Success—Is There a Formula?

T he voyage through time presented in this book began with first steps in a Delta town on the banks of the Nile and ended with discovery in science at Caltech in the California city of Pasadena. My journey had a happy ending—the awarding of the Nobel prize in 1999—though I certainly hope that the prize will not be the end of the road for further achievements in science and life. In this exposé I charted the path to that happy ending and the seemingly complex walks of life—I explored the landscape of molecules glimpsed on the scale of their lives in the split-second world of the femtosecond, a millionth of a billionth of a second, and the landscape of personal events glimpsed at the important stations of my life. Faith, fate, and intuition were forces influencing this voyage.

Throughout the journey, I found that passion characterizes my involvement in the three areas of this book—science, life, and vision for the future. Passionate optimism convinces me that the world can be a better place through science and global partnerships. It also allows me to see the simplicity of life and appreciate its multifaceted aspects. In the words of my father, "Life is too short—enjoy it!"

My passion in science is for knowledge, which is the cornerstone of progress. Knowledge is power and it empowers; information only helps us obtain knowledge. We are what we know. The human species is privileged with the capacity for thinking about thinking, and some gifted humans go so far as to change the way we think about nature. But the ocean of knowledge is deep and unlimited in its breadth. Isaac Newton put it well when he said: "To myself I seem to have been only like a boy playing on the seashore, and diverting myself in now and then finding a smoother pebble, or a prettier shell than ordinary, whilst the great ocean of truth lay all undiscovered before me." New knowledge allows us to understand ourselves, what goes on around us, and the universe we are part of. For me, the thirst for knowledge was evidenced throughout the journey, from the days of primary school until today. That is why the university is a *haram*, a sacred place, that I have enjoyed all my life. It is the place of light, liberty, and learning.

Equally important is my passion for work, which I consider one of life's gifts. By the same token, I feel that drive for success should not come at the expense of respect for others or personal contentment. We have a saying, *al-qana'a kanz la yufna*, which means "Contentment is a treasure forever." With passion, contentment, and optimism, I cannot see how anyone can fail. It may seem that I am offering a formula for success. I don't know an exact formula that applies universally, but one thing is clear to me—we must have a dream, if we are to cross the boundaries of the ordinary.

Christopher Columbus (1451–1506) realized a dream in his navigational endeavor. He was certain that "India," if not "China," was located about 3,900 miles west of the Canary Islands. Of course, this is not where India is, or China for that matter. The dream, however, led Columbus to new territories. With the knowledge of the time, he started with an intuition, but dedication to his vision propelled him to what seemed impossible. Even though his original scheme was not realized, his discovery opened up a new world. Was Columbus brilliant, mad, or lucky? Some historians have commented: all of the above! Whatever the ingredients, Columbus changed the picture of the world that is in everybody's mind. He changed the way humans think and made a difference in our world. Leonardo da Vinci (1452–1519), a contemporary of Columbus, outlined new ways of looking at nature in his book *Vision of the End of the World*. He reflected on the secret to success—it was *saper vedere*, "to know how to see."

Success in life may come to anyone at any level in any walk of life, but whatever the degree or the profession, one's success is shaped by the help of a multitude of other people—a team effort. Recognizing this fact, the haves should help the have-nots. To be part of a civilized country and a civilized planet, every human should matter. When a human being or a country or even a region does not enjoy the benefits of knowledge and attains an underdeveloped status, the consequences are ugly, not only because of the human costs and suffering, but also because of their negative impact on the world as a whole; these consequences include a degradation of social and cultural values as well as an increase in violence and terrorism. In the sections of this book detailing my vision for the future I have attempted to address these issues, identifying some key questions and possibly some answers. At the heart are poverty, illiteracy, and the repression of liberty.

In reflecting on the totality of my voyage to this point, I am awed by the scale of humans in the space and time of the universe. Our human lifetime, say one hundred years, in comparison with that of the universe, nearly 10 billion years, is as short as one second is to 100 million seconds, or three years—life is a transition state that is ephemeral on the time scale of the universe. In space, the size of our Earth is to the universe (within an order of magnitude) as the size of an atom (0.000 000 01 cm) is to that of the Earth—we live on a speck of dust in a corner of a vast universe. Even though our lives are short and we are tiny in relation to the universe, scientifically we know a great deal about the very small and the very big as well as the realm in between, which includes human life. From the extremes—atoms to cosmology—to everything in between, we are now exploring new frontiers of knowledge in the sciences and, as with the explorations of Christopher Columbus, these discoveries have a profound impact on culture, philosophy, and the humanities in general.

But with all these gains in knowledge and achievements in technology we must not forget that such gains and achievements are for the betterment of humanity. And we must all remember while on the way up to help those who are at the bottom or on the way down.

When I was a child, I thought of my Delta town as the center of the universe, but now I realize how little I know about the universe. As a child, I thought I was immortal, but now I recognize how limited a time we all have. As a child, success meant scoring A on every exam, but now I take it to mean good health, close family and friends, achievements in my work, and helping others. My voyage through time, with its walks of life to the Nobel prize, has taught me a great deal. Throughout, to paraphrase Harry S Truman, I have tried not to forget who I am and where I came from. With our smallness in the universe at large, I also bear in mind the important role of faith and scholarship. Although I am concerned about injustice in the world today, I am an optimist. I believe that with the power of knowledge and rational thinking, we can—and should—build bridges between humans, between cultures, and between nations.

Further Readings

R eferences below are given in alphabetical order by first author; a section at the end includes some works by the author of this book. This list is not exhaustive by any means; its purpose is to provide further reading on some of the topics discussed in the text.

H. Abraham and J. Lemoine, "Disparition instantanée du phénomène de Kerr." *Comptes rendus hebdomadaires des séances de l'Académie des Sciences,* 129, pp. 206–208, 1899.

Philip Ball, *Designing the Molecular World.* Princeton, NJ: Princeton University Press, 1994.

James Henry Breasted. *A History of Egypt, from the Earliest Times to the Persian Conquest.* New York: Charles Scribner's Sons, 1909; reprinted 1937.

A. Welford Castleman, Jr., and Villy Sundström, "Ten Years of Femtochemistry" a historical perspective and an introduction to the Third Femtochemistry (1997) Conference. *The Journal of Physical Chemistry A,* 102 (23), pp. 4021–4030; June 4, 1998.

Joel E. Cohen, *How Many People Can the Earth Support?* New York: Norton & Co., 1995.

Stephen Dalton, *Split Second.* London: J. M. Dent & Sons, 1983.

Lawrence Durrell, *The Alexandria Quartet: Justine, Balthazar, Mountolive, and Clea.* New York: Pocket Books, 1957.

Freeman J. Dyson, *The Sun, the Genome, and the Internet: Tools of Scientific Revolutions.* Oxford: Oxford University Press, 1999.

Derek Adie Flower, *The Shores of Wisdom: The Story of the Ancient Library of Alexandria.* Ramsey (Isle of Man), UK: Pharos Publications, 1999.

The Galileo Project. http://es.rice.edu/ES/humsoc/Galileo/

Peter Galison, *Image and Logic.* Chicago: University of Chicago Press, 1997.

J. Gribbin, *Schrödinger's Kittens and the Search for Reality: Solving the Quantum Mystery.* Boston: Little, Brown & Co., 1995.

Michael H. Hart, *The 100: A Ranking of the Most Influential Persons in History.* New York: Citadel Press/Carol Publishing Group, 1998.

Friedrich Hund, *The History of Quantum Theory.* New York: Barnes & Noble, 1974.

V. K. Jain, "The World's Fastest Camera." In *The World and I.* News World Communication Inc., October, pp. 156–163, 1995.

Thomas Kuhn, *The Structure of Scientific Revolutions.* Chicago: University of Chicago Press (second ed.), 1970.

Eadweard Muybridge, *Animals in Motion.* New York: Dover Publications, 1957.

Otto Neugebauer, *The Exact Sciences in Antiquity.* Providence, RI: Brown University Press, 1957.

Isaac Newton, *Mathematical Principles of Natural Philosophy,* translated by Florian Cajori. Berkeley, CA: University of California Press, 1934.

Bengt Nordén, in *Les Prix Nobel* (The Nobel Prizes 1999), Stockholm: Almqvist & Wiksell Intl., pp. 20–21; 2000.

Robert Paradowski, "Ahmed H. Zewail—A Scientist of Two Cultures." An essay, Rochester Institute of Technology, 2001.

J. R. Partington, *A Short History of Chemistry*. New York: Dover Publications (third ed.), 1989.

Colin A. Ronan, *Science: Its History and Development among the World's Cultures*. New York: Facts on File, 1982.

Helaine Selin (ed.), *Encyclopedia of the History of Science, Technology, and Medicine in Non-Western Cultures*, Boston: Kluwer Academic Publishers, 1997.

Douglas L. Smith, "Coherent Thinking." *Engineering & Science* (Caltech), 62:4, pp. 6–17, 1999.

Dava Sobel, *Longitude*. New York: Penguin Books, 1995.

M. M. Soliman. *Tarikh al-'ulum wa-l-tiknulujya fi al-'usur al-qadima wa-l-wusta* ("History of Science and Technology in Ancient and Middle Ages"). Al-Hiy'a al-Misriya li-l-Kitab, Cairo, 1995 [in Arabic].

F. Sherwood Taylor, *Galileo and the Freedom of Thought*. London: Watts & Co., 1938.

Charles H. Townes, *How the Laser Happened: Adventures of a Scientist*. Oxford: Oxford University Press, 1999.

———. *Making Waves*. Woodbury, NY: American Institute of Physics Press, 1995.

Charles van Doren, *A History of Knowledge: Past, Present, and Future*. New York: Ballantine Books, 1991.

Hans Christian von Baeyer, *Taming the Atom*. New York: Random House, 1992.

H. E. Winlock, "The Origin of the Ancient Egyptian Calendar," *Proceedings of the American Philosophical Society*, 83, pp. 447–464, 1940.

By the Author

Over the years at Caltech my group and I have published some 400 scientific papers. The following list, in chronological order, is a selection of these works that may be of interest for further reading.

Ph.D. Dissertation

"Optical and Magnetic Resonance Spectra of Triplet Excitons and Localized States in Molecular Crystals." University of Pennsylvania, Philadelphia, 1974.

Articles

"Laser Selective Chemistry—Is it Possible?" *Physics Today*, 33, pp. 2–8, 1980.

"Energy Redistribution in Isolated Molecules and the Question of Mode-Selective Laser Chemistry Revisited" (feature article). With N. Bloembergen. *The Journal of Physical Chemistry*, 88, pp. 5459–5465, 1984.

"Real-Time Laser Femtochemistry: Viewing the Transition States from Reagents to Products." With R. B. Bernstein. *Chemical & Engineering News*, 66, pp. 24–43; November 7, 1988.

"Laser Femtochemistry." *Science*, 242, pp. 1645–1653; December 23, 1988.

"The Birth of Molecules." *Scientific American*, 263 (6), pp. 76–82; December, 1990 [also published in Arabic, Chinese, French, German, Hungarian, Indian, Italian, Japanese, Spanish, Russian].

"Discoveries at Atomic Resolution (Small is Beautiful)." *Nature* (London) 361, pp. 215–216; January 23, 1993.

"Direct Observation of the Transition State." With J. C. Polanyi. *Accounts of Chemical Research*, 28, pp. 119–132, 1995.

"What is Chemistry? 100 Years after J.J. Thomson's Discovery." *The Cambridge Review*, 118 (2330), pp. 65–75; November, 1997.

"Mustaqbal al-'ilm fi Misr: ra'y shakhsiya" ("The Future of Science in Egypt: A Personal Vision"). *Al-Ahram*, No. 40,745, pp. 1 and 14; Saturday, June 27, 1998 [in Arabic].

"Femtochemistry—Atomic-scale Dynamics of the Chemical Bond Using Ultrafast Lasers." In *Les Prix Nobel* (The Nobel Prizes 1999), Stockholm: Almqvist & Wiksell,, pp. 110–203, 2000.

"Freezing Atoms in Motion." With J. S. Baskin. *Journal of Chemical Education*, 78 (6), pp. 737–751, 2001.

"The Uncertainty Paradox—the Fog That Was Not." *Nature* (London) 412, p. 279; July 19, 2001.

"Science for the Have-Nots." *Nature* (London), 410, p. 741; April 12, 2001.

"The New World Dis-Order—Can Science Aid the Have-Nots?" In *Proceedings of the Jubilee Plenary Session of the Pontifical Academy of Sciences* (Vatican), 99, pp. 450–458, 2001.

Books

Femtochemistry: Ultrafast Dynamics of the Chemical Bond (two vols.). River Edge, NJ: World Scientific, 1994.

The Chemical Bond: Structure and Dynamics. A. H. Zewail (ed.). Boston: Academic Press, 1992.

Appendix

Press Release: The 1999 Nobel Prize in Chemistry

KUNGL. VETENSKAPSAKADEMIEN
THE ROYAL SWEDISH ACADEMY OF SCIENCES

12 October 1999

The Royal Swedish Academy of Sciences has awarded the 1999 Nobel Prize in Chemistry to

Professor **Ahmed H. Zewail**, California Institute of Technology, Pasadena, USA

for showing that it is possible with rapid laser technique to see how atoms in a molecule move during a chemical reaction.

The Academy's citation:
For his studies of the transition states of chemical reactions using femtosecond spectroscopy.

This year's laureate in Chemistry is being rewarded for his pioneering investigation of fundamental chemical reactions, using ultra-short laser flashes, on the time scale on which the reactions actually occur. Professor Zewail's contributions have brought about a revolution in chemistry and adjacent sciences, since this type of investigation allows us to understand and predict important reactions.

Development of femtochemistry rewarded

What would a football match on TV be without "slow motion" revealing afterwards the movements of the players and the ball when a goal is scored? Chemical reactions are a similar case. The chemists' eagerness to be able to follow chemical reactions in the greatest detail has prompted increasingly advanced technology. This years laureate in Chemistry, **Ahmed H. Zewail**, has studied atoms and molecules in "slow motion" during a reaction and seen what actually happens when chemical bonds break and new ones are created.

Zewail's technique uses what may be described as the world's fastest camera. This uses laser flashes of such short duration that we are down to the time scale on which the reactions actually happen - femtoseconds (fs). One femtosecond is 10^{-15} seconds, that is, 0.000000000000001 seconds, which is to a second as a second is to 32 million years. This area of physical chemistry has been named *femtochemistry*.

Femtochemistry enables us to understand why certain chemical reactions take place but not others. We can also explain why the speed and yield of reactions depend on temperature. Scientists the world over are studying processes with femtosecond spectroscopy in gases, in fluids and in solids, on surfaces and in polymers. Applications range from how catalysts function and how molecular electronic components must be designed, to the most delicate mechanisms in life processes and how the medicines of the future should be produced.

How fast are chemical reactions?
Chemical reactions can, as we all know, take place at very varying velocities - compare a rusting nail and exploding dynamite! Common to most reactions is that their velocity increases as temperature rises, i.e. when molecular motion becomes more violent.

For this reason researchers long believed that a molecule first needs to be activated, 'kicked' over a barrier, if it is to react. When two molecules collide, nothing normally happens, they just bounce apart. But when the temperature is high enough the collision is so violent that they react with one another and new molecules form. Once a molecule has been given a sufficiently strong 'temperature kick' it reacts incredibly fast, whereupon chemical bonds break and new ones form. This also applies to the reactions that appear to be slow (e.g. the rusting nail). The difference is only that the 'temperature kicks' occur more seldom in a slow reaction than in a fast one.

The barrier is determined by the forces that hold atoms together in the molecule (the chemical bonds) roughly like the gravitational barrier that a moon rocket from Earth must surmount before it is captured by the Moon's force field. But until very recently little was known about the molecule's path up over the barrier and what the molecule really looks like when it is exactly at the top, its 'transition state'.

Hundred years of research
Svante Arrhenius (Nobel laureate in Chemistry 1903), inspired by van't Hoff (the first Nobel laureate in Chemistry, 1901) presented just over a hundred years ago a simple formula for reaction speed as a function of temperature. But this referred to many molecules at once (macroscopic systems) and relatively long times. It was not until the 1930s that H. Eyring and M. Polanyi formulated a theory based on reactions in microscopic systems of individual molecules. The theoretical assumption was that the transition state was crossed very rapidly, on the time scale that applies to molecular vibrations. That it would ever be possible to perform experiments over such short times was something no-one dreamed of.

But this is exactly what Zewail set out to do. At the end of the 1980s he performed a series of experiments that were to lead to the birth of the research area called *femtochemistry*. This involves using a high-speed camera to image molecules in the actual course of chemical reactions and trying to capture pictures of them just in the transition state. The camera was based on new laser technology with light flashes of some tens of femtoseconds. The time it takes for the atoms in a molecule to perform one vibration is typically 10-100 fs. That chemical reactions should take place on the same time scale as when the atoms oscillate in the molecules may be compared to two trapeze artists "reacting" with each other on the same time scale as that on which their trapezes swing back and forth.

What did the chemists see as the time resolution was successively improved? The first success was the discovery of substances formed along the way from the original one to the final product, substances termed *intermediates*. To begin with these were relatively stable molecules or molecule fragments. Each improvement of the time resolution led to new links in a reaction chain, in the form of increasingly short-lived intermediates, being fitted into the puzzle of understanding how the reaction mechanism worked.

The contribution for which Zewail is to receive the Nobel Prize means that we have reached the end of the road: no chemical reactions take place faster than this. With femtosecond spectroscopy we can for the first time observe in 'slow motion' what happens as the reaction barrier is crossed and hence also understand the mechanistic background to Arrhenius' formula for temperature dependence and to the formulae for which van't Hoff was awarded his Nobel Prize.

Femtochemistry in practice
In femtosecond spectroscopy the original substances are mixed as beams of molecules in a vacuum chamber. An ultrafast laser then injects two pulses: first a powerful *pump pulse* that strikes the molecule and excites it to a higher energy state, and then a weaker *probe pulse* at a wavelength chosen to detect the original molecule or an altered form of this. The pump pulse is the starting signal for the reaction while the probe pulse examines what is happening. By varying the time interval between the two pulses it is possible to see how quickly the original molecule is transformed. The new shapes the molecule takes when it is excited - perhaps going through one or more transition states - have spectra that may serve as fingerprints.

The time interval between the pulses can be varied simply by causing the probe pulse to make a detour via mirrors. Not a long detour: the light covers the distance of 0.03 mm in 100 fs!

To better understand what happens, the fingerprint and the time elapsing are then compared with theoretical simulations based on results of quantum chemical calculations (Nobel Prize in Chemistry 1998) of spectra and energies for the molecules in their various states.

The first experiments
In his first experiments Zewail studied the disintegration of iodocyanide:
ICN -->I + CN. His team were able to observe a transition state exactly when the I-C bond was about to break: the whole reaction takes place in 200 femtoseconds.

In another important experiment Zewail studied the dissociation of sodium iodide (NaI): NaI --> Na + I. The pump pulse excites the ion pair Na+ I - which has an equilibrium distance of 2.8 Å between nuclei (Fig. 1) to an activated form [NaI]* which then assumes covalent bonding. However, its properties change when the molecules vibrate; when the nuclei are at their outer turning points, 10-15 Å apart, the electron structure is ionic, while at short distances it is covalent. At a certain point on the vibration cycle, just when the nuclei are 6.9 Å apart, there is a great probability that the molecule will fall back to its ground state or decay into sodium and iodine atoms.

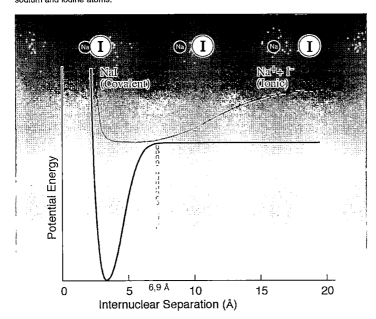

Figure 1
Potential energy curves showing ground state and excited state for NaI. The upper curve shows the molecule vibrations in excited NaI. When the distance between the sodium nucleus and the iodine nucleus is short the covalent bond dominates, while the ion bond dominates at a greater distance. The vibrations may be compared to those of a marble rolling back and forth in a dish. As the 6.9 Å point is passed there is a chance that the marble will roll down to the lower curve. There it may end up in the pit to the left (return to ground state) or fly out to the right (decay into sodium and iodine atoms respectively).

Zewail also studied the reaction between hydrogen and carbon dioxide:

H + CO2 --> CO + OH a reaction that takes place in the atmosphere and in combustion. He showed that the reaction crosses a relatively long state of HOCO (1 000 fs).

A question that has occupied many chemists is why certain chemical bonds are more reactive than others and what happens if there are two equivalent bonds in one molecule: will they break simultaneously or one at a time? To answer this kind of question Zewail and his co-workers studied the disassociation of tetrafluordiiodethane (C2I2F4) into tetrafluorethylene (C2F4) and two iodine atoms (I):

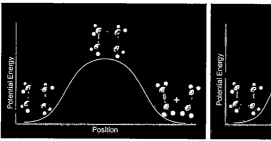

They discovered that the two C-I bonds, despite their equivalence in the original molecule, break one at a time.

Research is extra interesting when the results are unexpected. Zewail studied what may be thought the simple reaction between benzene, a ring of six carbon atoms (C6H6) and iodine (I2), a molecule consisting of two iodine atoms. When the two molecules become sufficiently close together they form a complex. The laser flash causes an electron to be shot from the benzene molecule into the iodine molecule. This then becomes negatively charged while the benzene molecule becomes positively charged. The negative and positive charges cause the benzene and the nearest iodine atom to be rapidly drawn to one another. The bond between the two iodine atoms is stretched when one of them is sucked in towards the benzene, whereupon the other atom breaks free and flies away. All this happens within 750 fs. Zewail found, however, that this is not the only way individual iodine atoms can be formed: sometimes the electron falls back onto benzene. But it is already too late for the iodine atoms: like a stretched rubber band breaking, the bond between the two atoms breaks and they fly apart.

Research explosion
A much studied model reaction in organic chemistry is the ring opening of cyclobutane to yield ethylene or the reverse, the combining of two ethylene molecules to form cyclobutane. The reaction may thus go directly via one transition state with a simple activation barrier as shown schematically on the left in Figure 2. Alternatively, it may proceed through a two-stage mechanism (right) so that first one bond breaks and tetramethylene is formed as an intermediate. After crossing another activation barrier the tetramethylene in turn is converted to the final product. Zewail and his co-workers showed with femtosecond spectroscopy that the intermediate product was in fact formed, and had a lifetime of 700 fs.

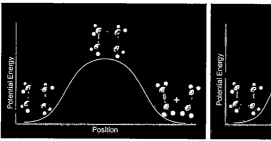
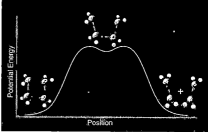

Figure 2
How does the reaction from the cyclobutane molecule to two ethylene molecules actually proceed? The left-hand figure shows how the state energy varies if both bonds are stretched and broken simultaneously. The right-hand figure shows the case where one bond at a time breaks.

Another type of reaction studied with femtosecond technology is the light-induced conversion of a molecule from one structure to another, *photoisomerisation*. The conversion of the *stilbene* molecule, which includes two benzene rings, between the *cis-* and *trans-* forms was observed by Zewail and his co-workers.

light

cis-stilbene   **trans-stilbene**

They concluded that during the process the two benzene rings turn synchronously in relation to one another. Similar behaviour has also recently been observed for the *retinal* molecule, which is the colour substance in rodopsin, the pigment in the rods of the eye. The primary photochemical step, when we perceive light, is a cis-trans conversion around a double bond in retinal. With femtosecond spectroscopy other researchers have found that the process takes 200 fs and that a certain amount of vibration remains in the product of the reaction. The speed of the reaction suggests that energy from the absorbed photon is not first redistributed but is localised directly to the relevant double bond. This would explain the high efficiency (70%) and hence the eye's good night vision. Another biologically important example where femtochemistry has explained efficient energy conversion is in chlorophyll molecules, which capture light in photosynthesis.

Femtosecond studies following Zewail's work are being performed intensively the world over, using not only molecular beams but also processes on surfaces (e.g. to understand and improve catalysts), in liquids and solvents (to understand mechanisms of the dissolving of and reactions between substances in solution) and in polymers (e.g. to develop new material for use in electronics). Another important research field is studies of biological systems. Knowledge of the mechanisms of chemical reactions is also important for our ability to control the reactions. A desired chemical reaction is often accompanied by a series of unwanted, competing reactions that lead to a mixture of products and hence the need for separation and cleansing. If the reaction can be controlled by initiating reactivity in selected bonds, this could be avoided.

Femtochemistry has fundamentally changed our view of chemical reactions. From a phenomenon described in relatively vague metaphors such as 'activation' and 'transition state', we can now see the movements of individual atoms as we imagine them. They are no longer invisible. Here lies the reason why the femtochemistry research initiated by this year's Nobel Laureate has led to explosive development. With the world's fastest camera available, only the imagination sets bounds for new problems to tackle.

Further reading

- "Extended version in English" by Professor Bengt Nordén.
- M.A. El-Sayed, I. Tanaka and Y. Molin *"Ultrafast Processes in Chemistry and Photobiology"* Blackwell Science 1995 306 pp, ISBN 0-86542-893-X.
- S. Pedersen, J.L. Herek and A.H. Zewail *"The Validity of the Diradical Hypothesis: Direct Femtosecond Studies of the Transition-State Structures"*. Science Vol 266 (1994) 1359-1364.
- A.H. Zewail *"The Birth of Molecules"* Scientific American December 1990 p 40-46.
- V.K. Jain *"The World's Fastest Camera"* The World and I, October 1995 p 156-163.
- Nobel Symposium: *Femtochemistry & Femtobiology: Ultrafast Reaction Dynamics at Atomic-Scale Resolution* (Editor: V. Sundström) World Scientific, Singapore 1996.

Ahmed Zewail was born in 1946 in Egypt where he grew up and studied at the University of Alexandria. After continued studies in the U.S.A. he graduated for PhD in 1974 at the University of Pennsylvania. After two years at the University of California at Berkeley he was employed at Caltech where he has the Linus Pauling Chair of Chemical Physics since 1990. Zewail is Egyptian and American citizen.

Professor **Ahmed H. Zewail**
California Institute of Technology
Arthur Amos Noyes Laboratory of Chemical Physics
Mail Code 127-72
Pasadena, California 91125
USA

The amount of the Nobel Prize Award is SEK 7, 900, 000.

Nobel Prize Address
by Professor Bengt Nordén

Stockholm, Sweden
Concert Hall
December 10, 1999
The 1999 Nobel Prize in Chemistry to Professor Ahmed H. Zewail

Your Majesties, Your Royal Highness, Ladies and Gentlemen,
We chemists want to understand molecules and their intrinsic essence, and to be able to predict what happens when molecules meet—do they attach weakly to each other or do they react passionately to form new molecules? Not least, we want to understand the complicated chemistry called life. Through a revolution in knowledge, molecules today take center stage in all fields, from biology and medicine through environmental sciences, and technology.

The heart of chemistry is the chemical reaction, meaning the breaking and formation of chemical bonds between atoms. How then do chemical reactions occur? We all know that they can proceed at different rates—compare the time it takes a nail to rust with explosion of dynamite! Alfred Nobel knew that reaction rates are important; dynamite reacts too rapidly to be used in cannons—they would blow up. He also knew that chemical reactions proceed at greater speed at higher temperatures, but he did not see why. This was, however, realized by the docent of physical chemistry in Uppsala, Svante Arrhenius. Inspired by the Dutch scientist Jacobus van 't Hoff (the first Nobel laureate in chemistry, 1901), Arrhenius presented the first theory on reaction rates and an equation for their temperature dependence that has been used for more than a hundred years now. Arrhenius was himself awarded the third Nobel Prize in Chemistry (1903), but for different achievements.

Science has always strived to see smaller and smaller things and faster and faster events. Since the time of Arrhenius a number of methods have been developed to measure increasingly faster reaction rates, many of them rewarded with Nobel prizes. However, no one had, until recently, been able to observe what actually happens to the reacting molecule as it passes through its so-called transition state, a metaphor for a kind of intermediate state of the reaction in which bonds are broken and formed. This remained a misty no man's land.

The molecule passes the transition state as fast as the atoms in the molecule move. They move at a speed of the order of 1000 m/second—about as fast as a rifle bullet—and the time required for the atoms to move slightly within the molecule is typically tens of femtoseconds (1 fs = 10^{-15} second). Only few believed that such fast events would ever be possible to see.

This, however, is exactly what Ahmed Zewail has managed to do. Twelve years ago he published results that gave birth to the scientific field called femtochemistry. This can be described as using the fastest camera in the world to film the molecules during the reaction and to get a sharp picture of the transition state. His "camera" is a laser technique with light flashes of only a few tens of femtoseconds in duration. The reaction is initiated by a strong laser flash and is then studied by a series of subsequent flashes to follow the events. The key to his success was that the first femtosecond flash or starting shot excited all molecules in the sample at once, causing their atoms to swing in rhythm. The first experiments demonstrated in slow motion how bonds were stretched and broken in rather simple reactions, but soon studies of more complex reactions followed. The results were often surprising, and the dance of the atoms during the reaction was found to differ from what was expected.

Zewail's use of the fast laser technique can be likened to Galileo's use of his telescope, which he directed towards everything that lit up the vault of heaven. Zewail tried his femtosecond laser on literally everything that moved in the world of molecules. He turned his telescope towards the frontiers of science.

Ahmed Zewail is being awarded the Nobel Prize in Chemistry because he was the first to conduct experiments that clearly show the decisive moments in the life of a molecule—the breaking and formation of chemical bonds. He has been able to see the reality behind Arrhenius' theory.

It is of great importance to be able in detail to understand and predict the progress of a chemical reaction. Femtochemistry has found applications in all branches of chemistry, but also in adjoining fields such as material science (future electronics?) and biology. The retinal molecule is an example—a substance that you are all making use of at this very moment, namely to see with. It has been found that light causes this molecule to twist like a hinge around a well-greased bond, which sends a nerve signal to the brain. The reaction takes only 200 fs, which explains the eye's sensitivity to light.

Femtochemistry has radically changed the way we look at chemical reactions. A hundred years of mist surrounding the transition state has cleared.

Professor Zewail, I have tried to explain how your pioneering work has fundamentally changed the way scientists view chemical reactions. From being restricted to describe them only in terms of a metaphor, the transition state, we can now study the actual movements of atoms in molecules. We can speak of them in time and space in the same way that we imagine them. They are no longer invisible.

May I convey to you my warmest congratulations on behalf of the Royal Swedish Academy of Sciences and ask you to come forward to receive the 1999 Nobel Prize in Chemistry from the hands of His Majesty the King.

Nobel Prize Address
by Ahmed Zewail

Stockholm, Sweden
City Hall
December 10, 1999

Your Majesties, Excellencies, Ladies and Gentlemen, let me begin with a reflection on a personal story, that of a voyage through time. The medal I received from His Majesty this evening was designed by Erik Lindberg in 1902 to represent Nature in the form of the goddess Isis—or *Izees*—the Egyptian Goddess of Motherhood. She emerges from the clouds, holding a cornucopia in her arms and the veil that covers her cold and austere face is held up by the Genius of Science.[1] Indeed, it is the genius of science that pushed forward the race against time, from the beginning of astronomical calendars six millennia ago in the land of Isis to the femtosecond regime honored tonight for the ultimate achievement in the microcosmos. I began life and education in the same Land of Isis, Egypt, made the scientific unveiling in America, and tonight, I receive this honor in Sweden, with a Nobel medal that takes me right back to the beginning. This internationalization by the Genius of Science is precisely what Mr. Nobel wished for more than a century ago.

In visionary words, Mr. Nobel summed up the purpose of the Prize: "The conquests of scientific research and its ever expanding field awake in us the hope that microbes—of the soul as well as of the body—will gradually be exterminated and that the only war humanity will wage in future will be war against these microbes." Mr. Nobel saw clearly what he wished for the world and the value of scientific discovery and advance-

---

[1] The inscription reads: *Inventas vitam juvat excoluisse per artes,* loosely translated: "And they who bettered life on earth by new-found mastery" (literally, "inventions enhance life which is beautified through art").

ment. Although there exist in the world today some microbes of the soul, such as discrimination and aggression, science was and still is the core of progress for humanity and the continuity of civilization. From the dawn of history, science has probed the universe of unknowns, searching for the uniting laws of nature. The world applauds your Majesties and the Swedish people for your appreciation, recognition, and celebration of discoveries of the unknown, which, according to Alfred Nobel will "leave the greatest benefit to mankind." I know of no other country that celebrates intellectual achievements with this class and passion.

To the world, the Nobel Prize has become the crowning honor for two reasons. For scientists, it recognizes their untiring efforts, which lead to new fields of discovery, and places them in the annals of history with other notable scientists. For science, the prize inspires the people of the world about the importance and value of new discoveries, and in so doing science becomes better appreciated and supported by the public, and, hopefully, by governments. Both of these are noble causes and we thank you. To me, there is a third cause as well.

If the Nobel Prize had existed six thousand years ago, when Egypt's civilization began, or even two thousand years ago, when the famous library and university (Museum) at Alexandria were established, Egypt would have scored highly in many fields. In recent times, however, Egypt and the Arab world, which gave to Science Ibn Sina (Avicenna), Ibn Rushd (Averroës), Jabir Ibn Hayyan (Geber), Ibn al-Haytham (Alhazen), and others, have had no prizes in science or medicine. I sincerely hope that this first one will inspire the young generations of developing countries with the knowledge that it is possible to contribute to world science and technology. As expressed eloquently in 1825 by Sir Humphrey Davy: "Fortunately, science, like that nature to which it belongs, is neither limited by time nor by space. It belongs to the world, and is of no country and of no age." There is a whole world outside the boundaries of the "West" and the "North" and we can all help to make it the microbe-free world of Mr. Nobel. I also hope that the prize will help the region I came from to focus on the advancement of science, the Science Society, and on dignity and peace for humanity.

Your Majesties, I do not know how to express my own personal feelings and those of my family about this recognition. Behind this recognition, there exists a larger community of femtoscientists all over the world who tonight declare themselves proud. My own science family at Caltech of close to 150 young scientists represents the true army that marched to victory and made the contribution possible; they, too, must be proud of their effort. Personally, I have been enriched by my experiences in Egypt and America, and feel fortunate to have been endowed with a true passion for knowledge. I am grateful that this highest crowning honor comes at a young age when I can, hopefully, enjoy and witness its impact on science and humanity. The honor comes with great responsibilities and new challenges for the future, and I do hope to be able to continue the mission, recalling the thoughtful words of the great scholar, Dr. Taha Hussein: *Wailu li-talib al-'ilmi in radia 'an nafsihi*, which can be paraphrased in the following words: The end will begin when seekers of knowledge become satisfied with their own achievements—Woe to the satisfied scholar.

Thank you, Your Majesties. Thank you, all who are celebrating science and scientists.

Order of the Grand Collar of the Nile (Qiladat al-Nil al-'Uzma) Address by President Mohammed Hosni Mubarak

Cairo, Egypt
Presidential Palace
December 16, 1999

Brothers and Sisters,

First I would like to express both for myself and on behalf of the great people of Egypt our sincere congratulations to the loyal son of Egypt, Dr. Ahmed Zewail, on his winning the Nobel Prize in Chemistry for 1999. You may agree with me that this precious occasion affords much wider implications beyond the winning by Dr. Ahmed Zewail of this prize; his success clearly complements the chain of accomplishments characteristic of the innovative contributions to civilization of the great people of Egypt.

As you all know, this is not the first time that Egyptians have been awarded international honors for their creative contributions to humanity. Earlier, President Anwar al-Sadat pioneered a peace-making process in a region destined to pay a high price for its long-standing ferocious conflict. This conflict had relentlessly drained off its energies. Hence, he was the first Egyptian to win the Nobel prize for his endeavors to achieve peace for the sake of humanity at large.

Next was Egypt's great novelist Naguib Mahfouz, whose splendid and comprehensive literary vision delved into the depth of Egyptian political and social reality. He soared high through vast horizons of elevated human values and connotations, and received worldwide recognition of his magnificent literary value in return.

With the winning by the distinguished scientist Dr. Ahmed Zewail of the Nobel Prize in Chemistry, the diversity of Egyptian contributions to civilization, with this international recognition thereof, has come full circle, offering implications for the present and the future.

The Egyptians and Arabs were most deeply thrilled by the great event because they instantly realized its significance—namely, we are capable with the help of God of contributing to the accelerating scientific revolution and its marvelous achievements.

Brothers and sisters, the splendid scientific achievement by Dr. Ahmed Zewail has completed world recognition of the chain of significant contributions of the Egyptian people to human civilization. Additionally, it underscores the continuing progress of these contributions since the beginning of history. Ahmed Zewail is the child of this ancient Egyptian civilization, whose achievements, based on advanced scientific knowledge, involving some secrets that still remain inaccessible to modern science, have continued to astound the world until today. He is also a son of the Arab Islamic civilization, in which scientific progress played an indisputable leading role that helped put Europe, in the early modern era, on a course in the transition from backwardness to renaissance, and full-scale development.

Brothers and sisters, what makes us more proud of this great event are a number of its implications: First, this scientist, whose unique and pioneering work has been recognized by the whole world, received his education up through his M.S. studies at Egyptian educational institutions. I believe that it is an undeniable testimony to the ability of these institutions to prepare generations of scientists under suitable circumstances. I also believe that the thousands of scientists who work in silence within Egypt and those outside their homeland who contribute to human progress with their scientific efforts present further proof of the ability of this homeland to provide major contributions to scientific progress.

Egypt had earlier expressed appreciation for the scientific accomplishments of Dr. Ahmed Zewail for his desire to maintain close ties with scientists and scientific research institutions in Egypt, by conferring the Order of Merit in the Sciences and Arts, First Class, on the day of celebration for scientific research in 1995. This initiative was indicative of my own personal desire as well as the state's keenness to give due care to our expatriate scientists and maintain strong ties between them and their homeland.

Secondly, the scientific career of Dr. Ahmed Zewail continued after completing his university education in Egypt in a scientific and institutional environment of deep-rooted traditions in university scientific research. This indicates that individual genius, no matter how singular, can reach the highest degree of distinction only within the framework of sound scientific and technological policies and institutions capable of implementing such policies with effective cooperation among the government, business people, and well-off categories of the Egyptian society.

The third of these implications is related to the sincere happiness that filled the hearts of all Egyptians on hearing the news that one of their compatriots had won such an outstanding science award. This happiness was triggered by our loyal people's awareness of the value of the relationship between this achievement and their country. Yet the sense of happiness transcended this country to cover the entire Arab world, of which Egypt has always been the heart.

It is not surprising, then, that such feelings of pride and admiration for Dr. Ahmed Zewail have prevailed over all the Arab world with the same force and sincerity as expressed in Egypt. This is an extension of our feeling of pride for the achievements of our Arab scientists, such as al-Khawarizmi, the most famous mathematician and astronomer of his time, al-Hassan Ibn al-Haytham in optics and physics, al-Razi, author of the first medical encyclopedia, Ibn Sina, Ibn Rushd, and many others.

Brothers and sisters, the real importance of this occasion is not to be found in regarding the winning by Dr. Ahmed Zewail of the Noble Prize in Chemistry at such a young age as an individual event to take pride in. Rather, we should regard it as a starting-point for enhancing national scientific research throughout Egypt, for pursuing true and persistent efforts in order to obtain a share of the current world scientific revolution. We should work toward solving problems and facing challenges that could hamper our progress toward our national aspirations. Here, we should proudly mention that one of the most precious national achievements during the second half of the twentieth century, the glorious October victory, was built on a sound scientific base, and it is a scientific base that will help us face our present challenges.

It was this scientific base that I referred to in my vision of the changes that should be made in the Egyptian national action campaign. In my address to the national conference on technology and information last September, I emphasized that a new national project for a comprehensive technological revival is to be added to Egypt's megaprojects. This project provides for rapid and ongoing implementation of an ambitious national program to mobilize efforts by all sectors of the community to use, produce, and make indigenous technology for application in all production sites and all walks of the Egyptian life. I also asserted in my address to the People's Assembly and Shura (Consultative) Council last October that I would personally follow up this vital project. In the same month, in the letter of assignment to the new cabinet, I referred to the prerequisites for this project's success, which included preparing all sectors of Egyptian society to enter the high-tech age, intensively reforming and continually upgrading the educational system, while giving special attention to high-flying and innovative students, and improving scientific research by all possible means.

Brothers and sisters, to succeed in attaining these ambitious goals, in addition to a clear-cut vision, we need an integrated policy, which I urge all competent bodies to collaborate in developing and implementing. To attain this vital goal, the best use of the energies of distinguished Egyptian scientists as well as the new generation of researchers must be made.

I call on the Egyptian scientists who migrated or left to work abroad to effectively contribute to this giant project not only with their ideas and inventions, but also by transferring advanced technology and training their colleagues in Egypt.

I also call on them to sponsor, as supervising professors, young scientists and researchers in Egypt who are working toward their Ph.D.s. For my part, I will never hesitate a moment in giving maximum possible support to make this ambitious project a success.

At the same time, I seize this opportunity to call for real Arab integration that will allow Arab countries to make giant strides in scientific research, since no one nation can do this single-handedly. I am aware of difficulties and sensitivities involved in putting this call into effect.

But the expected fruits and the challenges facing us all with the advent of a new century are worthy of our maximum efforts. Egypt will always be ready to provide its best ideas and expertise to proceed forward with this call.

Brothers and sisters, I reiterate my congratulations to the devoted son of Egypt and its distinguished scientist, Dr. Ahmed Zewail, for his winning this distinguished prize. I am confident in the ability of our people and our nation to attain the progress we deserve. I am sure that there will be gatherings like this in the future to celebrate further achievements of the loyal children of Egypt for the sake of their homeland and future of their descendants. By so doing, they are fulfilling lofty human principles laid down by their ancestors at the dawn of human civilization.

Translation from the Arabic primarily made by the Office of the Presidency; extracts quoted in the text may appear in slightly different form.

Order of the Grand Collar of the Nile Address by Ahmed Zewail

Cairo, Egypt
Presidential Palace
December 16, 1999

Your Excellency Mr. President, Mrs. Mubarak; Mr. Prime Minister; distinguished Ministers, scientists, and guests:

Kull 'am wa-antum bi-khayr [Greetings] on the special occasions of the holy month of Ramadan, the blessed Christmas, and the beginning of the seventh millennium in the history of Egypt. This is a day I will cherish forever. It is a great honor for me to stand before you to receive the Order of the Grand Collar of the Nile, the highest decoration in our beloved Egypt. This honor symbolizes an award to all of science and to all fellow scientists.

I left the country more than a quarter of a century ago, and from the beginning my goal has been to acquire knowledge—knowledge of science and the universe. The awarding of the Nobel prize in the sciences— a first in the history of Egypt and the Arab world—underscores what the people of this nation can achieve on the international level, if they have the proper milieu for utilizing their skills and abilities.

I am only one of the many sons of Egypt, inside and outside the country, who have made significant advances in science, medicine, literature, art, economics, politics, and other fields. Ever since the dawn of history, Egypt has continuously contributed an enormous amount to the world's store of knowledge.

As I said earlier this month in Stockholm, if the Nobel prizes had been awarded six thousand years ago at the beginning of Egyptian civilization, or even two thousand years ago when the Library of Alexandria served as the beacon of knowledge to the world, Egypt would surely have received a significant portion of these prizes. Nor can we forget the pivotal role played by Arab scientists, whose research was like a shining torch for the dark pre-Renaissance age in Europe.

Mr. President, with this honor you have reconfirmed your strong desire to develop and support the sciences in Egypt. The world today stands on two primary supports that are the foundation for power, influence, and progress. These two supports are advanced scientific knowledge and the productivity of the people in line with this knowledge base. The developed world of today relies on science and productivity to change the standard of living and to be positioned as a world force on this planet.

For developing states to attain a similar level of progress and development requires the building of a science base and a scientific culture. With these keys, it is possible to escape the 'import mentality,' the trap of relying on importing goods only for consumption, and it is possible to join in technological competition with the outside world in the new system of globalization. Such a powerful scientific base needs true and unified participation—the Egyptian people need to believe in the role of science in creating a new and advanced position for the country.

Egypt now has the ability to take that great scientific and technological leap forward that will boost it into the twenty-first century, because of the success of your wise leadership, Mr. President, in courageously embarking on the difficult task of building the infrastructure and strengthening Egypt's political position in the world. In my opinion, the scientific renaissance in the time of President Mubarak has an important historical dimension for prosperity and peace for Egypt and for the Middle East. It is the foundation for preparing healthy generations in a society that can be guided by rationalism and can cope successfully with the age of globalization.

Mr. President, the telephone call I received from Your Excellency at my home and the thousands of messages I received from the people of Egypt and from the Arab world, after the announcement of the prize, have kindled in me feelings of joy and pride in belonging to this nation. In many of these letters and in meetings with young people, I noted an overwhelming thirst to acquire knowledge and achieve excellence on the international level. For the sake of these national treasures—our youth—I hope that I can help by encouraging them and by inspiring them to the benefits of science as a means to serve the country and humanity at large.

I have been honored by many scientific and international organizations for what I have achieved with my research group at Caltech, but the honor I am receiving today has a special meaning for me. It underscores the strong bond I have to this great country. It also opens wide the doors of hope for a renaissance in scientific and technological development in Egypt. This is not much to ask for such an ancient country, whose historical roots have blossomed into many great civilizations. Moreover, Egypt has multitudes of capable people eager to achieve at the best level possible. Although the complete scientific base is not in place at the present time, I am sure that within a very short time it would be possible to establish it on a world-class level. When this scientific and intellectual power is achieved, it will become the base for a modern renaissance, which will be not less than that which took place in Europe and Asia, where science played a dominant role in leading those nations from the dark ages into the luminous age of science.

Mr. President, I cannot find words that can express my real feelings to thank you for such a special honor. I can only offer you my sincere gratitude, and hope that Allah will protect your work and achievements for the betterment of our beloved Egypt. I would also like to convey my sincere thanks and appreciation to the loyal people of Egypt. Finally, I believe that we all should work together as a team with persistence and integrity and with a positive and optimistic attitude to raise high the flag of Egypt, the mother of civilizations, among the civilizations of the modern world.

Translated from the Arabic.

THE WHITE HOUSE

WASHINGTON

October 28, 1999

Ahmed H. Zewail, Ph.D.
Arthur Amos Noyes Laboratory
   of Chemical Physics
California Institute of Technology
Mail Code 127-72
Pasadena, California 91125

Dear Ahmed:

I am delighted to congratulate you on receiving
the 1999 Nobel Prize in Chemistry.

This prestigious award is a fitting tribute to
your groundbreaking research using femtosecond
spectroscopy to study chemical reactions. By
discovering chemical events that previously were
invisible, you have greatly advanced our knowledge
regarding what occurs during chemical reactions.
Your work has fundamentally altered the field of
chemistry and holds great promise for improving
the lives of people everywhere.

You can take great pride in this remarkable
achievement. I commend you for your commitment
to scientific exploration and send my best wishes
for continued success and every happiness.

Sincerely,

Bill Clinton

New Initiative for Science and Technology in the Twenty-first Century

Foundation of Science and Technology
University of Science and Technology (UST)
and
Technology Park (TP)

Chairman of the Board of Patrons
H. E. President of Egypt

Proposed Plan and Structure
by Ahmed Zewail
January 10, 2000

Synopsis

Under the patronage of H.E. President Mohammed Hosni Mubarak, it is proposed to create a nonprofit Foundation of Science and Technology, with the mission of establishing the University of Science and Technology (UST) and the related Technology Park (TP). This project offers a means for building an advanced science base in this age of science and globalization, which requires the integration of human resources, technology, and capital. It is clear that a strong science base forms the foundation for technological advances, and both are the driving force for prosperity of the nation and for secure peace in the Middle East.

UST and TP are to provide the nucleus for a center of excellence, with the aim of: 1) the education of the young generation in world-class science and technology; 2) the development of new technologies in the country and the region; and 3) the participation in the technology-based global economy, regionally and internationally. The founding research/education institutes are unique in their focus and represent twenty-first century frontiers: genetic medicine, energy and water resources, femto- and nanotechnology, information technology, and others.

In order to be successful, this historic undertaking requires the following three essentials: *new academic and administrative plans*, which include the development of a new education and research curriculum for a select number of students and researchers; a *new law*, which permits this center of excellence to achieve its goals; and a *new capital endowment*, which should be devoted to the project without any personal-profit motive.

The academic and administrative planning of the project has been structured in detail, and is outlined below. As for the capital, it is anticipated that support will come from two sources without any burden on the government: tuition charged for undergraduate education (similar to the American University in Cairo) and income from an endowment raised especially for the advanced research and high-tech endeavors of UST and TP.

The site for the UST and TP project on a parcel of 300 acres in October 6 City has already been apportioned by the government of Egypt (the groundbreaking ceremony was held on January 1, 2000). The fundraising campaign can only begin after the approval of the new law. Already some prominent people, Egyptians and non-Egyptians, have expressed willingness to participate in supporting this project. Equally importantly, prominent scientists from around the world have offered their help in this new initiative. The patronage of President Mubarak is essential for the success of this project, which should propel Egypt and the Arab world into a renaissance in science and technology.

Historical Perspective

Egypt and the Arab world have historically made major contributions to the advancement of human thought and civilization. Over many millennia, Egypt, the birthplace of scientific thought, made discoveries and inventions in science, engineering, medicine, and other fields. Nearly a millennium ago, Arab civilization and its scientific advances reached

Europe and Asia; without doubt this contact was significant to the birth of the European Renaissance. In recent times, however, the contributions from Egypt and the Arab nations to world science have been modest. This situation has resulted in a "brain drain" of many able scientists to the West and the necessity of importation of technology from the West. The brain drain coupled with the absence of a solid and sustained science base locally has defined the current technological status of Egypt and other Arab countries and hence their impact on the world market. However, the Arab world is rich in resources, both human and, in many countries, financial. Thus, there should be no fundamental barrier to building an essential science base here. Moreover, such a science base is critical to the future of the Arab world, especially in the context of any hoped-for peace in the Middle East.

The twentieth century has witnessed revolutions in science and technology. The invention of lasers, computers, and transistors has resulted in new technologies that have transformed our society. Discoveries have spanned the entire universe, from the world of the very small to the world of the very large and the very complex. Quantum theory, relativity, new dimensions in time and space (femto and nano), black holes and the expanding universe, and the deciphering of the genetic code are examples that have transformed human thought and are the basis of new quests for new frontiers. In the twenty-first century, new discoveries will surely be made and will affect society in every respect—human health (medicine), human informatics (Internet, etc.), and human existence (environment). Globalization drives the integration of human resources, capital, and technology, making it impossible for any nation to influence the global economy in a significant way without a strong science base.

The University of Science and Technology and the associated Technology Park constitute a focused new concept designed to bring about a serious participation in twenty-first century science and to advance local technologies to the world-class level. With the first Nobel prize in science for Egypt and the Arab world and the desire of the respective governments and their peoples to reach this level of accomplishment, excellence is a goal that can be achieved in a relatively short time. What is needed is a commitment to excellence within a new system capable of providing present and future generations with the opportunity to build a science and technology base of international stature. The ultimate goal is to advance the means for the betterment of human health and defense and to acquire new knowledge, from atoms to outer space. The science base is the basis for endless frontiers. UST is not a luxury—it is of vital importance to the nation and to the region.

UST Goals and Uniqueness
The concept behind UST and its partner TP can be realized only if a *highly select* group of faculty and students form the University. The plan is to build a campus, housing a maximum of up to five thousand students and faculty, that is equipped with state-of-the-art facilities and research laboratories. The campus will be self-sufficient and will provide a true scholarly environment to nurture new ideas and make new contributions. UST will emphasize learning and communicating scientific ideas and technology at the level of the advanced nations (the United States, Europe, Japan, etc.), but it will maintain an equal focus on the home culture, pride, and ethics. UST will be unique for several reasons:

First, UST will prepare a new generation of students with versatile and up-to-date qualifications in science and technology. The current state university system is less than able to provide such critical preparation at the international, competitive level.

Second, UST will put Egypt and the Arab world on the international map in research and development, permitting serious participation in world science and technology and exchanges with world cultures. The current university system is less able to provide such participation in a significant way.

Third, UST will have an enormous impact on society and the world, seeding the "scientific society" of the future. As an enlightening center of excellence, UST will engender a special pride in the population, help other institutions achieve excellence through mutual interactions, and communicate advances on the new frontiers of science and technology to all segments of society, including the vital industrial, economic, and agricultural sectors. It will forge new links between scientists and laypersons, merging scientific and societal values. These contributions will be of significance nationally and internationally, as they will build bridges and establish rational dialogues.

UST Structure
The basic structure of UST is as follows:

• The undergraduate program will, initially, emphasize the basics of science (mathematics, physics, chemistry, engineering, economics, etc.) at the highest level, along with a multidisciplinary curriculum. In addition, it will introduce, especially at the freshman level, some courses in languages and humanities with cultural, historical, and artistic appeal. With this curriculum, the initial preparation of students of different backgrounds will end with candidacy for admission to the UST advanced program. This program provides specialization in different areas of multidisciplinary science, engineering, medicine, and related areas.

• For the graduate schools, institutes are to be established at the highest level possible, similar in spirit to the Max-Planck Institutes. Ideally, these institutes should be devoted to new fields to ensure originality and encourage creative thinking. This means aiming at new frontiers that have special relevance to problems in Egypt and the region, such as energy, information, and genetics.

• The founding institutes should not exceed five to seven in number, and all should be twenty-first century frontiers: molecular medicine, genetic engineering, informatics, materials, lasers, water resources, global changes, space exploration, etc. International programs should be established to encourage student and faculty exchanges.

UST Organization and Support
UST is a nonprofit organization administered by the Foundation of Science and Technology. Both the foundation and the university should function under the umbrella of a new law, signed by President Mubarak and approved by the People's Assembly, which gives them independence as a nonprofit, nongovernmental organization. The operational structure

of UST must be free of bureaucratic hindrances, but with careful accountability for 1) resources and expenses and 2) the level of excellence. Support for UST and its TP should derive mainly from two income streams: tuition and endowment. Tuition should cover the operating costs of UST, and the income from the endowment should maintain the research and development activities at the institutes. The initial endowment should be the result of a fundraising campaign for one billion dollars, secured in full at the end of the first five-year phase. It will fund a grant system that supports research with an emphasis on creative ideas and teamwork. A fellowship program will also be established from the endowment for exceptional students.

The world will take note of UST's significance when it is fully operational within its first five-year period; in another five years the university should stand out as a distinguished world-class institution. In time, after the first decade, the addition of new institutes will need to be addressed, with an eye to maintaining UST's unique size, structure, and excellence.

The Technology Park

The interface of UST with society will be through a Technology Park (TP) that will provide young entrepreneurs with the opportunity to develop new technologies and industries; laboratory space and financial support from UST and its parent foundation will be provided on a contractual basis. Equally importantly, the TP will provide a problem-solving body (a research corporation), important to different sectors of high-tech industries. The realization of both objectives in UST's TP will cement the link to society by keeping the young entrepreneurs in the country and advancing new technologies; moreover, in the long run it will bring in valuable income resources for UST and the foundation through joint agreements.

Administrative Structure

A distinguished Board of Trustees will be formed to oversee the foundation. The trustees will include distinguished personages, including Nobel prize winners from all over the world, distinguished Arab scholars, and distinguished members of the business community and other sectors in the region and the world. Patrons include heads of state, prime ministers, and ministers. President Mubarak has kindly agreed to chair the patrons' board. The foundation will appoint the UST and TP presidents and approve their boards of directors.

The Site
The land for UST has been assigned by the government of Egypt on a 300-acre parcel in October 6 City. A groundbreaking ceremony was held on January 1, 2000, under the patronage of President Mohammed Hosni Mubarak, and in the presence of the prime minister, the ministers of higher education and housing and land reclamation, myself, and other dignitaries. A building was assigned to the Foundation, but was later proclaimed invalid.

The above text was prepared in January 2000 for a brochure; all detailed documentation of what has followed since then is available and will be part of the archive of the Foundation.

Curriculum Vitae
Ahmed H. Zewail

California Institute of Technology
Linus Pauling Chair Professor of Chemistry and Professor of
    Physics
Director, NSF Laboratory for Molecular Sciences
Editor, *Chemical Physics Letters*

Personal

Married to: Dr. Dema Zewail
Children: Maha, Amani, Nabeel, and Hani

Academic Degrees

B.S., First Class Honors, Alexandria University, Egypt (1967)
M.S., Alexandria University, Egypt (1969)
Ph.D., University of Pennsylvania, Philadelphia, USA (1974)

Honorary Degrees

Oxford University, United Kingdom (1991): M.A., h.c.
American University in Cairo, Egypt (1993): D.Sc., h.c.
Katholieke Universiteit, Leuven, Belgium (1997): D.Sc., h.c.
University of Pennsylvania, USA (1997): D.Sc., h.c.
Université de Lausanne, Switzerland (1997): D.Sc., h.c.
Swinburne University, Australia (1999): D.U., h.c.
Arab Academy for Science & Technology, Egypt (1999): H.D.A.Sc.
Alexandria University, Egypt (1999): H.D.Sc.
University of New Brunswick, Canada (2000): Doctoris in Scientia,
    D.Sc., h.c.
University of Rome "La Sapienza," Italy (2000): Dottore *honoris*
    causa, D.Sc., h.c.
Université de Liège, Belgium (2000): Doctor *honoris causa,* D., h.c.
Queen of Angeles-Hollywood Presbyterian Medical Center, Los

Angeles (2000): Honorary Medical Doctor, Member of the
Medical Staff
Jadavpur University, India (2001): D.Sc., h.c.
Concordia University, Montreal, Canada (2002): Honorary Doctor of Laws
Heriot Watt University, Scotland (2002): Honorary Doctor of Science

Orders And Distinctions
Order of Merit (OM), First Class (Sciences and Arts), conferred by
President M. H. Mubarak, Egypt (1995)
Order of the Grand Collar of the Nile, Highest Honor of Egypt, con-
ferred by President M. H. Mubarak (1999)
Order of Zayed, Highest Presidential Honor, State of United Arab
Emirates (2000)
Order of Cedar, Highest Rank of Commander, from President Emile
Lahoud, State of Lebanon (2000)
Order of ISESCO, First Class, from Prince Salman Ibn Abdel Aziz,
Saudi Arabia (2000)
Order of Merit (OM) of Tunisia, Highest Honor, from the President
of the Republic, Zine el-Abdine Ben Ali (2000)
Insignia of Pontifical Academy, from Pope John Paul II, Vatican (2000)

Special Honors
King Faisal International Prize in Science (1989)
First Linus Pauling Chair, Caltech (1990)
Wolf Prize in Chemistry (1993)
Robert A. Welch Award in Chemistry (1997)
Benjamin Franklin Medal, the Franklin Institute, USA (1998)
Egypt Postage Stamps, with portrait (1998); the "fourth pyramid"
stamp (1999)
Dr. Ahmed Zewail High School, Desuq City (1998)
Dr. Ahmed Zewail Street, Damanhur City (1998)
Dr. Ahmed Zewail Intellectual Salon, Opera House, Cairo (1998–)
Nobel Prize in Chemistry (1999)
The Ahmed Zewail Fellowships, University of Pennsylvania, (2000–)

Dr. Ahmed Zewail Square, City of Alexandria (2000)
Ahmed Zewail Prize, American University in Cairo (2001–)
The Zewail Prize, Femtochemistry V Conference, Spain (2001)
Exhibition, Nobel Museum, Stockholm, Sweden (2001)
BBC documentary, "The End of the Race against Time" (2001)

Awards and Prizes (partial list)
Alfred P. Sloan Foundation Fellow (1978–82)
Camille and Henry Dreyfus Teacher-Scholar Award (1979–85)
Alexander von Humboldt Award for Senior U.S. Scientists (1983)
National Science Foundation Award for especially creative research
    (1984; 1988; 1993)
Buck-Whitney Medal, American Chemical Society (1985)
John Simon Guggenheim Memorial Foundation Fellow (1987)
Harrison Howe Award, American Chemical Society (1989)
Carl Zeiss International Award, Germany (1992)
Earle K. Plyler Prize, American Physical Society (1993)
Medal of the Royal Netherlands Academy of Arts and Sciences,
    Holland (1993)
Bonner Chemiepreis, Germany (1994)
Herbert P. Broida Prize, American Physical Society (1995)
Leonardo da Vinci Award of Excellence, France (1995)
Collège de France Medal, France (1995)
Peter Debye Award, American Chemical Society (1996)
National Academy of Sciences Award, Chemical Sciences, United
    States (1996)
J. G. Kirkwood Medal, Yale University (1996)
Peking University Medal, Beijing, China (1996)
Pittsburgh Spectroscopy Award (1997)
First E. B. Wilson Award, American Chemical Society (1997)
Linus Pauling Medal (1997)
Richard C. Tolman Medal (1998)
William H. Nichols Medal (1998)
Paul Karrer Gold Medal, University of Zurich, Switzerland (1998)

E. O. Lawrence Award, U.S. Government (1998)
Merski Award, University of Nebraska (1999)
Röntgen Prize (the 100th anniversary of the discovery of x-rays),
    Germany (1999)
Faye Robiner Award, Ross University School of Medicine,
    New York (2000)
Golden Plate Award, American Academy of Achievement (2000)
City of Pisa Medal, City Mayor, Pisa, Italy (2000)
Medal of "La Sapienza" ("Wisdom"), University of Rome (2000)
Médaille de l'Institut du Monde Arabe, Paris, France (2000)
Honorary Medal, Université du Centre, Monastir, Tunisia (2000)
Honorary Medal, City of Monastir, from the Mayor, Tunisia (2000)
Distinguished Alumni Award, University of Pennsylvania (2002)

Honorary Academies and Societies
American Physical Society, fellow (elected 1982)
National Academy of Sciences of the United States of America
    (elected 1989)
Third World Academy of Sciences, Italy (elected 1989)
Sigma Xi Society (elected 1992)
American Academy of Arts and Sciences (elected 1993)
Académie Européenne des Sciences, des Arts et des Lettres, France
    (elected 1994)
American Philosophical Society (elected 1998)
Pontifical Academy of Sciences (elected 1999)
American Academy of Achievement (elected 1999)
The Royal Danish Academy of Sciences and Letters (elected 2000)
American Association for the Advancement of Science (AAAS),
    fellow (elected 2000)
Chemical Society of India, honorary fellow (elected 2001)
Indian Academy of Sciences, honorary fellow (elected 2001)
The Royal Society, London, foreign member (elected 2001)
Gezira, Alexandria Sporting, Cairo Capital, and Automobile clubs,
    Egypt (honorary life memberships)

Professional Activities

Member of boards of trustees

Member of advisory and editorial boards

Current editor of *Chemical Physics Letters*

Chairman and member of organizing committees of international
conferences

Invited lecturer for 480 occasions and events, more than 150 of which
are named or plenary lectures, such as the Nobel, Celsius, Faraday,
Röntgen, Franklin (Benjamin), Perrin, (J.J.) Thomson, Planck,
Schrödinger, London, Lawrence, Condon, Watson, Aimé Cotton,
Debye, Pauling, Hinshelwood, Karrer, Eyring, Noyes, Kirkwood,
Tolman, Kistiakowsky, Pimentel, Bernstein, Wilson, Berson,
Roberts, Polanyi, and Onassis

Publications and patents: At the end of 2001, 400+ articles and eight
books have been published, and one patent has been issued (U.S.
Patent 4,227,939, dated October 14, 1980) for "Solar Energy
Concentrator Devices"

Visiting Professorships

John van Geuns Stichting Visiting Professor, University of Amsterdam,
Holland (1979)

Visiting Professor at the University of Bordeaux, France (1981)

Visiting Professor, École Normale Supérieure, France (1983)

Visiting Professor, University of Kuwait, Kuwait (1987)

Visiting Scholar, University of California, Los Angeles (1988)

Distinguished Visiting Professor, the American University in Cairo,
(1988)

Rolf Sammet Professor, Johann Wolfgang Goethe-Universität,
Frankfurt, Germany (1990)

Christensen Professorial Fellow, St. Catherine's College, Oxford,
United Kingdom (1991)

Visiting Professor, Texas A&M University (1992)

Visiting Professor, University of Iowa (1992)

Visiting Professor, Collège de France, Paris, France (1995)

Visiting Professor, Katholieke Universiteit, Leuven, Belgium (1998)
Röntgen Visiting Professor, University of Würzburg, Germany (1999)
Honorary Chair Professor, University of Lausanne, Switzerland (2000)
Linnett Professorship, Cambridge University, United Kingdom (2002)

Academic Positions
Director, NSF Laboratory for Molecular Sciences, LMS, California
    Institute of Technology, Pasadena, (1996–present)
Linus Pauling Chair Professor of Chemistry and Professor of Physics,
    Caltech (1995–present)
Linus Pauling Professor of Chemical Physics, Caltech (1990–94)
Professor of Chemical Physics, Caltech (1982–89)
Associate Professor of Chemical Physics, Caltech (1978–82)
Assistant Professor of Chemical Physics, Caltech (1976–78)
IBM Postdoctoral Fellow, University of California, Berkeley (1974–76)
Predoctoral Research Fellow, University of Pennsylvania (1970–74)
Teaching Assistant, University of Pennsylvania (1969–70)
Instructor and Researcher, Alexandria University (1967–69)
Undergraduate trainee, Shell Corporation, Alexandria (1966)

Index

motion of, 2; observing movement
of, 164; photographing, 105,
115–16, 163; size of, 100
atomic nuclei, measuring, 116
attosecond resolution, 164
Averroes (Ibn Rushd), 4
Avicenna (Ibn Sina), 4
Avogadro, Amadeo, 154
Axis armies, 12
al-Azhar University, 12

Bab Zeweila, 12
al-Badawi, Ahmed, 15
Bagush, camping at, 38
Baker, W.O., 178
Baldeschwieler, John, 85, 91, 96
Baltimore, David, 89, 183
Barari, Ahmed, 26
basketball, 19
Basov, Nikolai, 128
Batisha, Omar, 32
El-Bayoumi, Ashraf, 44
Behira, governorate of, 11
Beirut, 81
Bell Labs, 128
Benjamin Franklin Medal, 179
Bernstein, Dick, 116, 141, 168, 171
Big Bang, 165
Binnig, Gerd, 105, 171
biology, lasers in, 162–63
"Birth of Molecules," 116
Blobel, Günter, 171
Bloembergen, Nico, 108, 111
Bohr, Niels, 104
Boyle, Robert, 154
Bragg, W. Lawrence, 10, 155
Bragg, William H., 102, 155
Bray, Bob, 59
Breasted, James Henry, 121
Breiland, Bill, 76
British Drug House (BDH), 41
British occupation of Egypt, 12, 217
British system of essays, 57
Brock, John, 76
Brown, Harold, 189

Browne, Malcolm W., 168
Buck-Whitney Medal, 98
Buggraf, Larry, 136
bureaucracy, reform of, 221, 223

Cairo University, 181
calendars, 119, 120–21
Caltech, 4, 7, 79, 85, 87–8, 162, 163,
171, 177, 189, 195, 196, 200, 216
camera obscura, 123, 124
carbon dioxide, shedding atoms, 142
Carnarvon, Lord, 165
Carter, Howard, 165
Castleman, Will, 168
cats, anatomy, 129; falling, 129, 131
Cecil Hotel, 111
censorship, 205–206
Champollion, Jean-François, 14, 157
Chan, Sunney, 85
chemia, 153
chemical bonds and lasers, 140
Chemical Physics Letters, 117
chemical reactions, observing in real
time, 152–53
chemistry, Arab contributions, 154; as
art of change, 153; word defined,
153
Christy, Bob, 97
Chu, Steven, 105, 171
Churchill, Winston, 13
Clauser, Francis, 97, 171
Clinton, Bill, 195, 196
clock, cesium atomic, 122; mechanical,
122; pendulum, 125
clubs, Alexandria, 28
Cohen, Joel, 204, 211
Cohen-Tannoudji, C., 105
coherence, 161, 162
Columbus, Christopher, 234–35
conferences, 216
constitution, rethinking national, 207
copper, use in Sinai, 153
Corey, E.J., 178
Cornell, Eric, 171
cotton, Egyptian, 99

crystals, 79
cultural bonding, 230
culture, science, 207–208
Curie, Marie, 179
Curl, Robert, 86
customs, Egyptian and American contrasted, 62–63

Dalton, John, 102, 154
Damanhur, 11, 13, 181; naming of, 11; street renamed, 182
Dar, Rawhia Rabi'e, 12, 17–18
Dar, Rizq, 21 , 31
Darwish Restaurant, 31
da Vinci, Leonardo, 235
Davis, Larry, 136
Davisson, C.J., 103
Davy, Sir Humphrey, 7
Davydov, A. S., 68
Dawson, Dan, 92
de Broglie, Louis, 101, 156
de Broglie wave length, 161
Dehmelt, H. G., 105
Delbruck, Max, 90
demotic, 14
Democritus, 100; atomic theory of, 101
Dervan, Peter B., 83, 178, 182
Desuq, Egypt, 12, 15, 26, 34, 99, 181; Zewail home in, 13–14
developed countries, responsibilities of, 210
developing countries, responsibilities of, 212
Dirac, Paul A.M., 105
discrimination, 36
Durrell, Lawrence, 28
dye laser, invention of, 128
Dym, Sally, 59
dynamics, evolution of, 155
Dyson, Freeman, 149

Eaton, Bill, 55, 59
Edgerton, Harold, 127, 132
education, in Egypt, 18, 20–21, 221, 222–23; in US, 215–16, 226

Egypt, compared to US, 214; economy, 221; history, 214, 217; honors author, 181; in science, 4; priorities, 222; response to Nobel Prize in, 191; role in author's career, 7
Egyptian blue, 153
Egyptian heritage, 220
Egyptian Order of Merit, 194
Eigen, Manfred, 127
Einstein, Albert, 91, 156, 179
Eisenthal, Ken, 168
electrodes, 103
electron, discovery of, 103, 154
electron beam, 163
electron-spin transitions, 79
English language, learning in, 7
Euclid, 29
evolution, teaching, 227
experiments, femtosecond laser, 137
Eyring, Henry, 155
El-Ezaby, Samir, 40, 41, 43

Faham, Bashar, 173
Faham, Chaker, 173, 174
Faham, Dema, 173–75; marriage to author, 174
Fahmy, Amal, 169–70
falafel sandwiches, 19
fanaticism, 206
Felker, Peter, 113
femtochemistry, 2, 142, 183; conferences in, 169; development, 109; in journals, 168; significance of, 152, 153; word origin, 116
femtolands (labs), 144
femtometer, 116
femtoscope, 134
femtoscopy, 134; compared to photography, 135
femtosecond, 2, 116; applications of, 145; initiating, 134–35
femtosecond lasers, 164
femtosecond resolution, 158, 159
femtosecond time scale, 124, 155, 160
Feynman, Richard, 84, 90, 103

Fitts, Donald, 45
Florida State University, 44
foreign policy, US, 229
Fowler, Willy, 90
Franklin, Benjamin, 165, 179–80
Franklin Institute, 180
Free Officers Revolution, 20
free speech movement, 75
freeze motion, 133
Friedman, Joel, 59
fullerenes, 86

Galilei, Galileo, 124, 126, 151, 187
Galison, Peter, 149
Gamal, Ahmed, 42
Gaweish, Fathy, 25
Geber (Jabir ibn Hayyan), 4, 154
Gell-Mann, Murray, 90
geology, 33–34
El Gibaly, Ragae, 32
glass, early Egyptian, 153
globalization, 204
Gold Rush, 73
Goldberger, Murph, 137
Goldstein, Joseph, 178
Gouda, Shehata, 33
Graduate Towers, 67
Grand Collar of the Nile, 4, 193, 201–202
Grand Hotel, Stockholm, 186
Gray, Harry B., 84, 85
Gregorian calendar, 121
Grente, Ingmar, 189
Gribbin, John, 122
gross national product (GDP), 203
Guggenheim grant, 98
Gutenberg, Bino, 91

Hackerman, Norman, 178
Hafez, Hani, 42
Hale, George Ellery, 89
Hamdan, Gamal, 219
Hamouda, 'Amm, 16
Hamouda, Mohammed, 26
Hardy, Godfrey, 149
Harris, Charles, 71, 76

Harrison-Howe Award, 175
Heeger, Alan, 58
Heisenberg, Werner, 104
Heisenberg uncertainty principle, 104
Herodotus, 14
Hochstrasser, Robin, 45, 54, 56, 57, 59, 62, 64, 71
"Horse in Motion," 115
horses, photographing movement of legs, 130
Horus, 11
human genome, mapping of, 201
human resources, building, 207
Hussein, Saddam, 81
Hussein, Taha, 31, 173, 200
Huygens, Christiaan, 125

IBM Zurich Lab, 105
Ibn al-Haytham (Alhazen), 81
Ibn Rushd (Averroës), 4
Ibn Sina (Avicenna), 4, 154
ICN reaction, 138–39
illiteracy, 204–5
indigo, 154
Inquisition, 126
institute system, 25
Institute for Scientific Information, 144
instrumentation, 57
insurance, 67
International Conference on Photochemistry and Photobiology (PAP), 112
intramolecular vibrational energy redistribution (IVR), 136
Iraq, author visit to, 80–81
Isied, Stephan, 75, 172
Iskander, Youssef, 39
Islam, 6–7, 206
Issa, Rafat, 37, 39, 40, 41
'Izzat, Enas, 36

Jabir ibn Hayyan (Geber), 154
Johnson, Richard, 178
joint uncertainty relations, 160
Jones, Kevin E., 92

Journal of Chemical Physics, 108
Journal of Physical Chemistry, 168
Julian calendar, 121

Kandil, Kamal, 39
Kafr al-Sheikh, 25
Kekulé, Friedrich August, 102
Kelvin, Lord, 162
Kepler, Johannes, 124
al-Khadem, Hassan, 39
Khalil, Omar, 65
al-Khamry, Atef, 181
King Carl XVI Gustaf, 187, 188
King Faisal International Prize, 6,
    170–71, 172
King Farouk I University (Alexandria
    University), 30
Kinsey, Jim, 168
Knee, Joe, 114
knowledge, passion for, 234
Koonin, Steve, 183
Kroto, Harry, 86
Kuhn, Thomas, 149
Kupperman, Aron, 84

laboratories, 41
Laboratory for Research on the
    Structure of Matter (LRSM), 58, 59
Lambert, Bill, 113
laser, acronym, 127; invented, 127;
    pulses, 133; chemistry and, 162; in
    controlling reactions, 162; integra-
    tion of, 151
laser, colliding pulse, 137
laser, femtosecond, 3, 137
laser, picosecond, 78, 80
laser, solid-state, 128
laser, titanium-sapphire, 128
Laser and Optics Research Center,
    Baghdad, 81
laser femtochemistry, lectures on, 170
laser strobes, 2
laser trapping, 105
lasers, in probing molecules, 93; inter-
    national conference on, 216

Lavoisier, Antoine, 154
law reform, 224
Lawrence, Ernest O., 77
Lawrence Berkeley Lab (LBL), 77–78
Lee, Yuan, 111, 178
Lemoine, J., 135
Leucippus, 100
Lewellyn, Mark, 76
Lewis, G. N., 105, 156
light, as electromagnetic wave, 156;
    coherence in, 157; duality of, 156;
    experiments with, 123
Lindberg, Erik, 188
Lindquist, Svante, 230
Linus Pauling Chair, 7
Lionaes, Aase, on Egypt, 221
Lipscomb, William, 178
Los Angeles Times, 168
Luminescent Solar Concentrator (LSC),
    93
Luxor, 37, 111

magnetic resonance imaging (MRI),
    113
Mahfouz, Naguib, 3
Maki, Gus, 71
Marcus, Rudy, 86, 111, 171
Marey, Etienne-Jules, 127, 128, 129,
    131
Marshall Plan, 211, 229
Martens, Craig, 168–69
maser, 162
mathematics, study of, 33
matter, behavior of, 1
Maugh, Thomas H., article by, 168
Måwe, Ann, 186
Max Planck Institutes, 216
Maxwell, James Clerk, 156
McClure, Don, 83
McDiarmid, Alan, 58
McKoy, Vince, 84, 95, 196
McMillan, Edwin, 77
mechanics, quantum and classical, 160
Mekawi, Sayyid, songs by, 23
memorization, in school, 18